The Business Strategy of Booker T. Washington

UNIVERSITY PRESS OF FLORIDA

Florida A&M University, Tallahassee
Florida Atlantic University, Boca Raton
Florida Gulf Coast University, Ft. Myers
Florida International University, Miami
Florida State University, Tallahassee
New College of Florida, Sarasota
University of Central Florida, Orlando
University of Florida, Gainesville
University of North Florida, Jacksonville
University of South Florida, Tampa
University of West Florida, Pensacola

The Business Strategy of Booker T. Washington

Its Development and Implementation

Michael B. Boston

University Press of Florida
Gainesville/Tallahassee/Tampa/Boca Raton
Pensacola/Orlando/Miami/Jacksonville/Ft. Myers/Sarasota

Copyright 2010 by Michael B. Boston
All rights reserved
Printed in the United States of America. This book is printed on Glatfelter Natures Book, a paper certified under the standards of the Forestry Stewardship Council (FSC). It is a recycled stock that contains 30 percent post-consumer waste and is acid-free.

First cloth printing, 2010
First paperback printing, 2012

Library of Congress Cataloging-in-Publication Data
Boston, Michael B.
The business strategy of Booker T. Washington: its development and implementation/Michael B. Boston.
p. cm.
Includes bibliographical references and index.
ISBN 978-0-8130-3473-7 (cloth: alk. paper)
ISBN 978-0-8130-4171-1 (pbk.)
1. Washington, Booker T., 1856–1915. 2. Washington, Booker T., 1856–1915—Philosophy. 3. African American business enterprises—History. 4. African American leadership—History. 5. African Americans—Economic conditions. 6. African American businesspeople—Biography. 7. Entrepreneurship—United States—Biography. 8. Success in business—United States. I. Title.
E185.97.W4B676 2010
370.929–dc22   2010001916

The University Press of Florida is the scholarly publishing agency for the State University System of Florida, comprising Florida A&M University, Florida Atlantic University, Florida Gulf Coast University, Florida International University, Florida State University, New College of Florida, University of Central Florida, University of Florida, University of North Florida, University of South Florida, and University of West Florida.

University Press of Florida
15 Northwest 15th Street
Gainesville, FL 32611-2079
http://www.upf.com

I dedicate this book to the loving memory of my father, David Boston Jr., and my brother, Gregory E. "Keith" Boston.

Contents

Acknowledgments ix

Introduction xi

1. The Setting That Shaped Booker T. Washington's Entrepreneurial Philosophy 1

2. Key Influences that Helped to Mold and Develop Washington's Entrepreneurial Ideas 28

3. The Entrepreneurial Ideas of Booker T. Washington 57

4. The Negro Farmers' Conference: Helping Those Near and Far 75

5. The National Negro Business League: A History and Analysis 91

6. Fundraising, Management, and Industrial Education: Booker T. Washington as a Business Executive and Promoter of the Tuskegee Spirit 114

7. Washington's Broad Economic Influence on African-American Life and History 129

Conclusion: Booker T. Washington, a Shrewd Strategist 145

Notes 153

Bibliography 197

Index 235

Acknowledgments

I would like to thank a number of extraordinary people who helped me to complete my book. I thank Dr. Rashid Hamid, who was a great teacher and mentor to me while I was an undergraduate student at Oneonta State College. I thank Dr. Mwalimu J. Shujaa for sharing with me his extensive knowledge of research methods. I thank the Tuskegee University archivists for guiding me through their archives; Daniel Williams introduced me to some of the descendants of Booker T. Washington, and Cynthia Wilson provided housing during the summer of 1998. I thank all of the librarians who assisted me at the Library of Congress, the Schomberg Center for Research, Cornell University, and the University of Buffalo.

I owe a great debt to my colleagues, Professors Henry Taylor, David Gerber, and Michael Frisch. These scholars scrutinized each of my chapters and helped me elevate them to a still higher level. I thank Professor Henry Taylor for providing encouragement in my moments of doubt. I thank Professor David Gerber for helping me to expand my knowledge of African-American history. I thank Professor Michael Frisch in particular for all his untiring work, his critical eye, and his thoughtful guidance.

Last but not least, I thank my mother for her guidance, encouragement, and the strong example she has exhibited throughout the years.

Introduction

Toward a New Framework for Understanding Booker T. Washington

Booker T. Washington, one of the most controversial leaders in African-American history, rose to prominence as head of Tuskegee Institute in Macon County, Alabama. Using Tuskegee Institute as a power base and launching pad for his efforts to improve the plight of African Americans, Washington became one of the most influential men in the United States. A major key to Washington's success and influence was his business philosophy, which was reflected in his entrepreneurial approach to developing, maintaining, and expanding Tuskegee Institute.

Unfortunately, even after the enormous amount of revisionist work that has been done, the average person still possesses a distorted image of Booker T. Washington. This misperception largely stems from the conflicts between him and W.E.B. Du Bois, as a result of which Washington has often been portrayed as the cowardly Uncle Tom, financed and controlled by white money, leading his people into a new form of slavery. Du Bois, on the other hand, is typically described as the antithesis of Washington. He has often been written of as a courageous, unappreciated, and underfinanced genius who attempted to lead his people to true freedom and equality while fending off formidable foes such as Washington. Both definitions of these two great men, however, are far too simple to hope to explain them or their roles in American history.

An extensive reading of primary source materials from 1900 to 1972 about and by African-American entrepreneurs reveals an image of Booker T. Washington at variance with the popular interpretation. Many of these entrepreneurs, who were respected leaders in their communities, admired Washington, naming their businesses or associations after him and incorporating aspects of his business philosophy into their own. The parents of

Motown Records founder Berry Gordy Jr., for example, named their grocery store after Booker T. Washington. Sherman L. Walker, a funeral hall director and Buffalo, New York's first African-American alderman, and Frank Merriweather Sr., the founder and editor of the *Buffalo Criterion*, named their political club after Booker T. Washington. They and many others clearly did not view Washington as cowardly, an Uncle Tom, or a puppet of white financial interests. They saw him not only as a great man but as a visionary.

This inconsistency led me again to begin a casual reading of literature about and by Booker T. Washington, but this time focusing on materials with entrepreneurship as a framework. Over time, my interest increased and my readings grew intense. As I reread *Up From Slavery*, Washington's business ideas seemed to literally jump out of the pages, and this was also true for other works that I read by him. In studying the standard secondary literature, it seemed that much of it was missing a critical component of Washington's leadership strategy—his business (or entrepreneurial) philosophy. Fragments were present, but none provided a composite, detailed view of Washington's entrepreneurial philosophy. This crucial gap in scholarship my book strives to fill.

Hence, this study examines the entrepreneurial ideas and practices of Booker Taliaferro Washington, which were the foundation of his uplift strategies for African Americans. Numerous works on Washington have been written, the best studies having been conducted since his death and the general publication of his extensive papers. Moreover, underscored below are gaps in the literature that my work addresses.

Most authors do not study Washington as an entrepreneur, nor do they spell out his entrepreneurial philosophy at any great length. In terms of the setting in which Washington operated, most stress the segregated environment but not so much the general economic state or the specific economic conditions in Macon County, Alabama, where Washington lived. Very few even briefly acknowledge Washington as a champion of African-American business development. Indeed, not much scholarly attention has been given to the profundity and dynamics of Washington's advocacy of African-American business development. Washington's entrepreneurial philosophy was much more intricate and complex than scholars have generally characterized it as being, and one of his crucial objectives was to encourage a significant number of African Americans to become "economic producers" rather than simply consumers. Washington functioned as a reform nationalist—one who seeks to reform the state and society—because he sought to correct the low status of African Americans by helping them to become valued assets integral to the state and society. In doing this he reasoned that his actions would reform the state. No scholars recognized Washington as the father of the extensive promotion of twentieth-century African-American business development. None traced Washington's economic progression, comparing and contrasting stages of his development.

In not covering these themes, most studies fail to uncover a crucial component of Washington's leadership program—his entrepreneurial philosophy. My book will cover these themes and in doing so, offer a very different interpretation of Booker T. Washington. Washington was neither an economic separatist nor an accommodationist but rather a strategist with a clear sense of the importance of business development for survival, change, resistance, advancement, and, ultimately, real freedom, empowerment, and equality. He operated shrewdly in a perilous setting.

My book will also reconstruct and evaluate the entrepreneurial ideas of Washington through his speeches and writings.[1] It will demonstrate how he implemented many of his pervasive ideas, and how the execution of them eventually made him a champion of African-American business development. More specifically, I argue that Washington aggressively promoted his entrepreneurial ideas, which were formed in response to the impact that Reconstruction and the nadir had on African Americans, as well as the lessons he learned from significant individuals and events that he dealt with during his formative years. Washington envisioned the implementation of his entrepreneurial philosophy as a progressive strategy for African-American advancement that was grounded in the realities of the nation, particularly the South. I further argue that Washington's school garnered tremendous respect from white citizens throughout Macon County, Alabama, as a result of its economic relationship with them. He reasoned that African Americans throughout the nation could grow to be of indispensable value to their respective communities by providing quality goods and services, thereby solving not only the race problem, but also ultimately freeing and empowering them. This was a crucial aspect of Washington's entrepreneurial philosophy.

This book is divided into two parts: part 1, which is titled "Influences and Ideas," and part 2, which is titled "Implementation: From Ideas to Practice." Part 1 consists of three chapters. Chapter 1 focuses on the political, economic, and social forces at work during Reconstruction (especially during the nadir) that helped to shape and develop Washington's entrepreneurial ideas. Chapter 2 focuses on significant events and individuals that impacted Washington's entrepreneurial philosophy, including those people who confirmed

Washington's entrepreneurial ideas once they had been put forth. Chapter 3, which is one of the most critical chapters in this work, presents Washington's entrepreneurial ideas as constructed from his speeches and writings. Part 2 explores the manner in which Washington promoted and implemented his entrepreneurial ideas, from his activities in the Negro Farmers' Conference to the actual operations of the Tuskegee Institute. Part 2 consists of four chapters. Chapter 4 analyzes the Negro Farmers' Conference that Washington founded, examining its purpose, growth, and its broad intent to make African-American farmers into entrepreneurs. Chapter 5 focuses on the National Negro Business League (NNBL), providing a history and analysis of this organization, which helped to further establish Washington as a champion of African-American business development. Chapter 6 examines Washington's role as an executive at Tuskegee Institute, covering how he raised funds and generated revenue, how he managed his expanding institution, and how he promoted entrepreneurial ideas to his students, hoping that they would continue in the Tuskegee tradition of helping those in need. In attempting to promote further research and argue for the pervasiveness of Washington's entrepreneurial philosophy, chapter 7 begins an examination of Washington's broad economic impact on African-American life and history by analyzing his influence on notable entrepreneurs, African-American leaders, and members of the intelligentsia. After all, Washington wanted his entrepreneurial ideas to aid his race over time, a sentiment that chapter 7 conveys. Finally, my conclusion revisits and highlights major themes and arguments presented throughout this book.

If at times my book seems too ardent in its defense of Washington, know that it is not intentionally so. This issue may arise simply because my study calls for a reinterpretation of the manner in which Washington is seen and presented. In my humble opinion, a significant portion of the secondary literature written about Booker T. Washington is skewed, and because of this some of my analyses and conclusions respond to the prevailing image of him—one that vastly contrasts to my primary source readings about and by Booker T. Washington. Hopefully, my findings can contribute to the revisionist work already done in the effort to uncover the "real" Booker T. Washington.

To date, volumes of scholarly materials have been written and published on Washington's educational philosophy and his supposed accommodationist leadership strategy, but little has been written about his entrepreneurial ideas and practices. Most scholars do not focus on this aspect of Washington's program. Accordingly, the purpose of my study is to further explore this important dimension of Washington so that he can be better understood, and, hopefully, to inspire further research about this American leader.

Listed below are some important abbreviations and their meanings:

ALHCTU	Albon L. Holsey Collection at Tuskegee University Archives
BTWCTU	Booker T. Washington Collection at Tuskegee University Archives
BTWPLC	Booker T. Washington Papers at the Library of Congress
HBTWPVN	Louis Harlan's Edited Booker T. Washington Papers and the Volume Number
JHPCTU	John H. Palmer Collection at Tuskegee University Archives
WLPTU	Warren Logan Papers at Tuskegee University Archives

1

The Setting That Shaped Booker T. Washington's Entrepreneurial Philosophy

The Reconstruction era strongly influenced Booker T. Washington's entrepreneurial ideas, and they were shaped, developed, and reinforced as a result of the political, economic, and social settings of the United States in the post-Reconstruction era, especially the general Southern milieu in the period from 1877 to 1915, specifically as reflected in Tuskegee, Alabama. By focusing on the political, economic, and social dimensions of the national and state settings that Washington lived in, this chapter will underscore and analyze the forces that helped to mold and develop Washington's entrepreneurial ideas. Washington was an optimistic pragmatist who believed that African-American advancement could be achieved more readily by addressing Southern racism than by engaging in Northern competition. He developed his entrepreneurial ideas in response to the racism and discrimination evident during what historian Rayford Logan has termed the nadir (1877–1901) of African-American history.

According to Logan, the period from 1877 to 1901 marked the lowest point in African Americans' quest for equal rights.[1] Logan does not, of course, argue or infer that the nadir was worse than slavery. Rather, he means that the early periods of freedom—the end of slavery leading into the beginning years of Reconstruction—gave African Americans the false sense that they were on the path to quickly being considered first-class citizens, in law and practice. The mid- and post-Reconstruction eras marked a drastic reversal of these hopes and achievements, creating what really was a low point in African-American history. These reversals occurred most observably along political, economic, and social lines and denote what Logan meant by the nadir. For the purposes of this text the nadir will extend from 1877 to 1914, the advent of World War I.

Booker T. Washington's public addresses and published writings usually focus on political events when they discuss the effects of Reconstruction on African Americans.[2] During Reconstruction he saw, heard, and most likely read of African Americans in political positions of power who were helping to make legislation. Simultaneously, he felt that unscrupulous white leaders were using African-American voters to gain political office.[3] These leaders, according to Washington, gained African Americans' confidence and thereby controlled their vote, then used their power to further their own aims regardless, in many cases, of the permanent well-being of African Americans.[4] Similarly, Washington considered it unfortunate that white Southern Democrats did not make more of an effort to gain the confidence and sympathy of African-American voters, who were their neighbors.[5] Consequently, in all political matters, according to Washington, African Americans and Southern Whites were completely alienated from one another. Because of these factors, Washington felt that African Americans would ultimately suffer the most, for he viewed their political power as artificial.[6] Moreover, he felt that Southern white supremacists, who represented the majority of white Southerners, would destroy African-American political power and lead a movement to make them pay for the results of Reconstruction. Thus, for Washington, who lived and worked in the heart of the South, placing greater emphasis on obtaining political power through traditional means was not an effective course of action. He came to see the need for a different strategy—one that he believed would not only make African Americans first-class citizens in law, but in practice as well.

Although Washington did not publicly write much about the endless violence perpetrated against African Americans during Reconstruction, he was acutely aware of it.[7] Unfortunately, no scholar has yet done a comprehensive study of this widespread violence, though it is certainly a story that needs to be told.[8] African Americans were murdered in untold numbers for being members of the Republican Party, voting Republican, being suspected Republicans, or, in essence, being perceived to step out, in any way, of their preordained societal place.[9] Washington, who strongly felt that no constitutional rights should be relinquished or taken away from African Americans, would eventually advocate an economic approach to circumvent the grievous setbacks African Americans suffered during Reconstruction and particularly the nadir.

Thus, as Washington foresaw, the Reconstruction era soon officially ended in 1877 after a compromise was reached regarding which political party would legally claim the deadlocked states of Florida, South Carolina, and Louisiana.[10] The Republican presidential candidate, Rutherford B. Hayes, was given the presidency over Democratic presidential candidate Samuel J. Tilden. In return, the control of the Southern state governments was given back to the ex-Confederate leaders as the few remaining Federal troops were ordered to evacuate the South. Washington was about twenty-one years of age when this compromise went into effect.[11] He had graduated from Hampton Institute and was teaching in Malden, West Virginia. Two years later, he would be called back to Hampton Institute to head an experimental program designed to acculturate Native Americans.

The Political Nadir

National and State Forces

As Booker T. Washington anticipated, the political aftermath of Reconstruction had a devastating impact on African Americans. In 1883 the Supreme Court of the United States declared the Civil Rights Act of 1875 unconstitutional.[12] "[The act had] declared that all persons within the jurisdiction of the United States should be entitled to the full and equal enjoyment of accommodations, advantages, facilities, and privileges of inns, public conveyances on land or water, theaters and other places of public amusement, subject only to the conditions established by law and applicable alike to citizens of every race and color, regardless of any previous condition of servitude."[13] This ruling ignited a storm of protest from African Americans throughout the nation. For instance, at a protest meeting in Washington, D.C., attended by ex-senator Blanche K. Bruce and former abolitionist Frederick Douglass, Douglass said, "the decision places the colored people again outside of the law, and places them, when on steamboats or railroads, or in the theater, restaurant or other public place, at the mercy of any white ruffian who may choose to insult them."[14] Booker T. Washington, unlike Bruce and Douglass, did not openly protest the loss of this civil rights measure.[15] In fact, in an 1884 speech in Madison, Wisconsin, before the National Educational Association, Washington expressed his lack of confidence in exclusively political efforts to improve the plight of African Americans:

> Brains, property, and character for the Negro will settle the question of civil rights. The best course to pursue in regard to the civil rights bill in the South is to let it alone; let it alone and it will settle itself. Good school teachers and plenty of money to pay them will be more potent in settling the race question than many civil rights bills and investigating committees.[16]

It is clear that, like Bruce and Douglass, Washington was against any measures that took constitutional rights away from African Americans. He made this evident years later in his Atlanta Exposition address of 1895 when he said, "It is important and right that all privileges of law be ours."[17] Yet he also felt that his race should make obtaining a solid economic foundation their top priority. That, according to Washington, would ensure all of their rights. Nonetheless, repealing the Civil Rights Act of 1875 signaled to the Democratic South that African Americans could again be relegated to a subordinate place through the use of Jim Crow legislation.

Washington was aware that with the official ending of Reconstruction and the overturning of the Civil Rights Act of 1875 Southern states would seek more sophisticated means of disenfranchising the African-American electorate.[18] Stuffing ballot boxes and throwing away those of African-American voters to ensure white supremacy disturbed the consciences of some Southerners,[19] so they sought legal means to achieve the same ends. In 1890 the state of Mississippi adopted a new constitution which embraced provisions for keeping African-American voters away from the polls. These measures consisted of two parts: Each voter was required to pay a poll tax of two dollars, which could be increased to three, depending upon the actions of local authorities; Each voter was required to read any section of the state constitution "or be able to understand the same when read to him, or to give a reasonable interpretation thereof."[20] Thus, even paying the poll tax did not guarantee the right to vote, for citizens still had to pass the literacy test or interpret aspects of the state constitution or both. Because these voting provisions were made to apply to both African Americans and whites, the Supreme Court approved them.[21] Isaiah T. Montgomery, an associate of Booker T. Washington and the only African-American delegate at the Mississippi State Convention, estimated that the poll tax and literacy requirements would disenfranchise one hundred and twenty-three thousand blacks but only eleven thousand whites.[22]

This plan not only disenfranchised a significant portion of the African-American electorate, but it served as a model for other Southern states to emulate.[23] A similar plan was adopted in South Carolina in 1895, Louisiana in 1898, North Carolina in 1900, Alabama in 1901, Georgia in 1908, and Oklahoma in 1910.[24] In Louisiana, for instance, historian C. Vann Woodward found that on January 1, 1897, there were 164,088 whites and 130,344 African Americans registered to vote, for a total of 294,432 potential voters; on March 17, 1900, only three years later and with Louisiana's new constitution, 125,437 whites and only 5,320 African Americans were registered.[25]

An analysis of the two data sets show 38,651 fewer whites registered to vote compared with 125,024 fewer blacks.[26] The grandfather clause also served to disenfranchise African-American voters. These registration results, as well as all of the plans detailed above, were clear violations of the Fifteenth Amendment of the United States Constitution, which declares, in part, that the right to vote should not be restricted in any way because of "race, color, or previous condition of servitude."[27]

In 1900 a convention was called in Washington's home state of Alabama to amend the state constitution created during Reconstruction. The Alabama Constitutional Convention dealt with numerous issues, but the main two were the disenfranchisement of the African-American electorate and "the division of the public school money between the two races, according to the amount of taxes that each paid."[28] According to Max Bennett Thrasher, a ghostwriter for Washington who interviewed participants at the assembly, the convention consisted of 155 delegates—all of whom were white, though the state was nearly equally divided between blacks and whites. Many of these delegates considered the African American inherently inferior, yet still claimed that they wanted to do justice by him, as well as all other Alabamians. "To deprive the negro of the right to vote or hold office," one Alabama state legislator said, "and then give him no money for his schools, is to put him in a well and cover him up."[29] This idea, according to Thrasher, was openly embraced by a majority of the legislators at the Alabama Constitutional Convention, but in practice, the nadir would continue.

According to Wilford H. Smith, a lawyer who fought legislation that violated the U.S. Constitution and was detrimental to African Americans, and who was secretly financed by Washington to fight the disenfranchisement measures in Alabama, the Alabama Constitutional Convention disenfranchised nearly the entire African-American population in the state. "And in the whole state of Alabama, with about two hundred thousand qualified negro electors," wrote Smith, "only about two thousand five hundred were allowed to register; while all the white men in the State who applied—183,232—were given certificates of qualification for life."[30] Moreover, some upstanding, educated, and relatively wealthy African-American citizens were still denied the vote.[31] To the consternation of some, Washington was permitted to exercise the franchise, but the majority of black Alabamians were not.[32]

In regard to public education, the Alabama Constitutional Convention did not alter the inequitable distribution of funds for African American and white children, although an intense debate did ensue between representatives of counties with high proportions of African Americans and those with high concentrations of whites.³³ It appears that some of the delegates at the convention concurred with Washington when he said, "If you deny the Negro the ballot, then open up the school houses."³⁴ However, they ignored his advocacy of, and belief in, suffrage for most, along with an educational test, property test, or both, but he held that, whatever test might be required, if any, should be applied with equal and exact justice to both races.³⁵

Aware of the unconstitutionality of the disenfranchising practices of the Southern Democrats, Henry Cabot Lodge, a young Republican from Massachusetts, introduced a bill into the House of Representatives in 1891 that called for federal supervision of national elections.³⁶ Although it did pass by a slim margin, Lodge's bill was heatedly debated in the House. The Southern Democratic leadership hated the bill and called it the "Force Bill." When it was introduced in the Senate, Congress adjourned before it could be acted upon, thereby killing the bill. In accordance with his thoughts concerning the overturning of the Civil Rights Bill of 1875—that, left to themselves, racism and voting issues would work themselves out—Washington was against Lodge's proposition.³⁷ He felt that its enforcement would come from outside of the South and would therefore exacerbate racial tensions, causing African Americans to ultimately suffer.

Consonant with the overturning of the Civil Rights Act of 1875 and the defeat of Lodge's bill, the nadir of African-American life and history continued with efforts to legally segregate public conveyances. Beginning with Tennessee in 1881, Southern states began to enact Jim Crow railroad laws: Florida in 1887, Mississippi in 1888, Texas in 1889, Louisiana in 1890, Alabama, Kentucky, Arkansas, and Georgia in 1891, South Carolina in 1898, North Carolina in 1899, Virginia in 1900, Maryland in 1904, and Oklahoma in 1907.³⁸ This segregation on railroad cars insulted and frustrated African-American patrons because their accommodations were generally unequal to those of whites, although their fare was the same. Complaint over this discrimination helped to ignite the *Plessy v. Ferguson* Supreme Court case of 1896, the results of which Booker T. Washington would respond to.

In Louisiana, Homer Plessy, a mixed-race person who could pass for white, was arrested for violating the state law requiring segregated accommodations for intrastate travel. Plessy challenged this law in court by arguing it was unconstitutional. Albion W. Tourgee, a Northerner who had lived in the South during Reconstruction and was critical of the role of ex-Confederates during that era, represented him.³⁹ The State Court of Louisiana rejected Plessy's contention, agreeing with the railroad company that he had violated a state law. Plessy then appealed this decision in the United States

Supreme Court. "With only Justice John Marshall Harlan dissenting, the Supreme Court held that the state law was [a] reasonable exercise of state police power and therefore constitutional."[40] The African-American populace and leadership were disgusted and frustrated with this decision because it meant that they would continue to be degraded on public conveyances and would have no legal means to redress this abuse.

Booker T. Washington was against the *Plessy v. Ferguson* decision because it was unfair and would foster discrimination against African Americans on trains. He was operating within the framework of the South when he said during his 1895 Atlanta Exposition address, "in all things purely social we [the races] can be as separate as the fingers." Although Washington meant interacting with whites on a social basis, which a train setting could certainly foster, he still expected and demanded that just service be granted to African Americans while they patronized public transportation. He wanted African Americans to "pull themselves up" by owning and cultivating land and establishing businesses, for example, but he did not want any unfair laws passed that would adversely impact their quality of life. Concerning who would be permanently hurt by the Supreme Court's momentous decision and in accordance with his view of letting the South settle its racial problems free of federal intervention, Booker T. Washington wrote:

> The United States Supreme Court has recently handed down a decision declaring the separate coach law, or "Jim Crow" car law constitutional. What does this mean? Simply that the separation of colored and white passengers as now practiced in certain Southern States, is lawful and constitutional. This separation may be good law, but it is not good common sense. The difference in the color of the skin is a matter for which nature is responsible. If the Supreme Court can say that it is lawful to compel all persons with black skins to ride in one car, and all with white skins to ride in another, why may it not say that it is lawful to put all yellow people in one car and all white people, whose skin is sun burnt, in another car. Nature has given both their color; or why cannot the courts go further and decide that all men with bald heads must ride in one car and all with red hair still in another. Nature is responsible for all these conditions. But the colored people do not complain so much of the separation, as of the fact that the accommodations, with almost no exceptions, are not equal, still the same price is charged the colored passengers as is charged the white people. Now the point of all this article is not to make a complaint against the

white man or the "Jim Crow Car" law, but it is simply to say that such an unjust law injures the white man, and inconveniences the negro. No race can wrong another race simply because it has power to do so, without being permanently injured in morals, and its ideas of justice. The negro can endure the temporary inconvenience, but the injury to the white man is permanent. It is the one who inflicts the wrong that is hurt, rather than the one on whom the wrong is inflicted. It is for the white man to save himself from this degradation that I plead.[41]

The legal segregation of train cars during the nadir, as anticipated by Frederick Douglass and articulated above by Washington, was undoubtedly a custom that degraded the African-American citizenry. Train vendors were known to store their excess goods in those cars provided for African Americans.[42] Sometimes these goods made the seating arrangements quite congested. Train cars for African Americans were often known to be abnormally uncomfortable, to have no sleeping quarters or bathroom facilities, to be next to smoker cars, where smoke fumes would drift amongst individuals who purchased first-class tickets, or to be in a smoker car comprised of whites, separated by a divider, such that spit and tobacco juice flowed abundantly along the floor on both sides of the car.[43]

Whenever Booker T. Washington's National Negro Business League held its annual conferences in a Southern locale, for instance, delegates were acutely aware of the potential discomforts that they faced while traveling there. Before the Atlanta NNBL meeting in 1906, Cyrus F. Adams, the NNBL transportation agent, sent out a letter to all NNBL delegates throughout the nation. Washington disapproved of a part of Adams's letter, which read: "Afro-American passengers on roads entering the new terminal station at Atlanta are not allowed to use the front entrance, but are compelled to enter and leave the station through a jim-crow [sic] side door, so it is important that when you buy your ticket to demand that it reads via either the following railroads into Atlanta: Seaboard Air Line Railway, Louisville and Nashville Railroad, Georgia Railroad, and Western and Atlantic Railroad."[44] Adams probably thought that he was honestly assisting in preventing further discomforts. Washington, on the other hand, felt that Adams's letter would prevent members from attending the Atlanta meeting.[45] "Besides, I do not think the expression 'Jim-Crowed,'" Washington wrote to Adams, "is a very dignified one to use when addressing a serious body of men like the members of the Business League."[46]

Washington, as a frequent train passenger, was no stranger to the abuses that existed on trains or at train stations. Eighteen years after the *Plessy v.*

Ferguson ruling, for example, Washington and a group of his friends and associates from Tuskegee were leaving Selma, Alabama, by train. Washington's party tried to get some coffee at the Selma station lunchroom. The lunchroom manager refused to serve coffee to any of them inside the lunchroom, which was unsurprising to Washington, who knew the folkways of the South. What was surprising was that this man would not let Washington or members of his party bring coffee into the railcar. In protest, Washington wrote a letter to Charles A. Wickersham, the chairman of the board of that railroad company, emphasizing the value of courtesy when attempting to profit from patrons. In concluding the narration of his experience to Mr. Wickersham, Washington wrote: "I believe you will agree with me that if the same amount of time and energy were spent in trying to be courteous to people, instead of discourteous, it would serve a much higher purpose and bring about a greater degree of success on the part of individuals. I hope you will find it possible to make some arrangement for colored people to be served at all of the eating houses where there is any considerable number of colored people patronizing the road."[47] These experiences and numerous others, in conjunction with the economic and social events occurring during Reconstruction and the nadir, would serve to shape, mold, and expand Washington's entrepreneurial outlook for African-American advancement.

The Economic Nadir

National Forces

The nadir impacted the American economic setting, making it difficult for African Americans to be successful. Compared to the political nadir, Booker T. Washington placed more emphasis on this dimension. Toward the end of the Civil War and during the early days of Reconstruction, freedpeople were given the impression that at the close of the conflict the government would grant them forty acres of arable land and a mule.[48] They, like most Southerners (and peasants everywhere), saw land as integral to obtaining freedom and a livelihood. Confederate slaveholders and Union representatives created this impression among African Americans.[49] Confederate slaveholders, in attempting to propel propertied whites to greater exertions and sacrifices, proclaimed broadly that if the Union Army won the war, Southerners' land would be confiscated and divided among their slaves. In January of 1865, General William T. Sherman issued Special Field Order No. 15, which set aside, for the exclusive use of freedpeople, forty-acre tracts of land between Charleston, South Carolina, and Jacksonville, Florida. Moreover, freedpeo-

Table 1. Statistics on the African-American population from 1880 to 1910

Year	Total population	Percentage of African-American population in the South	Percentage of entire U.S. population
1880	6,580,793	90.5	13.1
1890	7,760,000	90.3	12.3
1900	8,833,994	89.7	11.6
1910	9,827,763	89.0	10.7

Source: U.S. Bureau of the Census, *Negro Population, 1790–1915* (Washington, D.C.: 1918), pp. 29 and 33.

ple were often assured that the forty acres and their mule would be given to them at Christmas time. Though no widespread distribution of land was given to freedpeople, a small number of plots were made available to some of them for purchase through the Homestead Act of 1866. Although Washington does not mention these ideas in his autobiographies, he must have been exposed to some of them.

The granting of forty acres and a mule turned out to be, for the vast majority of freedpeople, including Washington and his family, an utter illusion. Nonetheless, freedpeople continued to strive to improve their condition, mainly remaining in the South, as depicted below in table 1.

The total African American population increased from 1880 to 1910 by 3,246,970 individuals, but their percentage of the overall U.S. population decreased by 2.4 points due to the significant influx of European immigrants into predominately urban Northern locales. Furthermore, the African-American population resided largely in rural areas, as illustrated in table 2 below. But from 1890 to 1910 (and beyond), they were constantly leaving rural areas and moving to towns and cities. In fact, Washington and his family also moved from a rural setting to a town immediately following the Civil War.

Whether in rural or urban locales, the growing African-American population aggressively sought employment. The type of work that they performed during the nadir, according to the U.S. Census reports for the years 1890 to 1910, was primarily agricultural. This can be partially explained by the fact that a strong demand existed for Southern farm laborers and most African Americans lived in rural Southern areas, where they worked as wage laborers, tenants (share or rent), or were landowners. The vast majority, however, were in the tenant category. In 1900, for example, about 557,174 African Americans were tenant farmers, while 187,797 actually owned their

Table 2. Percentage of the African-American population in urban and rural locales from 1890 to 1910

Year	Percentage in urban areas	Percentage in rural areas
1890	19.8	80.2
1900	22.7	77.3
1910	27.4	72.6

Source: U.S. Bureau of the Census, *Negro Population, 1790–1915* (Washington, D.C.: 1918), p. 90.

farms, and in 1910 about 672,964 were tenant farmers, while 218,972 owned their farms.[50] Even Washington farmed during the Tuskegee Institute's early days. Furthermore, in comparing African Americans to whites for the year 1910, about 75 percent of African-American farmers were tenant farmers, while roughly 25 percent were farm owners; among white farmers, about 33 percent were tenant farmers, while approximately 66 percent were farm owners.[51] Table 3 below displays the occupations that African Americans were engaged in from 1890 to 1910, while table 4, for the middle census year of 1900, illustrates the number of African Americans and whites gainfully employed by the industrial sector.

Table 3 reveals, as Washington was fully aware,[52] that the number of African Americans involved in agricultural pursuits steadily increased from 1890 to 1910, with the greatest increase occurring between 1900 and 1910.

Table 3. Numbers (in 1000's) of gainfully employed African Americans by industrial sector, 1890–1910

Sector	1890	1900	1910
Agricultural pursuits	1,728	2,143	2,881
Professional service	34	47	66
Domestic and personal service	957	1,318	1,358
Trade and transportation	146	209	334
Manufacturing and mechanical pursuits	208	275	553
All occupations	3,073	3,992	5,193
Percentage involved in agricultural pursuits	56	54	55
Percentage involved in nonagricultural pursuits	44	46	45

Source: Adapted from *Competition and Coercion* (Cambridge, Mass.: 1980), p. 81, and U.S. Bureau of the Census, *Negro Population, 1790–1915* (Washington, D.C.: 1918), p. 526.

In all other sectors there was steady growth as well. In the professional service sector, which consisted of actors, clergymen, musicians, and teachers, clergymen and teachers comprised the largest subgroups. The domestic and personal service sector consisted of such workers as barbers and hairdressers, unspecified laborers, launderers and laundresses, and servants and waiters, with these last two groups containing the largest number of employees. The trade and transportation sector consisted of numerous types of laborers, with draymen, hackmen, teamsters, porters, and steam railroad employees constituting the largest groups. The number employed by the manufacturing and mechanical pursuits sector was modest, with miners, quarrymen, iron and steel workers, saw and planing mill employees, dressmakers, and tobacco and cigar factory operatives making up some of the most significant categories.[53]

Table 4 reveals that African Americans were predominantly concentrated in agricultural and domestic pursuits, while whites were distributed broadly throughout the five occupational categories. Although about 90 percent of African Americans resided in the South, with a little over 77 percent of them living in rural areas, racism and discrimination undoubtedly affected this skewed labor distribution. In his important work, *The Roots of Black Poverty* (1978), economist Jay R. Mandle, following his in-depth analysis of African-American tenancy, wrote:

> [F]our mechanisms have been identified that tended to confine black laborers to plantation work. Within the South, blacks had little access to land ownership, and industrial employment grew but slowly. Outside of the South, discriminatory hiring practices probably worked to the detriment of blacks, and northern employers were legally discouraged from recruiting black workers. Each of these tends to work in the same direction: to deny southern blacks access to alternative employment opportunities to plantation labor.[54]

Whites in professional services, trade and transportation, and manufacturing and mechanical pursuits proportionately far outnumber African Americans. Though the data in table 4 reflect a national comparison, not a sectional one, considering Mandle's summary, some interesting findings are made—most importantly that African Americans were mainly tenant farmers or domestic laborers.

In addition to being relegated to these unfruitful pursuits, African Americans who migrated to cities found conditions there almost as difficult as those they left.[55] They generally had more trouble finding employment, par-

Table 4. Numbers (in 1000's) of gainfully employed African Americans and whites by industrial sector, for the year 1900

Sector	Blacks	Whites
Agricultural pursuits	2,143	8,179
Professional service	47	1,210
Domestic and personal service	1,318	4,191
Trade and transportation	209	4,541
Manufacturing and mechanical pursuits	275	6,793
All occupations	3,992	24,914
Percentage involved in agricultural pursuits	54	33
Percentage involved in nonagricultural pursuits	46	67

Source: Adapted from W.E.B. Du Bois, "The Negro American Artisan," *The Atlanta University Publication* (New York: Arno Press and *New York Times*, 1968), p. 41, and the U.S. Bureau of the Census, *Negro Population, 1790–1915* (Washington, D.C.: 1918), p. 526.

ticularly as their numbers increased. A white charity worker in the Seventh Ward of Philadelphia, for example, expressed the following concerning poor, unemployed African Americans:

> We do have a hard time in helping colored people; and permanent relief seems often most discouraging. If we send a man to a place where he can get work, the white men are apt to object.[56]

She then told Richard R. Wright Jr., a social scientist who published numerous scholarly articles in the *Southern Workman*, of a skilled mechanic she had sent to seek work from a certain firm. "A few days later the manager said he was sorry, but white men would not work with the Negro."[57]

African Americans were also generally unwelcome in labor unions. From the early stages of his life, Washington did not place much faith in them. The American Federation of Labor (A.F.L.), an organization of mainly self-governing craft unions, became influential around 1886. In its early years, the A.F.L. took a strong position against racial discrimination, but being a confederation of unions, it eventually capitulated to the demands of many local unions that preferred an exclusionary policy.[58] Thus, the new manufacturing jobs opening in cities were not commonly made available to African Americans until the advent of World War I, as the war caused a white male labor shortage and precipitated the first Great Migration.[59] Even so, the jobs which became available were usually poorly remunerative, dirty, and dangerous; in essence, they were the jobs that whites were reluctant to take. Hence, finding gainful employment in either the South or the North was no easy task for the African American of the nadir.

Rather than seek employment, some African Americans became entrepreneurs during the nadir. Washington met many of them on his national speaking tours following his Atlanta Exposition address. However, many of these entrepreneurs were compelled to cater almost exclusively to African-American consumers. According to recent research, this was not the case for free blacks from the colonial-American period up until the Civil War.[60] Free blacks conducted business in the open market in such places as New York City, Chicago, Philadelphia, and Cleveland. It was only after slavery that they slowly began to be forced to engage in business strictly amongst themselves, ultimately limiting their revenues and profits. Despite the obstacles, African Americans did form businesses, mainly in urban locales where their market was largest.[61]

At the turn of the century, W.E.B. Du Bois and his associates at Atlanta University conducted the best study available on late-nineteenth-century African-American entrepreneurs—one which Washington would make great use of. Titled "The Negro in Business," the research was published in 1899. The U.S. Census Report of 1890 indicated that there were 8,216 African-American entrepreneurs; Du Bois, deducing that significant errors existed in these calculations, estimated that there were 5,000 African-American businesses in the United States.[62] Du Bois' estimation was based on his analyses and the surveys that Atlanta University sent out to determine the number of African-American businesses nationwide. Of these surveys, which covered 30 different states and territories, 1,906 were returned and analyzed. The majority of them are summarized below in table 5.

As table 5 indicates, most African-American businesses were small and capitalized with an initial investment of between $100 and $2,500. Seventy-nine percent of the initial capital invested was less than $2,500 per business, with only 12 businesses representing investments of $50,000 or more. The total actual amount invested, as reported by the survey participants who reported their initial capital investment, was $5,691,137, while $93,500 was the estimated capital of the unknown cases. Regarding the 3,094 businesses not included in the study or the remaining portion of the 5,000 African-American-owned businesses that Du Bois estimated operated in the United States in 1899, the possible aggregate startup capital of these unreported businesses was estimated to be $3,000,000. Thus, with the total actual amounts invested summed, the estimated total capital invested by African Americans in business, according to Du Bois and his associates at Atlanta University,

Table 5. Summary of capital invested to start African-American businesses since the abolition of slavery

Capital invested	Number of businesses
Under $100	16
$100–500	312
$500–1,000	415
$1,000–2,500	586
$2,500–5,000	183
$5,000–10,000	115
$10,000–50,000	45
$50,000 and over	12
Total actual amount invested	$5,691,137
Capital unknown	170
Estimated capital of the unknown cases	$93,500
Possible capital of 3,094 unreported businesses	$3,000,000
Estimated total capital invested by African Americans in business	$8,784,637

Source: Adapted from W.E.B. Du Bois, "The Negro in Business," *The Atlanta University Publication* (New York: Arno Press and *New York Times*, 1968), p. 19.

was $8,784,637. This is a small figure when set beside business startup expenditures in the overall American economy,[63] as some of the most common African-American businesses were retail merchants, grocers, saloon keepers, hotel keepers, livery stable keepers, druggists, and publishers, all of which were mainly small enterprises. Nevertheless, Du Bois, like Washington later would, still considered the $8,784,637 figure a great accomplishment considering the poverty and educational background of freedpeople.[64]

As noted earlier, one reason why this figure was relatively small is that most African-American entrepreneurs, during and after the nadir, were generally beginning to be excluded from conducting business in the open market by restrictive governmental legislation, or more specifically, *Plessy v. Ferguson*.[65] John Sibley Butler, in his work *Entrepreneurship and Self-Help Among Black Americans: A Reconsideration of Race and Economics* (1991), used "Economic Detour Theory" as an explanation for the effects of segregation on African-American entrepreneurs in Southern and Northern settings. The components of Economic Detour Theory are theoretical constructs that Butler derived from Merah S. Stewart's *An Economic Detour: A History of Insurance in the Lives of American Negroes* (1940). Economic Detour Theory argues that African-American entrepreneurs, especially in the period following the Civil War, were restricted by law or social customs from operating their businesses in the open market. This restriction limited the potential growth of African-American-owned-and-operated businesses, which in turn limited profits earned and payroll size.[66] Thus, because this economic detour was generally restricted to a single market, African-American entrepreneurs were placed at a disadvantage—in short, the plea Washington made in his Atlanta Exposition address for fair play was summarily ignored.

State Forces

Similar patterns are evident when the focus is shifted from the national economic setting to the state in which Booker T. Washington's career flourished. According to the U.S. Census reports, Alabama's total population for the years 1890, 1900, and 1910 was 1,512,207, 1,828,697, and 2,138,093 respectively. In 1890 and 1900, African Americans comprised about 45 percent of the total population, while in 1910 the figure was about 42.5 percent. As depicted in table 6 below, African Americans made up a significant portion of Alabama's population.

Furthermore, the number of people migrating to urban locales in Alabama increased with the population. Growing urbanization was a trend occurring throughout the nation. African Americans, like Americans in general, were steadily migrating to towns and cities. Hence, in 1890, 10.3 percent of Alabama's African-American population lived in urban settings, while in 1900 the figure had grown to 11.9 percent, and by 1910, 17.2 percent.[67] According to U.S. Census data for black Alabamians 10 years of age and older, for the year 1910, 90.6 percent of males were gainfully employed, as were 63.7 percent of females.[68] Entire families were compelled to work merely to survive, and the vast majority of both males and females unsurprisingly worked in agricultural pursuits.[69] Out of 262,901 farmers in Alabama in 1910, 110,387 were African-American, while the remaining 152,458 were white.[70] Of these 110,443 African-American farmers, 17,047 were actual farm owners, with 58.3 percent of those holding no mortgages on their property. Ninety-three thousand two hundred and eighty-eight were tenant farmers (share or rent), and 52 were listed as managers of farms.[71] An Alabama State Commission sent to evaluate Tuskegee Institute in 1914 gave similar figures concerning African-American farmers.[72]

Census data on African-American tenant farmers for the years 1900 and 1910 reveal that significant growth took place, which reflects more of the effects of the nadir. In 1900 there were 79,887 tenant farmers in Alabama, and,

Table 6. Alabama's population from 1890 to 1910

Racial group	1890	1900	1910
Black	678,489	827,307	908,282
White	833,718	1,001,152	1,228,832
Indian	no data	177	909
Other	no data	61	70
Total	1,512,207	1,828,697	2,138,093

Source: U.S. Bureau of the Census, *Negro Population, 1790–1915* (Washington, D.C.: 1918), pp. 43 and 44. The "Other" category includes Chinese, Japanese, and all other racial groups.

as mentioned above, 93,288 in 1910, yielding a difference of 13,401.[73] This trend also occurred in other Black Belt states such as South Carolina, Georgia, Mississippi, Arkansas, Louisiana, and Texas.[74] After agricultural pursuits, African-American males were clustered in the categories of domestic and personal service and manufacturing and mechanical pursuits.[75] After agriculture, females were concentrated in domestic and personal service occupations.[76]

Washington lived in Tuskegee, Alabama, in Macon County, most of his adult life. When he first arrived there in early June of 1881, he made a personal tour of the county.[77] In his view, the people of Macon County exhibited patterns similar to those found elsewhere in the state. First of all, the African-American population of Macon County, like that of the state, made up a significant portion of the total. In 1910 there were 22,039 African Americans in Macon County, comprising 84.6 percent of the total population.[78] In the town of Tuskegee, Washington wrote that when he first arrived, there were "about 2,000 inhabitants, nearly one half of whom were coloured."[79] By 1910, 29 years later, the African-American population had increased to 2,803 individuals.[80] Most African Americans in Macon County were engaged in agricultural pursuits. They were wage laborers, sharecroppers, renters, or landowners.[81] Wage earning was a practice that began immediately after the Civil War.[82] Former slaves were paid a wage to work on farms and plantations, usually on a daily, weekly, or monthly basis. Freedpeople in the South disliked this practice, because they longed for their own land and feared the very real possibility of being cheated by their former owners. Sharecropping was the next labor arrangement to emerge during Reconstruction. It occurred mainly between former slaves and their ex-owners and involved farmers sharing at least half of their crop yields with their landlords.[83] During Washington's lifetime, this practice was pervasive in Macon County. Farm operators in Macon County who advanced beyond sharecropping often became land renters or owners, and those who owned land belonged to the most respected and desirable labor class.[84]

Of the four categories of farm operators listed above, according to Thomas J. Edwards, a farm field agent for Tuskegee Institute in the early 1900s, most in Macon County were sharecroppers or land renters.[85] Renting, according to Edwards, was a step up from sharecropping.[86] In 1890 one thousand sixty-eight African-American and white renters lived in Macon County, as well as 1,113 sharecroppers.[87] According to the agricultural census for 1900, the first census in which white and African-American renters and sharecroppers were counted separately, there were 2,097 African-American renters in Macon County and 760 African-American sharecroppers.[88] Nevertheless, as Washington often pointed out, whether farmers in Macon County were sharecroppers or renters, they generally were in debt as a result of liens on their crops or exorbitant charges for credit from landlords, merchants, or other financiers.[89] As will be conveyed in chapters 4 and 5, Washington would later employ various strategies to fight the effects of the economic, political, and social nadirs.

The Social-Cultural Nadir

In the social (or cultural) environment, which was affected by the political and economic setting of the nation, the effects of the nadir are evident as well. Immediately after the United States slavery era, a change in the social relationship between African Americans and whites occurred. During slavery no confusion existed among slaves and whites regarding their social status. Whites were free and had their own class structure; slaves and even free blacks were generally in a caste state beneath all whites, rich or poor, and lacked federal constitutional rights. White society by and large perceived slaves and free blacks to be in their "place" as long as they behaved according to their norms and were deferential to all whites. Moreover, for poor whites, as Washington was well aware, this racial caste system was even more important, because they were at the bottom of the white class structure.[90] Slaves and free blacks that did not conform to these norms were punished, often severely.

During Reconstruction, the political positions and influence gained by African Americans on the federal, state, and local levels were a novelty to both them and the whites. Many African Americans felt that they were now citizens, involved in the process of shaping their own destinies and that of society in general. Many whites, particularly Southern whites, held a different view. They felt that African Americans were inferior to them and thus should not be in leadership positions over them. To suggest otherwise was going against not only the customs of society but, in their minds, nature as well. In addition, many of them were only comfortable with African Americans being second-, third-, or even fourth-class citizens; after all, this is what they had grown accustomed to. Consequently, during Reconstruction and the nadir, Washington witnessed or learned of many whites working incessantly to relegate African Americans to a low stratum in the social order, effectively a racial caste station similar to that which existed during slavery.

Many African Americans, Washington included, also witnessed or learned of the racial caste system's effects—that is, the creation of a "color line" or a racial divide.[91] For example, during the nadir and even afterward, it was customary that adult African-American men and women were generally not addressed by Southern whites as Ms., Mrs., or Mr., especially those individuals employed by whites, which as a group included most African Americans. "The women [were] called, 'Cook,' or 'Nurse,' or 'Mammy,' or 'Mary Jane,' or 'Lou,' or 'Dilcey,' as the case might be, and men [were] called 'Bob,' or 'Boy,' or 'Old Man,' or 'Uncle Bill,' or 'Pate,'" for example.[92] And it was not unusual, even in the presence of their employees, for white employers to refer to African-American employees as their "niggers."[93] Historian Edward L. Ayers, author of *The Promise of the New South* (1992), even cited an incident in which a Southern youth referred to a respected African-American man as Mr. Jones. The boy's aunt quickly corrected him. "No, son. Robert Jones is a nigger. You don't say 'mister' when you speak of a nigger. You don't say 'Mr. Jones,' you say 'nigger Jones.'"[94] Even before Washington was about to present his famous Atlanta Exposition address in 1895, Rufus B. Bullock, the ex-governor of Georgia, hesitantly introduced him as a great Southern educator and "a representative of Negro enterprise and Negro civilization." Upon seeing that he was an African American, the majority of the white audience immediately stopped applauding, as though wondering to themselves, "What's Washington doing up on that stage?"[95] Moreover, during his address, Washington's daughter, Portia, "remembered seeing a mob of rednecks [poor, racist whites] formed up beside the stage waiting to set upon [her father] if he had said but one word against the South."[96] In this instance he was perceived to be not only out of his societal place but also in violation of the color line. African Americans experienced more overt discrimination in the South than in the North, though the racial caste system became more evident there when African Americans started populating the area in greater numbers, during and after the first Great Migration.[97]

Lynching and race riots were two of the most notorious and memorable aspects of the nadir, and Washington knew they were employed as control mechanisms to make African Americans stay in their "preordained" societal place.[98] Lynching is defined as the putting to death of a human being by mob action without legal sanction.[99] African Americans were lynched for a multitude of supposed reasons, such as being involved in political activities, debating the price of strawberries, not answering to "boy," and refusing to compel one's wife to work in the fields. The charge of "raping" a white woman, however, was the justification most often used to lynch an African-American male.[100] The alleged act of rape inspired the thought of an African-American male having sexual relations with a white woman and drove the predominately white male mobs into a frenzy, causing them not only to kill the alleged perpetrator but also to wreak havoc on the local African-American community as further retribution.[101] An expression commonly used after a lynching was, "The niggers are now much better behaved and show the proper deference to whites."[102]

Numerous African Americans were lynched during the nadir. Tuskegee Institute's research department, under the direction of Monroe N. Work, compiled excellent records on lynching rates.[103] Booker T. Washington must have examined a number of these reports. During the 1880s, the lynching of African Americans occurred at a steady rate. From 1882 to 1915, the Tuskegee Institute records indicate that 2,783 African Americans were lynched by mobs, mostly in the following states, ranked in descending order of deaths, of which all but one were in the Black Belt: Mississippi, Georgia, Texas, Louisiana, Alabama, Arkansas, South Carolina, and Kentucky.[104] More specifically, in 1882, 49 African Americans were lynched, while in 1885 that figure had grown to 74; by 1899, it was 94. The 1890s marked the high point of lynchings, with the average per year around 111. Within that decade, 1892 was the year in which the most lynchings occurred: 161. This statistical peak was probably related to the events that led to the Panic of 1893, which in turn caused an agricultural depression that reduced the price of farm goods. Records show that most lynching took place in the months of May, June, July, and August, with November, January, February, and April having the fewest lynchings.[105] This pattern was probably due to increased human interaction during the summer period, and, among several other factors, cyclical demand for labor in the agricultural South (lynching was also a form of labor control).[106]

Some of Washington's biographers have written of his outspoken stance against lynching and his disgust for the practice.[107] For example, according to Basil Mathews, Washington was scheduled to address an audience in Jacksonville, Florida, where two African Americans had been accused of murdering a white person.[108] These African Americans had been apprehended, and it was expected that they might be lynched. Washington's friends begged him to cancel his address, but Washington, knowing that a lynching could possibly take place, was all the more determined to give his address. "As he and his friends were being driven to the hall in Jacksonville to address a mixed audience, an excited gang of white men stopped one car and demanded furiously that Booker Washington should be handed over to them. Finding that the occupant of the car was a Negro of their own city whom they respected, they let him pass."[109] If Washington had in fact been in that car, he may have been lynched, especially considering that, of the Southern states, Florida had the highest number of lynchings per 100,000 African Americans—79.8, which was 27 more than the next-ranked state, Mississippi.[110] Nevertheless, as Washington was speaking, howls from the frenzied mob could be heard in the hall as they rushed to the city jail, desperately hoping to lynch the accused. Upon hearing this, to the dismay of his friends, Washington boldly spoke out against the horror and lawlessness of lynching.[111] Instead of being attacked, Washington was enthusiastically applauded by the mixed audience. Moreover, Washington wrote articles criticizing this widespread practice. In a 1904 article, he wrote: "Is it not possible for pulpit and press to speak out against these burnings in a manner that shall arouse a public sentiment that will compel the mob to cease insulting our courts, our Governors and legal authority; cease bringing shame and ridicule upon our Christian civilization?"[112] Washington, who lived in the South all of his life and had no intentions of leaving, unlike many of the more outspoken critics of lynching (Ida B. Wells-Barnett and W.E.B. Du Bois, for example), championed anti-lynching but simultaneously appealed to the morals of influential whites to help abate the lawless practice. He reasoned that since African Americans were mainly Southerners and would most likely have to work out their salvation in the South, they needed to develop a healthy working relationship with white Southerners, their neighbors. Washington's approach was nonconfrontational.

Washington's reasoning, along with his profound words, was lost on individuals like Mississippi's racist governor, James K. Vardaman, who openly promoted the subjugation of African Americans through extralegal and legal means. After Washington had completed his lecture tour through the state of Mississippi, which Vardaman vehemently disapproved of, lynching victims' bodies were left hanging by the railroad tracks. Allegedly, many of the lynchers hoped that Washington would view them as his train passed.[113] Vardaman himself proclaimed that there would be more African-American lynching victims if Washington made any further speeches in Mississippi.[114]

Although lynchings occurred during the nadir mainly in the South, the North was no haven for African Americans, as Washington had often written and exclaimed. As long as African Americans existed in small numbers in Northern locales, not much attention was paid to their presence. When their numbers significantly increased, however, they began to be seen as a threat, and restrictive covenants and gentlemen's agreements were formulated between realtors to confine them to limited areas.[115] In such urban settings, conflicts usually arose between African Americans and whites on the borders of their separate communities. When the African-American population sought to find quarters beyond their areas of confinement, attempting to spread into white communities, conflict arose and often escalated into race riots. Moreover, white realtors, along with the white population, generally prohibited the natural expansion of a growing African-American population, which further increased the population density of African-American communities.

The Springfield, Ohio, Riot of 1904 is an excellent example of the issue mentioned above.[116] As more African Americans migrated into Springfield, Ohio, their presence grew to be a concern, and racial tensions heightened. An African American got into an altercation with a white police officer, ultimately shooting and killing him. After he was apprehended and placed in jail, a white mob broke into the jail and killed the African-American prisoner within. They then hung his body upon a telegraph pole and riddled it with bullets. However, even this action did not satisfy the mob, so they proceeded to wreak havoc on the African-American section of town, injuring people and destroying property.

The race riot that "shook and shocked" America and sparked the formation of the National Association for the Advancement of Colored People (NAACP) was one which occurred in Springfield, Illinois, in 1908.[117] In a case similar to the Rosewood, Florida, massacre,[118] a white woman claimed that she had been dragged from her bed and raped by an African-American man, George Richardson, who had been working in her neighborhood. Richardson, who insisted upon his innocence, was nonetheless arrested and jailed. Though the white woman who cried rape later admitted to Richardson's innocence, as well as that she had been severely beaten by a white man whose identity she refused to disclose, it did not matter—Richardson's blood was desperately wanted. A mob formed in front of the jail and demanded that the sheriff turn Richardson over to them. The sheriff sternly refused. A restaurant owner who knew that the sheriff was the type of man who would rather die than surrender a prisoner agreed to transport Richardson and another African-American prisoner to Bloomington, Illinois. Fire trucks were driven past the jail to divert the mob's attention so that the prisoners could be taken safely out the back door. When the people in the mob realized that they had been duped, they grew furious. Since the restaurant owner had transported the prisoners to safety, they demolished his restaurant in retaliation and then proceeded to the African-American section of town, killing two people, destroying thousands of dollars worth of property, and forcing numerous African Americans to leave town. When Washington first heard of the Springfield, Illinois, race riot, he was again disgusted and issued the following statement from Baltimore, Maryland, while attending a NNBL meeting:

> Mob justice undermines the very foundation upon which our civilization rests, viz., respect for the law and confidence of its security. There are, in my opinion, two remedies—First of all, let us unite in a determined effort everywhere to see that the law is enforced, that all people at all times and all places see that the man charged with a crime is given a fair trial.
>
> Secondly, let all good citizens unite in an effort to rid the communities, especially the large cities, of the idle, vicious and gambling element. And in this connection I would not be just and would not be frank unless I stated that the betters of the black race could use their influence, especially in the cities, to see that the idle element that lives by its wits without permanent or reliable occupation or place of abode is either reformed or gotten rid of in some manner. In most cases it is this element that furnishes the powder for explosions.[119]

Washington's identification of a segment of the African-American population that could potentially incite racial conflicts was not applicable to the Springfield, Illinois, case since Richardson was innocent of any wrongdoings.

State Forces

As in much of the nation, the racial caste system was evident throughout Alabama, and those African Americans, including Washington, who did not adhere to the social norms could be severely punished. Nate Shaw, a cotton farmer born in Alabama in 1885, constantly informed readers of his autobiography of the deference that African Americans were compelled to give whites as a result of the Jim Crow system they lived under: "It's stamped in me, in my mind, the way I been treated, the way I have seed other colored people treated—couldn't never go by what you think or say, had to come up to the white man's orders."[120] This deference not only applied at work as Shaw alludes to, but in the social arena as well. In the state of Alabama, African Americans were expected to yield to whites while walking on sidewalks; they were not encouraged to shop in town at random, but only on a designated day and time; if they were allowed to attend certain theaters, they were compelled to sit in separate sections, usually in the balcony; they were excluded from public parks while whites were there; and they were buried in separate cemeteries or separate sections of cemeteries. Besides referring to African Americans as "niggers," it was also a common practice for whites to refer to them as "darkies" or "coons."[121]

Regardless of these facts, Washington publicly proclaimed before the Alabama State Negro Business League that there was very little discussion of the race problem in Alabama:

> The Negroes in the state of Alabama have this advantage as compared with members of our race in other parts of the country. Here in our state one hears very little discussion of the race problem, especially on the part of politicians and public men. It is very seldom that in any campaign, the race question is raised in a way to create bitterness and to disturb the friendly relations between the two races. This is a matter for great congratulation and satisfaction on the part of both Negroes and white people.[122]

Although Washington was one who measured his words to fit his audience, why he articulated this idea is not clear, especially considering that he spoke before an African-American audience. Perhaps he was thinking that Alabama did not have outspoken demagogues such as Hoke Smith of Georgia, James K. Vardaman of Mississippi, or Ben Tillman of South Carolina. If so, he was correct. The uproar, however, even in Alabama, that Booker T. Washington's meal in the White House with President Theodore Roosevelt caused, or the disenfranchisement efforts of the Alabama Constitutional Convention of 1900 attest that racial tensions were evident and easily aroused. Furthermore, the fact that a bill was introduced in the state legislature designed to separate African American and white passengers in train sleeping cars,[123] or that another was proposed crafted to exclude African Americans from the Republican Party in Alabama cast even further doubt on Washington's claim.[124] Nonetheless, Washington vigorously fought to defeat these bills.

Furthermore, the lynching issue in Alabama was reflective of discussions and ideas about race. As mentioned earlier, lynching was pervasive in Alabama. The Tuskegee Institute's lynching records reveal that from 1882 to 1968, 299 African Americans were lynched,[125] while from 1880 to 1930, Tolnay and Beck's records maintain that 262 African Americans met that fate.[126] Most of the lynching took place during the nadir of African-American history, as an examination of the Tuskegee records reveals. More specifically, according to Ray Stannard Baker, author of *Following the Color Line* (1908), there were 5 lynchings in Alabama in 1906 and 13 in 1907.[127] A black Alabamian was lynched in 1910 for having a secret relationship with a white woman of which a mixed-race child was born.[128] As a result of these kinds of events as well as other factors, the National Colored Immigration and Commercial Association of Montgomery, Alabama, which was located within forty miles of Washington's hometown of Tuskegee, adopted a petition for President Roosevelt and Congress to appropriate one hundred million dollars to the organization "to secure transportation of members of their race who desire to settle in Liberia."[129] This kind of information should make one seriously question Washington's above statement. Again, he perhaps was comparing racial tensions in Alabama to those in other states where conditions seemed worse, though the nadir's effects were prevalent in all the Southern states. Moreover, publicly, Washington preferred to remain positive, and being cognizant of Southern white racism, he may not have wanted to say or do anything that would antagonize whites, at least not until African Americans became a strong, indispensable asset to the nation. The other possibility is that he actually believed the statements he made before his African-American audience.

The norms of Tuskegee, Alabama, like those of the state in general, mandated that African Americans give deference to whites. When Washington arrived in Tuskegee in 1881, the first facility he acquired for his school was a dilapidated shanty near an African-American Methodist church.[130] He learned at some point that three African-American men were murdered in that building simply because it was believed that they were discussing politics.[131] Even so, Washington used the shack and the Methodist church (which still stands today). One day, Washington was walking along a road, headed to his school, when a white woman saw him and, taking him for one of her servants, ordered him to chop wood.[132] Washington, who was dressed in his school attire, rolled up his sleeves and began chopping the wood as the woman had demanded. When a female servant eventually told the woman who Washington was, after he had completed the task and left, she was extremely embarrassed. She went to Washington's school, found him, and apologized. As a result of this interaction, she became a friend of the school and a supporter of its expansion efforts. Washington was sensitive to the fact that whites in the Tuskegee community had fears and doubts about a growing African-American school in their midst.[133] Consequently, as mentioned earlier, he did not want to do anything to antagonize them.

Unsurprisingly, segregation existed in the town of Tuskegee and throughout Macon County. African Americans and whites that attended school went to separate ones. They attended different places of worship, and often had voting records which were diametrically opposed to one another.[134] They, as a rule, were buried in separate cemeteries, as noted by a writer: "Just outside of the village [of Tuskegee] is the white folks' cemetery, of which they are very proud, for it is full of monuments and receives constant care."[135] Commenting further, he wrote:

> The negroes have a separate cemetery. If a colored person was to be buried among the whites, the latter would all rise from their graves in indignation. How they tolerate the "niggers" in heaven is a mystery, unless there is a kitchen there.[136]

There was strict punishment for those African Americans who stepped out of their "designated place." Thomas Harris, an African-American lawyer, barely escaped being lynched by a white mob because many in the white community felt that he was arrogant.[137] George W. Lovejoy, a student at Tuskegee Institute, wrote a letter to a Mississippi African-American newspaper protesting lynching and the double standards of interracial relationships.[138] As a result, many whites in the Tuskegee community who had read or heard of the letter advised Lovejoy to leave the school and the town, and he did so. Some whites in the surrounding community questioned the intent of Tuskegee Institute after the Lovejoy incident. "Washington was away, but the teachers hastily sent word that they 'rebuked Lovejoy for his folly and advised him to leave school.' On return, Washington sent a card to the newspaper. 'It has always been and is now the policy of the Normal School to remain free from politics and the discussion of race questions that tend to stir up strife between the races, and whenever this policy is violated it is done without the approbation of those in charge of the school,' he wrote."[139] Although Washington's response seems somewhat muted, in the larger context, he believed that his economic program would help redefine and equalize the unhealthy black-white interactions stemming from slavery, Reconstruction, and the nadir, thereby ending belief in the African-American's inferiority.

Hence, as demonstrated above, Booker T. Washington's entrepreneurial ideas and practices would be largely shaped and developed by the political, economic, and social forces that dominated the national and state arenas during Reconstruction but especially during the nadir of African-American history. These forces acted as hegemonic ones upon him. Washington—observing that political participation alone, without a solid economic foundation, left his race at the mercy of their enemies—would search for a strategy that he felt would be people-friendly and proactive and would ultimately lead his race to real freedom and equality. In attempting to counter the adverse effects of Reconstruction and the nadir, Washington would develop an economic program that he believed, if practiced on a broad scale, would ultimately make African Americans an economic force to be reckoned with. In his mind, he equated economic power with true freedom and equality.

Consequently, Washington was not the simple accommodationist that historians have characterized him as—he was a vastly more complex figure. In the heart of the South, he would examine the results of Reconstruction and the nadir and propose an uplift and empowerment strategy. More concisely, he operated as a judicious, proactive leader who believed that African Americans could advance, despite numerous barriers, and greatly improve race relations by significantly contributing to the well-being of their surrounding communities. This, he believed, would make them an integral component of the South.

Washington was undoubtedly profoundly influenced by the political, economic, and social forces evident during Reconstruction and the nadir. We shall focus next on specific individuals, groups, and other forces that served to further shape, develop, reinforce, and expand Washington's entrepreneurial ideas and practices. This approach will contribute toward an even greater understanding of Washington's economic ideas and practices and how he hoped they would be implemented to obtain genuine freedom and empowerment.

2

Key Influences that Helped to Mold and Develop Washington's Entrepreneurial Ideas

Booker T. Washington's entrepreneurial ideas were influenced by a multitude of individuals and events throughout his relatively short life. By his early adult years, twenty-eight to thirty-two, his entrepreneurial philosophy had been established. Influences after these years extended his essential philosophy but mainly just reinforced it. In analyzing Washington's growth, it is not always clear which individuals or events influenced him the most profoundly. It is clear, however, that certain people and happenings impacted his outlook regarding business development, especially as related to uplifting African Americans during the nadir.

Thus, in providing a conceptual framework to begin to describe and understand the influences that shaped, developed, and reinforced Washington's entrepreneurial ideas, a dual-dimensional and multi-thematic analytical approach is employed. In the first dimension, I focus on influences that helped to mold and shape those core values within Washington that are at the root of his entrepreneurial philosophy, such as maintaining an organized system for working, a philosophy of labor, and high moral standards. Analyzing Washington's sense of group consciousness, his initial introduction to the Protestant work ethic, and his exposure to business expansion in the South is necessary to help underscore his core values. In the second dimension, practical business influences on Washington are analyzed, such as his observation and evaluation of local and national entrepreneurs and his exposure to accounting methods and procedures. Washington's early Tuskegee business influences, his business influences from captains of industry, and ideas garnered from key associates in the NNBL are the themes analyzed in the second dimension. Accordingly, this dual-dimensional and multi-thematic approach serves to accentuate key influences that contributed to the formation of Washington's entrepreneurial philosophy.

Moreover, using this approach serves well because a critical examination of Washington's life discloses that his entrepreneurial philosophy contained a strong group component that developed during his youth and young adulthood, compelling him to always be conscious of and concerned about the plight of his race. Washington's entrepreneurial philosophy was also highly influenced by the Protestant work ethic, business expansion throughout the nation (but mainly in the South), his relationships with key individuals who helped shape his budding business philosophy, and later by his relationships with important individuals who expanded or reinforced his established entrepreneurial philosophy. Hence, Washington's core values and practical business influences, along with Reconstruction and the nadir, helped to establish his entrepreneurial philosophy.

Core Value Influences on Washington

Group Consciousness

The experiences that Booker T. Washington shared with the rest of his race and his drive for upward mobility caused him to develop a "group-advancement" philosophy in regard to African-American entrepreneurship (along with his industrial educational program).[1] He was never an advocate of pure individualism, even during an age of laissez-faire capitalism. He always promoted the progress of his race and assistance for its least fortunate members. The formation of this mindset extends back to Washington's early years, when he first became aware that his race was an oppressed group.

Reflecting on his youth during the Reconstruction period, Washington wrote of its effects not on himself but on his race: "In many cases it seemed to me that the ignorance of my race was being used as a tool with which to help [elect] white men into office, and that there was an element in the North which wanted to punish the Southern white men by forcing the Negro into positions over the heads of the Southern whites. I felt that the Negro would be the one to suffer for this in the end."[2] Washington was right, because the nadir's effects in the South were largely in response to African-American advancements during Reconstruction. Even in Washington's adolescent years, which were still during Reconstruction, the sense of group consciousness was evident. When he wrote of his decision to go to Hampton Institute, he made it clear that members of his community supported him. Even some of the older members, who had been slaves most of their lives and had never thought that they would live to see a member of their race leave home to attend a boarding school, gave Washington a nickel, a quarter, or a handkerchief.[3] These impoverished people gave whatever they could spare to help him, and Washington was touched by their gestures; throughout the remainder of his life he held older people in high regard.[4] After a two-year absence, Washington returned to visit his community in Malden, West Virginia. He understood that his educational achievements were not just his, but belonged to the entire community. The community expected him to visit each household, share his experiences at Hampton Institute, and speak before the Sunday school and church.[5] Washington performed these duties because he understood that he was an emissary of the collective community that aspired to education and a better life.

When Washington opened Tuskegee Institute in July of 1881, he never sought to run or expand the school on his own. He considered it the duty of his race, his prospective staff, and himself. In his view, it was to be a group effort. Before opening the school, Washington canvassed Macon County seeking support and students. He visited numerous churches and homes, speaking to citizens about his goals for the new school.[6] As expected, in all cases the entire African-American community seems to have supported him. For example, Washington once saw an old man come along driving his mule wagon. Washington spoke to him about what Tuskegee Institute was going to do for African Americans and the institute's current needs. Then he said, "Now, Uncle, you can help by bringing your wagon and mule round at nine o'clock Saturday morning for me to go off round the country telling the people about the school."[7] Not only was the old man there the next morning, he was right on time. Later, when Washington and his small staff held a fundraising meeting to secure money for the construction of a building, an old, antebellum African-American man—a man who had lived part of his life as a slave during the period from 1820 to 1861—stood up to speak.[8] The old man stated that he did not have any money to give but that he had raised two fine hogs and brought one to contribute to building expenses. In concluding, he said, "Any nigger that's got any love for his race, or any respect for himself, will bring a hog to the next meeting."[9] This deeply impacted Washington and the other folks at the meeting. Perhaps as a result of this, a number of men in the community volunteered several days' work constructing the building.[10]

Though these many examples of group solidarity touched and inspired Washington and ultimately helped to mold his business philosophy, they did not match the effects of a special gift of six eggs. At another school fundraising meeting, an old woman of about seventy years of age hobbled into Washington's office using a cane and spoke these words to him:

> "Mr. Washin'ton, God knows I spent de bes' days of my life in slavery. God knows I's ignorant an' poor; but," she added, "I knows what you an' Miss Davidson is trying' to do. I knows you is tryin' to make better men an' better women for de coloured race. I ain't got no money, but I wants you to take dese six eggs, what I's been savin' up, an' I wants you to put dese six eggs into de eddication of dese boys an' gals."[11]

Washington was greatly impressed by this gesture because the old woman did not have much but nonetheless gave something that she needed dearly. Of all the gifts that Tuskegee Institute received during Washington's life, he wrote that none touched him so deeply as the gift of these six eggs. Furthermore, in speaking and writing of Tuskegee Institute and its work, Washington never solely referred to what he was doing for the school, but what the school workers and he were doing together to uplift the group.[12]

Washington's role as a race leader, like that as a student and school builder, also reflected his sense of group consciousness. When he was asked by the Board of Directors of the Atlanta Exposition to speak at the opening ceremony of the event, he agreed to the request, knowing that it carried a heavy burden. He was to speak before three very different groups: Southern whites, Northern whites, and African Americans. This was something Washington had not done before. He knew that one wrong word would negatively affect his race and would probably prevent another African American from being invited to speak before any prominent, white Southern forum for years to come. Yet he still wanted to be truthful. He was aware that he had to operate like a skillful technician to be successful. With this in mind, Washington wrote his speech, and his wife, along with the Tuskegee Institute faculty, listened to his speech and gave him helpful pointers.[13] This strengthened Washington's resolve and eased his fears a little.

After Washington gave his Atlanta Exposition address, he was shocked by the generally positive national reaction that it received, as most of the white press proclaimed him the new leader of his race.[14] Washington never envisioned himself in such a position, replacing a historical figure as giant as Frederick Douglass.[15] Yet, after many hours of long contemplation, and because he felt that prominent leaders of the Reconstruction era had not offered an economic component in their programs, he willingly submitted to the request that he become "the leader."[16] In doing so, Washington continued his lifelong practice of doing whatever he could to help his race advance, but now on a larger, national scale. In reflecting on his Atlanta address fifteen years later, Washington wrote: "I felt that we [African Americans] needed a policy, not of destruction, but of construction; not of defense, but of aggression; a policy, not of hostility or surrender, but of friendship and advance. I stated, as vigorously as I was able, that usefulness in the community where we resided was our surest and most potent protection."[17] Furthermore, Washington noted, "in my opinion, the Negro should seek constantly in every manly, straightforward manner to make friends of the white man by whose side he lived, rather than to content himself with seeking the goodwill of some man a thousand miles away."[18]

The examples above, which focus on Washington's observations during Reconstruction, his school days, the building up of Tuskegee Institute, and his role as the leader of his people, represent his strong sense of group consciousness. He was aware of the plight of his race during slavery, Reconstruction, and the nadir and devoted his life to elevating their condition, always deeming it a privilege to serve his race and in turn humanity.[19] A favorite lifelong comment of his was, "I learned that assistance given to the weak makes the one who gives it strong; and that oppression of the unfortunate makes one weak."[20] This mindset was ingrained in him as a child as he looked around and saw his race's plight. The realities of slavery, Reconstruction, and the nadir caused him to develop a group-advancement outlook that influenced his entire philosophy. Thus, these broad historical phenomena, along with key individuals, developed in Washington his sense of group consciousness, which became an integral part of his entrepreneurial philosophy.

Protestant Work Ethic Principle

In terms of the development of a group consciousness, Booker T. Washington credited his mother, Jane Ferguson, as the major influence in his life.[21] She, more than anyone else, taught him the lessons of truth, honor, and thrift, which Washington considered among his most precious possessions.[22] After his mother, according to Washington, the person who reinforced his lessons in thrift and honesty and who taught him the value of "developing a system for working" was Viola Ruffner, a Yankee from Vermont.[23] Since Washington's arrival in Malden, West Virginia, in 1865, he, his stepfather, and his brother worked alternately in the salt furnaces and coal mines in the area. Washington was no enthusiast of this type of labor, especially the dangerous coal mines, in which many miners lost their lives or were permanently injured. One day, with his mother's guidance and his stepfather's approval, Washington sought work as a house servant for Ruffner. He had heard many unpleasant stories from boys who had previously worked for Ruffner but had quit because of her strictness and the systematic way in which she demanded that the work be done. According to Washington, when he first met this woman, he trembled at the knees. As the boys who had worked for her had told him, she was indeed a very stern taskmaster, so much so that Washington also quit her service.[24] Eventually, though, he came back, confessed his inefficiencies, and asked for another chance.

In Ruffner's employment he worked hard and learned that she wanted her household and yard cleaned in a certain, extremely detailed fashion. Things had to be cleaned constantly, necessitating a system of laboring. Moreover, she required honesty and promptness.[25] In time, according to Washington, after he learned Ruffner's labor requirements, he had no more problems working for her and eventually became a valuable employee. Years later, while visiting Malden, West Virginia, Washington paid special homage to Viola Ruffner: "Not far from here, in the family of a noble white woman whom most of you know, I received a training in the matters of thoroughness, cleanliness, promptness and honesty, which, I confess to you, in a large measure, enables me to do the work for which I am given credit. As I look over my life I feel that the training which I received in the family of Mrs. Viola Ruffner was a most valuable part of my education."[26] "Employing a system of working" and "working hard without complaints" were the greatest lessons that Washington received from Ruffner. He took these lessons and applied them to all realms of his work life, including his entrepreneurial philosophy, through which he would advocate operating businesses—including his own Tuskegee Institute—with a system.

Besides reinforcing principles of hard work, thriftiness, honesty, promptness, and systematized laboring, Ruffner allowed Washington to obtain valuable training in salesmanship.[27] Around her house, Ruffner grew a great volume of fruits and vegetables, more than she and her family could consume. Being the thrifty woman that she was, according to Washington, she had him get up early each morning to sell the surplus to families in her community. These people, who mostly worked at the salt furnace or coal mine, were of a lower class than she. At first Washington felt that Ruffner did not trust him handling goods and cash, but eventually, as she saw him constantly accounting for "everything to the penny," she began to trust him implicitly.[28] Washington not only sold Ruffner's surplus goods regularly, but he prevented friends and older boys from stealing goods that did not belong to him.[29] In Washington's view, his early sales experience was another lesson in honesty and the performance of conscientious duty.[30]

Washington left Ruffner in 1872 when he went on to Hampton Institute. She may not have had another employee as good as Washington, as they corresponded long after Washington left her employment.[31] Notwithstanding, Washington reached Hampton Institute in the fall term, when school was already in session. Since there was an overabundance of African Americans attempting to enter Hampton Institute on a regular basis, school authorities could handpick those they considered worthy of their institution.[32] When Washington first arrived, he was neither admitted immediately nor denied entrance. Miss Mary Mackie, "the lady principal," left him in a state of limbo, which greatly disturbed Washington, especially since he saw other students being admitted. It was probably Washington's attire that gave Miss Mackie a negative impression of him, because when he initially arrived he looked dirty and shabby and had only one set of clothes, those upon his body. Nevertheless, perhaps since students were expected to not only study books but do manual labor, Miss Mackie gave Washington an assignment sweeping the recitation room in Academic Hall, Hampton Institute's only building in 1872. Washington considered this task his entrance examination and was adequately prepared. From his experience of working at Mrs. Ruffner's house he knew how to sweep. He swept the recitation room three times and dusted the furniture off four times. When Miss Mackie returned to inspect his work, she rigorously examined the recitation room for dirt. When she was unable to find one bit of dirt on the floor or a particle of dust on any of the furniture, she quietly remarked to Washington, "I guess you will do to enter this institution."[33]

While attending Hampton Institute from 1872 to 1875, Washington learned many valuable lessons that either added to his growing entrepreneurial philosophy or reinforced earlier lessons that he had learned from his mother or Ruffner. The "philosophy of labor" and the "philosophy of working with real things," however, were tremendously valuable lessons that he learned at Hampton Institute. He had learned how to work hard and be thrifty from his mother and Ruffner, but he had not learned an in-depth philosophy supporting these principles. That all changed when he arrived at Hampton Institute. The entire institution was run in such an industrial manner that no student could escape its influence.[34] From the time students awoke at 5:00 A.M. to the time they retired at 9:00 P.M., there was an established school routine that allowed virtually no time for idleness. School authorities taught that an idle brain was the devil's workshop and idle hands were his best tools.[35] "A man had better work for nothing and find himself," they further stressed, "than to spend his time in idling and loafing."[36] In this setting, Washington was taught that African Americans held their destiny in their own hands, and that in order to improve their social standing, they had to work hard and persistently, beginning with the common daily labors, and ridding themselves of notions that labor was bad. On the contrary, he was taught that all honest labor was honorable, even godlike.[37] Moreover, Washington was instructed that many African Americans had an aversion to work because in slavery they had been forced to work, and there was a difference between being forced to work and choosing to.[38] Hence, "Two hundred years of forced labor," Washington learned, "taught the colored man that there was no dignity in labor but rather a disgrace."[39] Speaking before the Hampton Institute student body in 1909 about the philosophy of work that he had learned at his alma mater, Washington proclaimed:

> Being worked means degradation; working means civilization. Every individual in this country who has to be worked is a slave. Every one who has learned to work is a free man or free woman; and through the medium of hand training or industrial education, it was General Armstrong's idea to teach the Negro to work so that he would not have to be worked.[40]

Samuel C. Armstrong was the founder and head of Hampton Institute, as well as the mind behind the philosophy of work principle and the principle of working with real things. He believed that an industrial education, coupled with a military regimen, the Protestant work ethic,[41] and morality training, were the best solutions for upward mobility among African Americans, especially for those individuals recently freed from slavery, for he believed that to succeed people had to do for themselves. However, following slavery, circumstances compelled African Americans to mainly do for themselves. Nonetheless, Washington greatly admired Armstrong and always spoke highly of him in his published literature.[42]

Armstrong preached to Washington and others to work hard and pray for good results, to not procrastinate, to always push and persevere, and that honest labor was the price of success.[43] Moreover, he taught students that industry and morality were interconnected. Industry produced moral development and moral development produced industry, which ultimately led to character-building and was an essential ingredient for true manhood and womanhood.[44] Armstrong, who seemed to have been religious, taught that when one was working hard, he was not only building character, but fulfilling God's divine will.[45]

Within Armstrong's philosophy of working with real things, which coincided with his philosophy of work, he taught Washington and his other students to not just concentrate on academics but to also focus on tangible "things" outside of books—real "things"[46] or practical items.[47] This was one of the main philosophical reasons why he required all of his students to do manual labor while they attended Hampton Institute, and to be at least exposed to the "industrial idea concept."[48] Armstrong further believed that working with real things—as in farming, carpentry, shoemaking, and janitorial work—not only helped his students to pay their tuition and board, but also helped stimulate self-discipline and gave them a practical education to accompany their academic one.[49] To Washington, this teaching had several meanings. For example, it meant combining academics with the acquisition of practical skills, such as a trade; it meant working hard to achieve the ownership of land and the building of a home on that land, even establishing businesses on it.[50] After all, both Washington and Armstrong thought that the African American's advancement was to come largely through farming the Southern soil.[51] Furthermore, for Armstrong and later Washington, land ownership meant the fulfillment of Biblical teachings (for example, working by the sweat of one's brow and reaping what one sowed). It meant independence, the exemplification of true manhood and womanhood, stability, a sense of security for children, freedom from rent, and the culturing of traits that would assist one in being a responsible taxpayer and wise voter.[52] Landowners, Armstrong taught, were the true American history-makers.[53]

Armstrong's philosophies of work and working with real things are evident throughout Washington's entrepreneurial ideas of racial uplift. As a leader, Washington typically preached that owning and operating a respectable, "visible" business would bring an individual the community's respect, especially if that individual sold much-needed goods and services not only to his race, but to other groups as well.[54] Washington, like Armstrong, taught that a sense of interdependency would thereby develop between African Americans and other groups, instead of the dependency being solely on the African-American side.[55] Washington felt that implementing these entrepreneurial ideas would improve race relations, for he saw them as a means of breaking down barriers. In addition, Washington had published *My Larger Education: Being Chapters from My Experience* (1911), a third autobiographical account of his life, in which he discussed how he learned by observing "men and things."[56] The theme of this book is an idea drawn directly from

Armstrong.⁵⁷ Washington wrote that he learned from many successful businessmen who not only worked hard, but used frugality and foresight in their daily business activities. Washington, echoing the lessons taught by Armstrong, stressed that he learned by actively studying these men's actions rather than by reading about them or by hearing what was said of them.⁵⁸ Ironically, although Armstrong viewed African Americans as inferior to whites, the above were critical lessons that Washington extracted from his teachings.

By the time Washington graduated from Hampton Institute in 1875, he had gained a philosophical understanding of the "gospel of hard work" and "men and things" to go along with his tendency to create a systemized way of working and his sense of group consciousness. And these lessons only solidified as he returned to Malden to teach and later pursue further studies in Washington, D.C.⁵⁹ Recognizing Washington's worth, in 1879, the Hampton Institute faculty invited him back to oversee the Native American living quarters and to do some postgraduate work. Washington consented. He remained working and studying successfully at Hampton Institute until 1881, when he was offered a job in Tuskegee, Alabama, opening a school similar to Hampton Institute. With Armstrong's blessings, Washington went off to Tuskegee with the core values that supported his budding entrepreneurial philosophy.

Influences from Business Expansion

Before discussing the economic factors of the state in which Booker T. Washington's career flourished, some attention must be focused on the general business arena of the nation and the ideology of late-nineteenth and early-twentieth-century entrepreneurs, by which Washington was influenced.⁶⁰ The general economic milieu in which Washington lived was relatively consistent, meaning that industry was constantly and rapidly expanding. The nation moved from an agricultural and commercial society into a new industrial era, as noted by historian C. Joseph Pusateri:

> The impressive expansion of American industry between 1860 and 1910 can be accurately measured. . . . Agriculture was the dominant sector in the economy in 1860 and contributed about 60 percent of total value added in commodity production, while industry contributed only 38 percent. But, by 1880, the two shares were roughly equal, and, by 1910, industry claimed three-quarters of the total. Since gross agricultural output actually grew in those years, industrial expansion was rapid. In

the early years of the twentieth century, the United States boasted one-third of the manufacturing capacity of the world.[61]

Moreover, railroad-serviced land area grew dramatically after 1860.[62] Northeastern businessmen were able to reach markets in remote areas of the United States, be they to the north, south, east, or west. No areas with substantial markets were now beyond the reach of entrepreneurs. With this railroad expansion, a professional business class of managers was created, and colleges and universities scrambled to establish "schools of management" to train would-be managers who would eventually run companies for particular families and shareholders.[63]

Philosophically and socially, successful entrepreneurs and even captains of industry (people such as Andrew Carnegie, John D. Rockefeller, and J. P. Morgan, who had amassed great fortunes during the Gilded Age and were dominant in their respective industrial fields) attributed their success to hard work, as the Protestant work ethic dictated.[64] Moreover, Herbert Spencer, a British philosopher, applied Charles Darwin's laws of evolution and natural selection to society,[65] arguing that if one had amassed great wealth, it was because he or she was the fittest and by that right should enjoy the fruits of their labor. From about 1870 until 1929, Spencer's philosophy was the dominant ideology held by American leaders of large enterprises as well as the general American public. Successful entrepreneurs and particularly captains of industry embraced Spencer's philosophy as a godsend, a justification of their place in society.

Besides Spencer's teachings and the influence of the Protestant work ethic noted above, Washington was also impacted by business expansion in the South in general, particularly in Alabama.[66] Following the Civil War, the South underwent an industrial revolution, and Washington was well aware of its expansion. Beginning gradually in the 1870's, four new economic activities emerged in the South: the iron industry, the manufacture of cotton cloth, expanded transportation via railways, and the increased trading of goods by organizations in different regions of the South.[67] In addition, North Carolina was an area in which the tobacco industry grew and flourished, with such entrepreneurs as Washington Duke leading the way.[68] The lumber industry, the South's largest industry, began in the states of Tennessee, Virginia, Georgia, and North Carolina, where plenty of timberland was available, and brick and tile factories were founded in Georgia, South Carolina, Tennessee, and Texas.[69]

In Alabama, the iron industry flourished. In 1880, 205,000 tons of pig iron, a crude iron that was the direct product of the blast furnace and was

Table 7. Number of manufacturing establishments in Alabama from 1870 to 1900 and the capital invested in them

Year	Number	Capital invested
1870	2,188	$5,714,032
1880	2,070	$9,668,008
1890	2,977	$46,122,571
1900	5,602	$70,370,081

Source: Donald B. Dodd and Wynelle S. Dodd, *Historical Statistics of the South 1790–1970* (Tuscaloosa: University of Alabama Press, 1973), pp. 4–5.

refined to produce steel, was produced in Virginia and Alabama combined, while in 1892, 1,568,000 tons were produced.[70] Birmingham, which was fewer than two hundred miles from Tuskegee, was a key Southern city involved in the iron industry, especially after the Tennessee Coal, Iron, and Railway Company purchased significant portions of the Birmingham iron mills and invested money in them.[71] Birmingham became the top pig iron producer in the South, supplying cast-iron pipe throughout the South and the nation and outcompeting Northern firms in such cities as Chicago, Cincinnati, Philadelphia, and New York; Birmingham even outproduced the nation of Britain.[72] Moreover, the number of manufacturing establishments generally increased from 1870 to 1900, as depicted in table 7 above.

Between 1870 and 1880, there was a decline in the number of established manufacturers. This was largely due to the Panic of 1873.[73] By 1890, the number of manufacturers in Alabama had again increased, while the capital invested constantly increased at an accelerating rate.

Washington experienced and read about the economic development occurring in the South, and it impacted his entrepreneurial ideas.[74] He knew that the economic revolution in the South was at a relatively early developmental stage. Moreover, he felt that for African Americans to gain economic leverage in the South and in the nation, they had to seize the opportunities right at their doorsteps. In an 1891 speech in Washington, D.C., concentrating on the Southern industrial revolution, Washington proclaimed:

> But let us for a few minutes take a somewhat different view of the subject and inquire what are the resources and inducements offered by the South as a field for business. Few I think will deny that the most important elements of wealth in any country are iron, wood, land, and climate. We do not I fear fully appreciate the rapidity and character of the material development that is taking place in the South and now

is the time for us to strike while this development is in comparative infancy. With all the disadvantages presented by the South we can find our way to the front sooner through Southern prejudice than through Northern competition.[75]

Not only did the economic trends of the South, and specifically Alabama, impact Washington's entrepreneurial ideas, but the ideology of the African-American leadership immediately after Reconstruction did as well.[76] In other words, African-American economic thought during the nadir stressed self-help, racial solidarity, and looking inward as opposed to placing emphasis on governmental or philanthropic aid.[77] The African-American leadership consisted of teachers, preachers, newspaper editors, and politicians—any individuals that wrote or spoke out publicly about what African Americans had to do to lift themselves up during the nadir. Washington was not oblivious to these activities.[78]

Examples of self-help and racial solidarity during Washington's early adult years that reflect African-American economic thought during the nadir are numerous. In 1883, Frank Wilkeson, the Southern correspondent of the *New York Sun*, impressed upon his readers, especially in the South, the value of buying land. He wrote that the time was right to buy land since it was relatively cheap and land speculators had not purchased it en masse. He further stressed that property owners were masters of their destinies.[79] In concurrence with this writer, Frederick Douglass counseled African Americans to buy land and accumulate wealth as a sign of racial progress and civilization.[80] The editors of the *New York Globe*, responding to a series of letters from a Southerner named Mrs. McDougall, wrote, "The only way for the Negroes of the South to improve their condition, to learn the industrial arts and become manufacturers, will be through their own exertions."[81] In the same year, a large meeting of African Americans was held in Muscogee County, Georgia, to oppose a Negro rights protest convention that was to be held in Louisville. The consensus reached at the meeting was that African Americans should not concentrate on protesting the political rights denied them but rather on being more successful farmers, manufacturers, merchants, doctors, lawyers, journalists, and so forth. When these objectives were achieved, they felt, "Negro office-holding would follow in abundance."[82] In response to another protest convention, which was presided over by Frederick Douglass, a writer contacted the editors of the *New York Globe*, protesting the convention and its outdated methods of appealing to the sympathies of liberal and paternalistic whites. He wrote: "But the convention is a thing of the past now, and at this safe distance I would say to the ex-delegates, 'Gentlemen, I cannot see why you were wont to meet, nor why you have met, and would ask most respectfully, what have you done different from previous National Colored Conventions? What practical thing have you done to elevate the condition of the Negro race?'"[83] Offering what he considered a more viable and practical solution, the writer proposed that African Americans mimic the Jews, at least insofar as becoming successful merchants and traders. "If the workshops will not open to us," the writer further emphasized, "must we stand outside and cry, and hold conventions? Would it not be more sensible to buy a few apples and peanuts and keep a stand on some corner; or a few shoestrings, matches and tin-pans and put a pack upon our backs and become peddlers?"[84] In this writer's opinion, "The commercial highway [was] the road to respectability."[85] Thus, before Booker T. Washington was proclaimed the new leader of his race in 1895, following the death of Frederick Douglass, from 1874 on, there was a strong tendency in African-American thought to focus on self-help efforts and racial solidarity.[86] It was still accelerating in 1899 at the Atlanta University Conference on the Negro in Business, when John Hope, in his paper "The Meaning of Business," wrote, "We must take in some, if not all, of the wages, turn it into capital, hold it, increase it. This must be done as a means of employment for the thousands who cannot get work from old sources."[87] These influences from business expansion contributed significantly toward Washington's budding entrepreneurial philosophy, which would become an integral component of his leadership program.

Practical Business Influences that Impacted Booker T. Washington's Entrepreneurial Philosophy

Early Southern Influences

Businesspersons whose entrepreneurial activities impacted Washington's thinking are what is meant by practical business influences. According to Washington, when he arrived in Tuskegee, Alabama, he met the African-American man who was largely responsible for the founding of Tuskegee Institute.[88] This man had a significant impact on Washington, like the business growth throughout the nation and in the specific state of Alabama. The man's name was Lewis Adams, and he was a former slave of "great intelligence and thrift," according to Washington, a "jack-of-all-trades" laborer.[89] In writing about Adams, Washington referred to him as "a mechanic, who had learned the trades of shoemaking, harness-making, and tinsmithing during the days of slavery."⁹⁰ Adams worked out an arrangement with two white Democrats who were in the Alabama legislature in which he assured them the African-American vote in Tuskegee provided that if they were reelected, they would fight for an annual appropriation of funds from the state to open the Normal School in Tuskegee. The two politicians won and got an initial appropriation of two thousand dollars.⁹¹

Lewis Adams was an extremely important influence because he was likely the first individual in Tuskegee who not only impacted Washington's initial entrepreneurial ideas, but reinforced his Hampton Institute teachings as well. Washington was very impressed with Adams and considered him the embodiment of genius and thrift.⁹² Adams, due to slavery, never spent a day in a classroom, but Washington still considered him a wise man. Commenting on him in a speech before an 1884 meeting of the National Education Association, Washington proclaimed:

> In Tuskegee a Negro mechanic manufactures the best tinware, the best harness, the best boots and shoes, and it is common to see his store crowded with white customers from all over the county. His word or note goes as far as that of the whitest man.⁹³

Adams exemplified for Washington what he had learned as a student at Hampton Institute and what he came to know after he graduated and taught school in Malden: "[there is a] real difference between studying about things through books and learning things themselves without the medium of books."⁹⁴ Adams opened a hardware store in the middle of downtown Tuskegee, starting small and expanding.⁹⁵ Black and white customers throughout the town of Tuskegee and the surrounding area were dependent on him for goods and services, making him valuable to the community. His business acumen allowed him to be considered an honored and respected citizen. Adams also represented for Washington that dying generation of former slaves who had learned numerous trades.⁹⁶ Adams was the epitome of Washington's entrepreneurial philosophy. He underscored what would occur when African Americans made themselves indispensable assets to their communities. Because of this, Washington not only referred to him extensively in his writings and speeches, but placed him on the initial Tuskegee Institute Board of Trustees and the Tuskegee Institute faculty.⁹⁷ Commenting further on Adams, Washington wrote:

> The leading citizen in Tuskegee is Mr. Lewis Adams, to whom the honor should largely be given for securing the location of the Tuskegee Normal and Industrial Institute in the town. Mr. Adams is not only an

intelligent and successful businessman, but is one who combines with business enterprise rare common sense and direction. In the most trying periods of the growth of the Tuskegee Institute I have always found Mr. Adams a man on whom I could rely for the wisest advice. He enjoys the highest respect and confidence of the citizens of both races, and it is largely through his power and influence that the two races live together in harmony and peace in the town.[98]

Another key individual who impacted Washington—also a member of Tuskegee Institute's Board of Trustees and a frequent visitor—was Cornelius N. Dorsette, a medical doctor who graduated from Hampton Institute in 1878 and from the University of Buffalo Medical School in 1882. He moved to Montgomery, Alabama, in 1884, and Washington placed him in contact with some of the influential citizens in that city to assist him in establishing his medical practice.[99] In time, according to Washington, Dr. Dorsette had perhaps the largest practice of any African-American doctor in the Gulf states.[100] Washington, in his writings and speeches, referred to him often as a successful African American who passed Montgomery's six-day medical examination rather easily. As a result, according to Washington, Dr. Dorsette was welcomed into the Montgomery community by his white peers. He was the first African-American physician in that city.[101]

It was at one time reported that Dr. Dorsette had made some comments about race relationships in Montgomery that upset many white citizens.[102] Tempers were apparently at a feverish pitch as discussions about a lynching and race riots ran rampant. Washington, assuming that he could be of some help to his friend, went to Montgomery and asked Dr. Dorsette what he was going to do. Dr. Dorsette explained that he was going to open a drugstore on one of the thoroughfares in Montgomery (which he did), a large three-story brick building near where Jefferson Davis delivered his Confederate inaugural address. With the opening of this drugstore, according to Washington, all talk about lynching Dr. Dorsette or race riots ceased.[103] Washington's brief explanation of how Dr. Dorsette solved his problem should not be accepted uncritically. There were probably other factors that contributed to the easing of tensions. Nonetheless, Dr. Dorsette worked toward making himself an integral part of his surrounding community of both African Americans and whites.

Again, Washington's rationale for the change in attitude was that Dr. Dorsette had offered to the Montgomery community something invaluable. African Americans and whites traded with the drugstore, which was highly visible on a busy thoroughfare. Those individuals who did not know Dr.

Dorsette got to know and respect him through their patronage. Thus, in opening the drugstore, Dr. Dorsette not only continued to be an entrepreneur, but also made himself an indispensable member of his community, further crystallizing and epitomizing Washington's entrepreneurial philosophy.

George W. Campbell, a white entrepreneur and initial Tuskegee Institute Board of Trustees member, was another whom Washington cited as having given sound business advice. Campbell, who lived in the town of Tuskegee, was the president of the board of trustees.[104] He was also a merchant and headed a local bank that financially aided Tuskegee Institute by providing loans in its times of dire need.[105] Moreover, he was the individual who actually wrote Samuel Armstrong requesting a teacher for the Tuskegee and Macon County African-American population.[106] His advice to Washington, in regard to running Tuskegee Institute, was: "Always remember that credit is capital."[107] Washington seemed to treasure this advice and never forgot it, as he cited it in his second autobiography and tried to make sure that Tuskegee Institute's treasurer always paid bills on time to preserve the institution's excellent credit rating.[108] This advice reinforced for Washington the lesson he had learned from Ruffner on the importance of maintaining a system of efficient labor. Moreover, he quickly learned that it was practical common sense and very much needed for goodwill. As principal of Tuskegee Institute, he demanded from his staff and himself a thorough "businesslike system" of conducting business with vendors.[109]

James F. B. Marshall, who was also white, was another individual who reinforced Washington's lessons on the importance of maintaining a system—in this case, a good bookkeeping system. Marshall was an instructor and the treasurer at Hampton Institute. He taught Washington and Tuskegee Institute's treasurer, Warren Logan.[110] When Washington needed funds to purchase the first grounds for Tuskegee Institute, it was Marshall who loaned him the two hundred and fifty dollars to make the initial down payment.[111] Marshall advised Washington during the early days of Tuskegee Institute, especially during the summer when Washington opened his school, and when Armstrong was vacationing in Europe.[112] He advised Washington to not just keep mental track of things but to also record them, especially financial transactions.[113] He stressed to Washington that as Tuskegee Institute expanded, there was no way that he would be able to keep track of everything mentally. He also emphasized that it would always help fund-raising if Washington could show donors, specifically, how each and every penny of their money had been spent.[114] Grateful for this advice, Washington wrote to Marshall: "I thank you for your advice in regard to keeping our accounts straight. We are making a special effort to keep every thing straight so that we can have detailed accounts of our recipts [sic] and expenditures printed and sent to each donor directly after the work is done."[115] Furthermore, in appreciation of Marshall's help and as a sign of respect, Washington and his wife made their daughter's middle name "Marshall."[116]

These early Southern influences are more than just simple stories about individuals who affected Washington. They are doors that allow us to view and understand Washington's entrepreneurial ideas more intensely. In fact, they could be interpreted as axioms. He would use these individuals (and others) to underscore basic aspects of his entrepreneurial philosophy, stressing that African Americans needed to follow the advice or example of these people, and that they could rise up if they just adhered to the adages exemplified in these stories.

By 1891, ten years after the establishment of Tuskegee Institute, with his influences from Malden, West Virginia, Hampton, Virginia, the Southern and national economic milieus, and Tuskegee and Montgomery, Alabama, Washington's entrepreneurial philosophy was established.[117] Significant traces of Washington's entrepreneurial philosophy are evident in his 1882 speech before the Alabama State Teachers' Association in Selma, Alabama, and his 1884 speech before the National Educational Association in Madison, Wisconsin. By the time of his 1886 address to the Unitarian National Conference at Saratoga, New York, however, Washington's entrepreneurial philosophy was in place, and by the time he delivered his 1891 address in Washington, D.C., "The South as an Opening for a Business Career," it was well developed. All ensuing business influences mainly reinforced or refined Washington's entrepreneurial ideas or else further expanded them.

Practical Business Influences that Served to Expand and Reinforce Booker T. Washington's Entrepreneurial Philosophy

Expansion

William H. Baldwin Jr. was an individual who reinforced and expanded Washington's entrepreneurial philosophy, specifically the component that called for employing a good work system.[118] According to Washington, Baldwin was the sole individual responsible for placing Tuskegee Institute's financial statements and operations on par with "generally accepted accounting principles," business methods that would be acceptable to any of the best banks on Wall Street.[119] After hearing of Baldwin's financial strengths and executive abilities, and knowing his father, who had been a New England abolitionist, Washington asked Baldwin to be on the Tuskegee Institute Board of Trustees. Baldwin, at first, carefully read the letter of introduction that his father had written for Washington, and then he looked Washington over. Finally, he told him, "No, I cannot become a trustee; I will not say I will become a trustee because when I give my word to become a trustee it must mean something."[120] As though he might change his mind, Baldwin did say that he would come to Tuskegee and see for himself how the Tuskegee staff was running the school, and that if it pleased him, he would consent to be a board member.[121]

On an unannounced visit, Baldwin showed up at the school grounds. He went into the classrooms to observe the pedagogical methods employed at Tuskegee Institute. He went into the trade shops and walked throughout the farm. He went through the dining room to observe the facilities and get a sense of how food was prepared. He even went to each table, taking pieces of bread, breaking them apart, and examining their internals to see how well they were cooked, even tasting some of it as he walked through the kitchen.[122] Following his thorough examination, Baldwin still did not consent to be a board member. Only after studying Tuskegee Institute's financial condition and after a number of months had passed did Baldwin consent to be a board member. "From the beginning to the end," according to Washington, "[Tuskegee Institute] never had such a trustee."[123]

Baldwin became a trustee in 1895, the year that Washington was catapulted into national prominence by his Atlanta Exposition address. Baldwin's influence was of critical importance not only for the further expansion of Tuskegee Institute but also for Washington's success as the national leader that he became. As a board member, one of Baldwin's first influential and important acts was to contribute toward the strengthening of Tuskegee Institute's financial condition. He strongly advised Washington, as principal of Tuskegee Institute, to hire a competent auditor, someone who could carefully examine the school's financial operations and offer concrete suggestions for improvement. Expressing concern over accountability to donors, Baldwin wrote to Washington: "You are handling sufficient funds to demand the greatest care, as any loss or improper accounting from any cause would strike a blow at your institution that you could not overcome in a great many years."[124]

The man who was chosen as auditor for Tuskegee Institute was Daniel C. Smith, an 1886 graduate of Princeton University and a certified public accountant whom Baldwin highly recommended and from whom Washington learned.[125] Smith's starting term of employment was October 1, 1898, to October 1, 1899, during which time he was to earn one thousand dollars, with Baldwin covering a significant portion of his traveling expenses from New York City to Tuskegee, Alabama, and back.[126] Smith's terms of employment could be renewed annually based on his performance.[127] The Tuskegee Institute bookkeepers were accountable to Smith as the auditor, while the treasurer, Warren Logan, was responsible for the management of the school's funds. With this new arrangement, the bookkeepers were technically no longer subordinates of Logan, as the auditor theory of distinct separation and accountability of duties was applied. Either Logan was upset with this new arrangement, or Washington presumed that he would be, because Baldwin had to reiterate to Washington a few times the importance of keeping critical financial operations separate. He emphasized also that the intent of the auditor's work was not to hurt Logan's feelings but to make the school function better financially and to improve its financial reports, especially those sent out to donors.[128] This was a basic accounting lesson for Washington, and it influenced and enhanced not only his entrepreneurial philosophy but his financial skills as well.

One of the first assignments that Smith undertook was the creation of a gains and loss statement for Tuskegee Institute's industrial department for 1896–97. This was done to examine the efficiency of its system.[129] He found that eight departments together lost $4,097.89, including the carpenter shop, sawmill, brickyard, wheelwright shop, printing office, tailor shop, industrial room, and the Marshall Farm. The carpenter shop and Marshall Farm contributed the most toward the losses.[130] Smith's advice was that Washington make each department a self-sufficient unit, and those incapable of such should be eliminated. Marshall Farm was one of the industries that Smith, Baldwin, and Washington tried to make self-sufficient. When all efforts seemed to fail, Baldwin suggested to Washington that it be abolished.[131]

Regardless of the Marshall Farm, Washington, with Baldwin's guidance, was satisfied with the way that the Tuskegee Institute accounts were shaping up.[132] He had written in his second autobiography that it was his intention to make Tuskegee Institute's financial operations so sound that any New York banking house would approve of them.[133] Furthermore, Baldwin advised Washington to see that Tuskegee Institute was run in a very cost-effective manner, perhaps the way he had operated the Long Island Railroad. In Washington's early years organizing and expanding Tuskegee Institute, construction of buildings was often started when adequate funds were not available, which caused Washington much stress when he and his staff had to meet bill due dates.[134] Baldwin wanted to discourage Washington from this sort of "building on faith" and encourage him rather to take the hardheaded businessman's approach of staying within a projected budget, especially since most of Tuskegee Institute's yearly funds came from donations.[135] For the most part, Washington adhered to this well-intended advice, but not always. When Washington made arrangements to improve the permanent plant from June 1st to February 25th of 1904, Baldwin, annoyed, wrote: "What special gifts did you have to pay for these improvements, and how much of it came out of the current income? The simple fact is, as I have told you so often, that you cannot afford to make such extensive improvements until you have the money in sight."[136] Washington, in response, sent Baldwin a letter apologetically attempting to justify the extra expenditure:

> I have your note regarding the large amount spent since June first in making permanent improvements. I realize that I was taking a terrible risk in doing this and may suffer for it, but the fact is the change from the Marshall Farm to the new tract was a greater undertaking than I had expected, but I am quite sure when you come here and really see what we have done that you will feel that we have been justified. For the first time we are now feeling that the people in this vicinity and visitors have real respect for our farming operations; they can actually see what is being done instead of having to imagine it.[137]

As a result of his input and that of Daniel C. Smith, Baldwin felt a great degree of confidence in the manner in which accounting was being handled at Tuskegee Institute. Regarding this issue, he told an audience at a New York City fund-raising meeting for Tuskegee Institute that, "the generous friends who made Tuskegee possible should know its exact business condition."[138] As a board member, Baldwin now felt that he could responsibly do this, as well as grant donors true and concise financial statements that reflected how their contributions were spent.[139] According to Washington, Baldwin's systematic method of requiring that Tuskegee Institute be operated according to generally accepted accounting principles was his greatest gift to the school and to himself.[140]

Evidence indicates that Baldwin was probably the individual who influenced Washington's systematic fashion of reporting how money was to be spent to the penny.[141] After all, Baldwin exercised this exact same practice in justifying monetary expenditures.[142] In fact, more than once Baldwin informed Washington to be ready to discuss specifics about Tuskegee Institute finances to donors or prospective donors. Implementing what he learned, after ten years of attempting to secure funds from Andrew Carnegie, Washington finally convinced him to contribute funds toward the building of a library, which cost twenty thousand dollars. He did this by showing Carnegie how effectively the money would be used and its widespread impact on the institute's students. "All of the work for the building," Washington wrote to Carnegie, "such as brick making, brick-masonry, carpentry, blacksmithing, etc., would be done by the students. The money which you would give would not only supply the building, but the erection of the building would give a large number of students an opportunity to learn the building trades and the students would use the money paid to them to keep themselves in school."[143] Carnegie was impressed with Washington's brisk business methods, and Washington was fond of projecting exact costs to fellow businessmen such as Carnegie because he felt that they were quick to grasp his point.[144] Carnegie later donated six hundred thousand dollars to Tuskegee Institute in U.S. Steel bonds.[145]

Baldwin helped Washington develop the business methods he used to impress a financially astute individual like Carnegie, especially business procedures that pertained to developing the best financial system. As acknowledgment of his aid to Tuskegee Institute, the board of trustees, along with the faculty, staff, and students, erected a bronze memorial tablet in memory of Baldwin in 1905, following his death.[146] It still stands today on the Tuskegee Institute campus.[147] Moreover, in conjunction with Washington's continuous experience of directing Tuskegee Institute, Baldwin's influence contributed significantly toward molding Washington into a businessman whose entrepreneurial ideas and skills would later be reinforced by others.

Reinforcements

After Washington's ten- to eleven-year business relationship with Baldwin, his associations with other captains of industry reinforced his already-established entrepreneurial philosophy. His second autobiography, *Up From Slavery* (1900), a fund-raising document,[148] even epitomized principles that the industrialists, financiers, and other businesspersons believed in.[149] In the narrative, a young slave boy is portrayed as rising from slavery to fame and honor through consistent hard work, industry, and fortitude, overcoming numerous obstacles along the way and embodying a true Horatio Alger success story, using pluck more than luck.[150] After reading *Up From Slavery*, even more businesspeople and philanthropists contributed money toward Washington's projects.[151] In their minds, *Up From Slavery* made him more legitimate, as Washington shrewdly manipulated language to appeal to the industrialists of his day while simultaneously inspiring and leading those of his race.[152]

Moreover, in the chapter of *Up From Slavery* titled "Raising Money," Washington appeases wealthy folks by writing that, regarding character, they are some of the best people in the world and that since they were wise and shrewd in earning their fortunes, he presumes that they would practice those same principles by giving some of it away.[153] For that reason, he writes that he always tries to present concrete facts concerning his work, on a highly dignified plane, rather than constantly begging.[154] Washington also claims that they are among his best audiences, because when it comes to business, many of them are as astute and sharp as Baldwin.[155]

Thus, when additional industrialists, financiers, and other businesspersons became acquainted with Washington, he was prepared for them. His past experiences had groomed him to be able to effectively interact with them; in a sense, he was their peer. Like them, he had been a major driving force responsible for building up an extensive facility that not only impacted his students, faculty, and staff, but also the economy of the surrounding community. He understood and used their business jargon, trying his best to ensure that Tuskegee Institute, like financially successful big businesses of his day, was always operated in the most efficient manner, with close attention paid to curbing wastefulness and expenses.[156] Consequently, Washington's experiences molded him into many roles, one of which was a businessman.

John D. Rockefeller Sr., the shrewd bookkeeper, businessman, and Standard Oil executive, agreed with Washington's Protestant work ethic principle. He began giving funds to Tuskegee Institute in the 1890s, and he and his descendants were among the principal philanthropic contributors to the school.[157] He once told Washington, while Washington was spending an evening at his home: "Always be master of the details of your work; never have too many loose outer edges or fringes."[158] Washington wrote that he was grateful for this advice, although he was well aware of it from his interactions with Ruffner. It was also reinforced at Hampton Institute through his sweeping examination, janitorial job, and the general environment. Finally, his early experience of helping to develop Tuskegee Institute, along with his lessons from Mr. Baldwin, had taught him well. Nevertheless, Washington probably listened attentively to Rockefeller's advice. He was not one to appear ungrateful, especially to powerful persons. To show Rockefeller how he mastered all loose outer edges or fringes, when Rockefeller gave Tuskegee Institute thirty-four thousand dollars for the construction of a building in his name, Washington and his staff so efficiently planned and constructed the building that they saved $249. Washington sent the unused balance back to Rockefeller, which impressed him deeply. He, in turn, had it sent back to Tuskegee Institute to be used as needed.[159] Moreover, Washington indicated that he had studied the business "methods of large business concerns" such as Rockefeller's firm, the Standard Oil Company, and had learned much from them.[160]

Collis P. Huntington, the millionaire railroad magnate, also began donating funds to Tuskegee Institute in the 1890s. His first donation was only two dollars.[161] Washington wrote that he did not get upset or become disappointed, but instead became more resolved to show Huntington the value of Tuskegee Institute's work. Employing a strategy learned from Baldwin, Washington sent Huntington a copy of the Tuskegee Institute's annual report. Huntington was very impressed with the businesslike precision with which Tuskegee Institute was operated, writing in his return letter: "Where shall we get another Booker T. Washington."[162] With Huntington's approval, his wife decided to donate fifty thousand dollars to Tuskegee Institute for the construction of a girl's dormitory in honor of the Huntingtons.[163]

Huntington informed Washington by letter in December of 1898, "You are doing a great work, and I think you will continue to do good work if you keep on the lines of economy which I believe you have followed all these years."[164] Moreover, he stressed to Washington to begin at the bottom and work up.[165] As Huntington deduced, Washington had been practicing economy for years and would continue to do so until his death in 1915, and, long before he met Huntington, his life epitomized moving up from the bottom. In exhibiting his economy for the Huntingtons, along with establishing a sound foundation, he stretched their fifty thousand dollars, creating a girl's dormitory which not only far exceeded their expectations but was one of the best and most attractive buildings on the Tuskegee campus—and it was built by students.[166]

George Foster Peabody, like Rockefeller and Huntington, also donated funds to Tuskegee Institute. He made a significant portion of his fortune in the banking and investing industry.[167] He served on the Tuskegee Institute Board of Trustees from 1900 to 1911.[168] Perhaps out of respect, Washington cautiously asked him to share some of his financial expertise with members of the NNBL at a 1905 gathering in New York City.[169] Peabody found time in his busy schedule to speak.[170] Notwithstanding, Peabody's most significant contribution to Washington's business philosophy, as well as to the progression of Washington's school, was his reinforcement of Washington's system of working to ensure success. He confirmed and extended what Washington had learned from Baldwin and his auditor Smith, as can be seen in a letter he wrote to Washington criticizing Tuskegee Institute's treasurer's method of calculating and reporting investments:

> I have your Sept. 4th enclosing Mr. Logan's letter respecting interest on endowment. I notice his method of calculation and call to your attention that it is highly improper in making such statement to include the principal amount of the sums on which annuities are paid as in case of the Carnegie fund and others noted in the memo. It is quite wrong to figure the Carnegie fund at 3.75—it pays 5% on $450,000 from which interest comes to the school. It is also absurd to quote an investment of $6,000 as a basis for criticism of investments running over $1,000,000. The income from the General Fund investments has been increasing by reason of the higher rate received upon investments of the last two or three years but all non-interest bearing securities, in the fund, should be carried at a nominal value in my judgment or else sold and the money invested. Mr. Logan seems to overlook in reference to the income statement of $48,000 in my letter that I stated it was calculated upon the present investments for the coming year. I do not think you need be concerned at all respecting rate of return upon the investments to the endowment fund.[171]

Washington valued Peabody's advice; he sought it, and it was offered to him.[172]

There were many other businesspeople besides Rockefeller, Huntington, and Peabody who reinforced Washington's entrepreneurial philosophy. Robert Ogden, a good friend of Samuel Armstrong and a member of the Tuskegee Institute Board of Trustees, confirmed for Washington, among many things, the value of offering honest labor. Washington had first learned this lesson from his mother and Mrs. Ruffner. As manager of the Wanamaker Store in New York City and as a devout Christian, Ogden believed in not manipulating people in order to make a profit.[173] His motto toward his customers, according to Washington, was always that "a good bargain is good to both buyer and seller."[174] Like Washington, he felt that "material prosperity was the basis of all sorts of progress."[175] Honesty, however, was critical. John Wanamaker, an associate of Washington's and head of the Wanamaker Store, said to members at one of Washington's NNBL meetings to "start at the bottom and work up" and that "merit was color-blind."[176] In 1910, he hosted an NNBL meeting in his Philadelphia department store.[177] Henry H. Rogers, an associate of

Washington's and a Standard Oil executive, also believed in helping people less fortunate than himself, provided that they were willing to help themselves. According to Washington, Rogers was touched deeply by his efforts to help those who were truly struggling to help themselves.[178] Julius Rosenwald, the wealthy Sears, Roebuck and Company owner and executive and member of the Tuskegee Institute Board of Trustees, contributed in a charitable manner. His gifts to the school and its students were contingent upon their continuous exhibition of signs that they were trying to help themselves.[179] He spoke to National Negro League members at the 1912 annual meeting held in Chicago, emphasizing the value of hard work and thrift.[180] Seth Low and William Wilcox were other board of trustees members who also reinforced Washington's entrepreneurial philosophy. Due to his financial relationship with these businessmen, Washington was an attentive listener and a shrewd operator who would use what he knew and what he had learned from these men to develop, expand, or reinforce an entrepreneurial philosophy that he hoped would serve to advance his own people.

Besides these businesspeople who served to reinforce Washington's business knowledge, he was also exposed to literature that emphasized Spencerianism and the Protestant work ethic,[181] as he likely at least browsed through books with such titles as, "How to Get Workmen," "How to Handle Workmen," and "How to Systematize Your Factory."[182] Perhaps in attempting to better understand the mind of Andrew Carnegie, a businessman, philanthropist, and supporter of Spencerianism, Washington read *The Gospel of Wealth* (1900) and claimed that it was an inspiring book.[183] Upon encountering W.E.B. Du Bois on a train, Washington recommended it to him as required reading.[184]

NNBL members, like the wealthy businessmen and the literature that Washington was exposed to, also reinforced Washington's established entrepreneurial philosophy, particularly those members who were seriously engaged in a business venture, many of whom had operated businesses long before they joined the NNBL or met Washington. The list of league members who met this criterion is extensive, but as illustrations, Isaiah T. Montgomery and Charles Banks are two excellent examples.[185] Isaiah T. Montgomery was born in 1847 and was a slave of Joseph Davis, the elder brother of Jefferson Davis, the president of the Confederacy. Montgomery, who was trained as a child to work in his owner's plantation office, experienced the effects of the Civil War and Reconstruction, or, in other words, the Union army's destruction of Mississippi's infrastructure and the backlash experienced by freed slaves following their emancipation. Through the kindness of Joseph

Davis, Montgomery and his family were allowed to purchase land from their former master and successfully cultivate it for a number of years.[186] When Joseph Davis died, however, his heirs illegally seized the land, compelling the Montgomery family to settle elsewhere.[187] In 1887, Montgomery worked out an arrangement with the Louisville, New Orleans, and Texas Railway that enabled him to purchase vast tracts of uninhabited land in Mississippi which the railroad wanted settled for commercial purposes.[188] This was the beginning of the town of Mound Bayou, which was incorporated in 1898. Mound Bayou grew rapidly and became a little city, inhabited and controlled exclusively by African Americans.

This self-help effort, initiated by Montgomery during the nadir, highly impressed Washington because it was an exemplification of his teachings.[189] As a result of the effects of Reconstruction and its aftermath on African Americans, Washington always advocated the duties that he felt African Americans had to fulfill to gain practical American citizenship. This was ingrained in him at Hampton Institute. Some noted historians, however, have misunderstood Washington's advocacy of self-help as tending to promote segregation, which was doomed to fail.[190] On the contrary, the ultimate aim of all Washington's philosophies was to bring about the inclusion of African Americans into the very fabric of mainstream American society. Thus, his complex activities in arduous times can easily be misconstrued. Washington behaved as a technician with humanly flaws, finding opportunities within disadvantages as historian John Flynn has so accurately suggested.[191] Montgomery, who was a strong supporter of African-American business development, probably worked with the same intent in mind, especially since he was a close ally of Washington's.[192] Ultimately, his economic activities reinforced Washington's entrepreneurial philosophy, particularly pertaining to self-help.

Charles Banks, like Montgomery, moved to the town of Mound Bayou. He came in 1903 from Clarksdale, Mississippi, a town a short distance from Mound Bayou. He had attended Rust University before coming, and after his graduation, he and his brother became successful entrepreneurs in Clarksdale. Unfortunately, his brother died shortly thereafter, so Banks decided to move to Mound Bayou and try his luck there. As in Clarksdale, he quickly became a successful and respected businessman. He organized and opened the Bank of Mound Bayou in 1904,[193] and he was later the driving force behind opening a cottonseed oil mill that began operations in 1913. Washington hailed these two efforts by Banks and the people of Mound Bayou not only because they were a confirmation of his ideas, but because they were perceived as signs of racial progress, especially the cottonseed oil mill.[194] Unfortunately, both these Mound Bayou businesses struggled to remain operational: the Bank of Mound Bayou failed in 1914, while the cottonseed oil mill suspended operations from 1915 to about July 12, 1919.[195] To combat the high interest rates charged by white banks in neighboring areas after the failure of Banks' institution, the Mound Bayou State Bank was opened in 1915 with his financial backing.[196]

Despite these events, Washington and his personal secretary, Emmett Scott, still seemed to hold Banks in high regard.[197] In Scott's 1917 biography on Washington, which was published a few years after the bank failure and two years after Washington's death, he still wrote favorably about Banks.[198] Since Scott was privy to many of Washington's innermost thoughts, it may be presumed that Washington felt the same. Scott referred to Banks as the J. P. Morgan of his race.[199] His respect for and devotion to Banks was evident in personal correspondence as well,[200] where Banks spoke of the late Washington in laudatory terms.[201]

In the early years of the NNBL, Washington was extremely impressed with Banks and his consistent hard work, and they kept up a steady correspondence with one another.[202] When Washington made his speaking tour of Mississippi, Banks was the architect behind it.[203] As head of the Mississippi Negro Business League, Banks saw to it that it was one of the most, if not the most, active and progressive state leagues in the country.[204] This all pleased Washington, as he saw his business ideas confirmed in Banks' actions. In his third autobiography, *My Larger Education: Being Chapters from My Experience*, Washington wrote the following concerning one of the things that he learned from Banks:

> I have learned much from studying the success of Charles Banks. Before all else he has taught me the value of common-sense in dealing with conditions as they exist in the South. I have learned from him that, in spite of what the Southern white man may say about the Negro in moments of excitement, the sober sentiment of the South is in sympathy with every effort that promises solid and substantial progress to the Negro.[205]

This lesson would be an integral part of Washington's entrepreneurial philosophy, and his respect for Banks continued to soar.[206] All of these individuals—the businesspeople on the Tuskegee Institute Board of Trustees, NNBL members, and others—confirmed to Washington that his entrepreneurial philosophy for the advancement of his people was the correct one.

Key influences upon the development of Washington's entrepreneurial philosophy have been analyzed, and as was the case with Reconstruction and the nadir, these key influences helped to mold and develop Washington's entrepreneurial philosophy. More specifically, a dual-dimensional and multi-thematic approach was employed in order to analyze various themes from two broad points of view: core values and practical business influences. These viewpoints have served not only to underscore key influences on Washington's entrepreneurial philosophy, but also to establish a relationship between the formation of Washington's early core values and his early and late practical business influences, all of which contributed toward the creation or progression of his entrepreneurial philosophy.

Washington's entrepreneurial philosophy was significantly influenced by the plight of his people, especially the unity that they displayed when helping one another under such adverse conditions. It was also affected by the Protestant work ethic, the national and Southern economic milieus, the self-help and racial solidarity schools of African-American economic thought evident during the nadir, and Washington's early Tuskegee business encounters. After Washington's core entrepreneurial philosophy became established, it was expanded and reinforced by Tuskegee Institute Board of Trustees members, large enterprise owners and operators, and members of the NNBL. All of these influences and reinforcements contributed not only toward compelling Washington to execute his ideas, but toward advocating their implementation on a local and national scale as a strategy to achieve real freedom and empowerment of African Americans during what was a trying period of American history.

3

The Entrepreneurial Ideas of Booker T. Washington

As noted earlier, most of the studies done on Booker T. Washington have concentrated exclusively on his views concerning industrial education or his supposedly accommodationist leadership stance, either supporting or opposing Du Bois' famous critique. These studies, however, do not even begin to fully explain another core aspect of Washington's leadership strategy—his entrepreneurial philosophy, a plan he had developed by 1891 that emphasized duties rather than rights. Most importantly, Washington's entrepreneurial philosophy has not been analyzed deeply from a business perspective. The aim of this chapter is to concretely present Booker T. Washington's entrepreneurial ideas by reconstructing their components from many of his speeches and writings and then explicating them. In addition, a summary and analysis effectively evaluate Washington's entrepreneurial philosophy.

Unlike many of the business leaders of Washington's era, the individual was never central to his entrepreneurial philosophy. As noted in chapter 2, "the group was primary." Although Washington never totally promoted the capitalist tenet of individualism, ideologies like the Protestant work ethic and social Darwinism greatly influenced him; he advocated individual development and racial solidarity and lauded captains of industry—successful individuals who would not only serve as role models, but would actively show others how to succeed. This mix of concepts characterized Washington's entire public life. He promoted individual successes, but once individuals became successful, he urged them to reach back and help others, because group progression was more meaningful for the advancement of his race and, ultimately, their happiness.

Washington, as a national leader, considered his business philosophy an operational, viable strategy. He passionately and consistently espoused it before African Americans throughout his public career. At its core, it was nothing more than a multitude of values, beliefs, and practices that, taken collectively, equaled his entrepreneurial philosophy—a plan for making a significant number of African Americans into producers instead of just consumers. Washington's entrepreneurial philosophy called for two things: adopting characteristics that were ingredients for success and boldly pioneering them. This becomes evident upon analyzing the basic components of Washington's entrepreneurial philosophy—his self-help plan for African Americans during and after the nadir.

Components of Washington's Entrepreneurial Philosophy

A controversial aspect of Washington's educational philosophy was his emphasis on industrial education.[1] Scholars have debated this issue extensively and because of that their arguments need not be reiterated here.[2] Nevertheless, industrial education played a significant role in Washington's entrepreneurial philosophy. At Tuskegee Institute, trades were taught along with academic course work.[3] Washington insisted that his faculty, especially the faculty in the Academic Department, teach their courses via the correlative method,[4] a pedagogical method that related course work to praxis.[5] Washington felt that the implementation of this methodology would assure that his students, upon leaving school, would be able to return to their respective communities and preferably create or at least successfully obtain employment (often as teachers), thereby making themselves productive, valuable citizens.

Washington stated that he was not against higher education but believed that African Americans in the post-Reconstruction and Jim Crow eras generally needed more than academic education,[6] especially since they had no foothold in the business world. He believed that they needed mental development that was tied to hand (trade) and heart (moral) training. Industrial education was an example of this for Washington. It gave an individual a skill to start a business, which he felt could ultimately help improve race relations. "Nothing else so soon brings about right relations between the two races in the South," Washington wrote, "as the commercial progress of the Negro."[7] He further felt that friction between the two races would pass away as soon as African Americans got something that whites wanted, "something that makes the white man partly dependent upon the Negro instead of all the dependence being on the other side."[8] In doing this, Washington argued that both groups would grow to exist on equal grounds, engaging in reciprocal relationships.

From a business perspective, Washington saw African Americans at a lower stage of development than Anglo-Americans.[9] He attributed this phenomenon to the experience of slavery. Making no excuses for this condition, Washington recommended and promoted industrial education for African Americans coupled with the correlative method of teaching as an uplift strategy. Provided this, Washington felt that the masses would be assured of practical education that would allow them to always be employed, and this, he believed, could eventually lead to self-sufficiency.[10]

Practical education, as opposed to strictly training in the liberal arts, was one of the first principles of Washington's entrepreneurial philosophy. Its purpose was to provide individuals with economic skills that were in demand in their respective communities. Washington often attested that individuals so trained were frequently considered elites of their communities primarily because the goods or services they provided were indispensable to their community's well-being.[11] In explaining how Tuskegee Institute became accepted in the surrounding community, Washington noted that some rural whites were at first skeptical because they did not know the staff, students, and faculty there. Many of them, however, needed bricks, which were produced at Tuskegee Institute's brickyard. Once they learned that the bricks were of high quality, according to Washington, many of them not only made purchases, but also got to know individuals at the school and its workings. They then began to see Tuskegee Institute as an asset to the entire community. Moreover, Washington noted, "Our institution own[ed] a better printing press for doing job work than that owned by the white printing offices. When the whites want[ed] a first class job of printing done, the difference in the color of our skin [did] not prevent their sending it to our office."[12]

After African Americans were equipped with practical education that was taught via the correlative method, in the late nineteenth and early twentieth centuries, Washington advocated finding economic opportunities in one's surrounding community. The order could also be reversed: one could find an economic opportunity first, then obtain the practical education in a formal or informal setting. Generally, finding economic opportunities was a theme consistently touched upon in Washington's speeches when he referred to obtaining a livelihood.[13] This idea was best exemplified in his Atlanta Exposition address of 1895. To the African Americans in the audience he said, "Cast down your buckets where you are. Cast it down in agriculture, mechanics, in commerce, in domestic service, and in the professions."[14] He meant that African Americans must stop looking in distant places for economic opportunities and take those in front of them. He felt that the South, where most African Americans lived during his lifetime, was a developing section of the nation, full of economic opportunities ready for the taking.

Furthermore, cognizant of discrimination and segregation in both the North and South, Washington in his speeches and writings consistently emphasized that African Americans should never allow their grievances to overshadow their opportunities and successes. He maintained that if they just continued to work hard and steadily, their situation would change. Although he thought it was important to be aware of wrongs that were done to African Americans, he felt more progress would be made by focusing on positive achievements among his race. He believed that protesting grievances without a constructive plan was futile and destructive. "In an increasing degree," he noted, "we must be an optimistic race. There is no hope for a despairing individual or a despairing race."[15] Always publicly depicting himself as the consummate optimist, Washington taught that there were advantages in disadvantages, and that the objective should always be to seize and promote those advantages.[16]

Washington also urged that, once an economic opportunity was seized, a niche should be created by not only practicing a learnt trade or some new entrepreneurial activity, but by doing it so well that it would be in high demand and capable of outpacing any potential competition. This meant performing an ordinary task in an uncommon manner. In presenting a speech to the National Educational Association in Madison, Wisconsin, Washington proclaimed:

> I said that the whole future of the Negro rested largely upon the question as to whether or not he should make himself, through his skill, intelligence, and character, of such undeniable value to the community in which he lived that the community could not dispense with his presence. I said that any individual who learned to do something better than anybody else—learned to do a common thing in an uncommon manner—had solved his problem, regardless of the colour of his skin, and that in proportion as the Negro learned to produce what other people wanted and must have in the same proportion would he be respected.[17]

To Washington, finding a niche meant not only offering a valuable product or service to one's surrounding community, but, more specifically, offering something that would attract the patronage of everyone in the community—blacks, whites, and everyone else. Washington saw the markets as color-blind when it came to purchasing something of high quality, something that the world wanted. "It is only as the black man produces something that makes the markets of the world dependent on him for something," he stressed, "[that] he will secure his rightful place."[18] Throughout his book *The Negro in Business* (1907), Washington cited numerous examples of African-American entrepreneurs who had faced difficult, even overwhelming, odds but had succeeded. Stories of individuals such as Junius Groves, a successful farmer who made a comfortable living as an entrepreneur, emphasized that African Americans' color had never been a hindrance to their business success.[19] Furthermore, in creating such a niche, provided that they offered high-quality goods and services, Washington felt that African Americans had an edge over others competing for the African-American market since they were an integral part of that community.[20]

In acknowledging this potential advantage, Washington was not recommending that African Americans conduct business exclusively amongst themselves (as has been argued).[21] He believed that individuals should conduct business in all markets—that is, the open market. (This issue will be explored further in chapter 5.) This would not only enhance their potential profits, he believed, but it would also display their worth to the surrounding community of blacks and whites.[22] This was a crucial aspect of Washington's uplift strategy for African Americans. "[W]hether in the North or in the South," Washington said, "wherever I have seen a black man who was succeeding in business, who was a taxpayer, and who possessed intelligence and high character, that individual was treated with the highest respect by members of the white race. In proportion as we can multiply these examples North and South will our problem be solved."[23] Further, Washington said, "no race that has anything to contribute to the markets of the world is long in any degree ostracized."[24]

To contribute to the markets of the world, Washington thought that it was imperative for individuals to begin their progression at the bottom and work their way up. This was one of the most dominant themes in his entrepreneurial philosophy, if not the most dominant. It appears in most of his speeches and writings concerning African-American business development. Furthermore, beginning at the bottom was what Washington did in his own life, as revealed in his autobiographies, *The Story of My Life and Work* (1900) and *Up From Slavery* (1901). Scarred by the failure of Reconstruction and the African American's experience during that epoch, Washington generally held that, "Ignorant and inexperienced, it is not strange that in the first years of our new life [the immediate aftermath of slavery] we began at the top instead of at the bottom; that a seat in Congress or the state legislature was more sought than real estate or industrial skills; that the political convention of stump speaking had more attraction than starting a dairy farm or truck garden."[25] And so, as alluded to in chapter One, to Washington, making political participation a higher priority than creating an economic foundation contributed toward the negative plight of African Americans during the Jim Crow era. The only sure remedy for this, in his opinion, was to begin small and grow large, which meant beginning at the bottom on a solid, real economic foundation.

Washington argued that all respected races first began at the bottom. "No people ever got upon its feet and obtained the respect and confidence of the world which did not lay its foundations in successful business enterprises."[26] For African Americans to do otherwise, he believed, was to begin on an artificial foundation, which would only lead to continued havoc. This was one rationale for Washington's consistent preaching of the benefits of farming, land ownership, and industrial education for African Americans. He thought that gaining economic strength would not only open other societal avenues to African Americans, but would also provide them a material foundation upon which they could stand and demand their rights. In responding to critics, Washington acknowledged that sacrifices would have to be made for fifty years, a century, or perhaps more until a solid foundation was acquired.[27] Moreover, he argued:

> I would set no limits to the attainments of the Negro in arts, in letters or statesmanship, but I believe the surest way to reach those ends is by laying the foundation in the little things of life that lie immediate about one's door. I plead for the Negro not because I want to cramp him, but because I want to free him. I want to see him enter the all-powerful business and commercial world.[28]

Washington even called upon the men and women in colleges and universities to lead the way in this direction.[29] Apparently, many heeded his call, because Tuskegee Institute was home to a significant number of college- and university-trained faculty. Emphasizing his vision, Washington stated, "We need education—industrial, technical, college and professional—but we must not forget to provide a medium through business and industrial enterprises for the services of a large proportion of our intelligent men and women."[30] He further noted that: "Without industrial development there can be no wealth; without wealth there can be no leisure; without leisure no opportunity for thoughtful reflection and the cultivation of higher arts."[31]

A material foundation, to Washington, like beginning at the bottom, was a tangible, visible reality. He abhorred theory, especially when practical examples were available; and to him they were always available. Some oft-repeated expressions of his were, "an ounce of application is worth a ton of abstraction"[32] and "an inch of progress is worth a yard of complaint." In his discussions on business and other aspects of his leadership platform, Washington generally asked that individuals give concrete examples. He stressed his appreciation for the man or woman who could show or tell him how to accomplish something tangible, the results of which were visible. One of the rules that he implemented as head of the Tuskegee Farmers' Conference and the NNBL was that all meetings be run simply, free of jargon. Speakers were required to explain their achievements and tell how they accomplished them. This, he believed, had more educational and motivational benefits than hearing some abstract explanation or an idea of what someone hoped to accomplish. For local branches of the NNBL, a pamphlet was published emphasizing this requirement.[33]

Washington respected such practices because he believed they led to results, and results brought about recognition. Results reflected industry, proved an individual's worthiness as a citizen, were hard to argue with, and if practiced on a large scale, could end prejudice. "Patiently, quietly, doggedly, persistently, through summer and winter, sunshine and shadow, by self-sacrifice, by foresight, by honesty and industry," Washington stressed, "we must reinforce argument with results."[34] Elaborating further, he wrote:

> I do not believe that the world ever takes a race seriously, in its desire to enter into the control of the government of a nation in any large degree, until a large number of individual members of that race, have demonstrated, beyond question, their ability to control and develop individual business enterprises. When a number of Negroes rise to the point where they own and operate the most successful farms, are among the largest tax-payers in the county, are moral and intelligent, I do not believe that in many portions of the South such men need long be denied the right of saying by their votes how they prefer their property to be taxed and in choosing those who are to make and administer the law.[35]

In writing about his experience in establishing Tuskegee Institute, Washington was aware that the surrounding community—black and white—would not have had faith in him had they not seen the fruits of his labor: purchased land, school buildings, on-campus businesses, students, teachers, and numerous farm animals.[36]

To obtain results and recognition, Washington constantly told individuals interested or involved in business ventures that they had to pay the price of success, "the price of sleepless nights, the price of toil when others rest, the price of planning today for tomorrow, this year for next year."[37] He cautioned individuals not to get involved in get-rich-quick schemes because one had to work for everything he or she acquired in the business world. No one would get something for nothing. It appears that Washington practiced what he preached.[38] A review of some of his numerous letters in the Library of Congress reveal that he made it a practice, for example, of not leaving his office in the evenings until every letter received that day had been responded to, and at the height of his career, Washington received numerous letters daily.

For Washington, the price of success had other specific meanings. For example, it meant developing characteristics that could lead to business success, such as being frugal, honest, thoughtful, and industrious; it meant saving, being prompt at one's place of work, keeping one's establishment clean and inviting, developing an effective system for operating one's business, getting the proper type of education (that which could be applied), obtaining property, and developing a Christian character.[39] Moreover, paying the price of success meant being persistent in a business endeavor through its ups and downs. "We have got to stick to what we undertake," Washington emphasized, "got to stick through failure and success when all the world sees failure looking us in the face."[40] Struggle and perseverance were important in Washington's outlook—to him these traits developed strength in an individual. Washington was fond of saying that an individual should be judged not by where he is but by the depths from which he has come. At the Ninth Annual Convention of the NNBL held in Baltimore, Maryland, Washington quoted a professor at Harvard University who had written that less than forty years from the Reconstruction era, African Americans had accumulated an aggregate taxable property of five hundred million dollars. To Washington, this was the reward for struggle and perseverance, which the price of success demands.[41]

Washington taught that, after having achieved a goal as a result of struggle and perseverance, to maintain success one had to continue paying the price of success. This meant always striving to do more and never becoming complacent. "Wherever you find a race that is easily satisfied, and one that has few wants," he noted, "there you will find a race that is of little value to its country, industrially, commercially or in any other direction."[42] In examining the life of Washington and those of the individuals generally whose occupations he discussed, it is evident that they started small and expanded. They pulled themselves up by their bootstraps (those who possessed any), and they were persistent in striving to achieve and maintain their goals. Washington's efforts at Tuskegee Institute were again evidence of this; he founded Tuskegee Institute in a shanty and nearby church on July 4, 1881. According to Emmett J. Scott, Booker T. Washington's trusted secretary and faithful friend, by the time of Washington's death, Tuskegee Institute's property and endowment were valued at almost four million dollars.[43] Washington secretly envisioned the school he started growing into a major institution—one of which his descendants would be proud and perhaps be encouraged to a still greater effort by.[44]

To Washington, maintaining success also meant staying abreast of the methods and practices involved in one's occupation.[45] This entailed reading pamphlets and journals and consulting individuals who had more knowledge and experience in a given field. Washington told the story of a man in Little Rock, Arkansas, who started off small and grew his business endeavors quite large.[46] This man, a Mr. Alexander, was fired from his job because he quarreled with a white man in another department. In searching for work, he agreed to paint a man's house, but unfamiliar with the painting trade, he felt lost. In Little Rock, Arkansas, in the early 1890s, white painters generally did not want to freely share their knowledge of the trade with him. He finally met an elderly white gentleman who agreed to teach him free of charge. From this humble beginning, he finished his first painting job and performed it so well that he was offered another, then referred to still other people. His business was so prosperous that in a relatively short period he hired a crew of workers. According to Washington, besides working hard, a significant part of this man's success was a result of staying abreast of new developments in his profession.

Washington further taught that keeping informed of the latest developments in one's field would help one be more competitive. He believed that the markets within the United States were competitive and merciless, and that for an individual to survive and prosper, he had to offer a product of superior quality, drawing customers for that reason and not strictly due to pleas of racial patronage. "Let any colored man enter any avenue of business," Washington declared, "and if he is capable, clean in his business methods, true to the race, not relying on his color for success, but on his superiority in his business, that man will be stood by and supported."[47] Washington could give examples of many different individuals throughout the nation who fit this description, particularly those who were members of the NNBL. Furthermore, to Washington, being competitive indicated personal merit.

Merit, another dominant theme in Washington's business philosophy and something he considered a key ingredient for success, was pervasive in his speeches and writings. To Washington, as alluded to above, an individual engaged in business had to constantly show that he was worthy of attracting and maintaining customers, and this could only come about through perseverance, hard work, and earnest toil. "Nothing ever [came] to one, that [was] worth having, except as a result of hard work."[48] In Washington's fundraising campaigns, for example, it sometimes took ten years to get a specific donor to contribute to Tuskegee Institute's educational fund (for instance, Andrew Carnegie). When discussing this fact, Washington let it be known that persuading these people to give funds was not just luck, but rather hard, consistent work.[49] Moreover, he felt and articulated that there was something in human nature that rewarded merit, regardless of skin color. "When an individual produces what the world wants," Washington related, "whether it is a product of hand, head or heart, the world does not long stop to inquire what is the color of the skin of the producer."[50] Something good that was tangible, in his view, went a long way in softening race prejudice. A great inventor, a productive farmer, a successful grocery-store owner, and a great painter would all be judged similarly based upon their work. If they were assets to their communities, they would always have a venue in which to conduct business. "In other words," Washington wrote, "a race, like an individual, becomes highly civilized and useful in proportion as it learns to use the good things of this earth, not as an end, but as a means toward promoting its own moral and religious growth and the prosperity and happiness of the world."[51] Thus, to be successful in Washington's view and to pay the price of success, one had to work hard at offering a high-quality product or service to all markets.

Washington thought the South was the best market for African-American entrepreneurs and laborers to first display their merit. After starting at the bottom, this was the second most dominant theme in Washington's entrepreneurial philosophy, which is evident in most of his public speeches and writings. To Washington—just as envisioned by Wilbur J. Cash,[52] author of *The Mind of the South* (1941)—the South was a new frontier, possessing numerous economic opportunities in which niches could be created and developed. The end of the Civil War had united the nation in purpose, strengthening the hegemony of the federal government. A result of this was that the South was industrializing, albeit at a slower rate than the North, and Northern industrialists were seeking to invest in Southern markets. Washington saw economic opportunities for African Americans in this Southern context. He believed and articulated that the white South would not generally be hostile to African-American business development, for most African Americans were already in the South and possessed keen knowledge of the environment and their white neighbors. Race prejudice, he believed, could sooner be conquered in the South. Millions of acres of unused, cheap land was available and European immigration was predominantly confined to the North. Furthermore, in Washington's view, the South was an oasis of opportunities for African Americans, whereas the North was potentially stifling, especially if African-American migrants were not able to make themselves valuable in Northern communities. Labor unions in the North discriminated against African Americans, especially those involved in skilled trades. From his fund-raising campaigns in the North, Washington noted: "Often it is easier in a Northern city to beg money than to find an opportunity to earn it. The facilities to spend money are wide open, but the avenues for earning it are too often closed because of race or color."[53] Morally, Washington also thought some Northern cities offered temptations that would corrupt newly arrived Southern men and women.[54]

In emphasizing what he thought were advantages in the Southern context, Washington was not oblivious to the oppressive conditions that African Americans faced in the post-Reconstruction and Jim Crow South. He was well aware of the effects of the Southern mortgage system, which kept many African Americans in perpetual debt; he was well aware of lynching and its effects, particularly in the states of Texas, Georgia, Alabama, and Mississippi. He was well aware of both the three-month school years which were common for African Americans in many Southern counties and the small amount of state funds appropriated for African-American education; and he was well aware of efforts on the part of some white Southern mobs to engage in "whitecapping," a practice of compelling successful African-American entrepreneurs to either shut down their businesses or leave town.[55] Notwithstanding these factors, as mentioned earlier, Washington publicly was a consummate optimist. He continued to emphasize the opportunities that existed in the South over the grievances, and he pleaded with respectable Southern whites, usually of the upper classes, for just and equal enforcement of the laws. To African-American migration advocates, Washington commented, "It is an unwise policy to encourage our people to leave the South, except from sections where they are not protected by the law, unless we are assured that the conditions will be permanently improved when they reach other sections."[56] However, regardless of Washington's public outlook, these grievances naturally served as barriers that prevented, limited, or slowed the upward mobility of African Americans, particularly whitecapping. Nevertheless, Washington's counsel to his people was to aggressively push on, in spite of the numerous barriers, to a better day that was just around the corner.

As a spokesperson for African Americans, Washington had access to a national forum to speak about such issues as the South being the best section for African Americans, migration, and overcoming obstacles. Northern industrialists and white Southern elites who were searching for some means of decreasing racial conflict and stabilizing markets in the South placed this national leadership responsibility first and foremost on Washington. They believed that Washington's Atlanta Exposition address was a workable, non-threatening compromise between the two dominant Southern races.[57] Taking on this responsibility, Washington spoke for his race, and, in time, his race generally acknowledged him as their leader.

As such, Washington believed in and advocated nationally the support of African-American enterprises that he deemed worthy. These included any that reflected merit, were successful, and proved useful.[58] As noted earlier, Washington was aware that individual advancement could lead to group advancement, which could ultimately lead to racial progress. Consequently, Washington strongly approved of racial cooperation for worthy ventures. To do any less, he thought, was to do his race a disservice. Racial cooperation for a worthy venture, in Washington's view, could potentially result in employment for African Americans. Moreover, he felt that the psychological effects of African Americans seeing members of their race in responsible positions or belonging to the entrepreneurial class would do the race a great service. In Washington's view, this would be especially true for those formerly enslaved African Americans who had been exploited most of their lives, shown and told that they were mere chattels and nothing more.[59]

As noted in chapter 2, Washington, in helping to establish Tuskegee Institute, frequently applied his principle of racial cooperation. He visited homes and churches and let it be known what Tuskegee Institute's purpose would be and the help needed from the surrounding community to make it a success. For example, he once informed a certain resident that Tuskegee Institute needed his labor for a particular period. The man replied that he had to harvest his crops. Washington reiterated to the man that his labor was needed and advised him to make an arrangement with his neighbors to harvest his crops. The man not only acceded to this request but also reported promptly for work at the time that he was needed, explaining later that, "I came same as everybody did what he told them."[60] Similarly, in 1914, Washington helped to establish the Baldwin Farms Colony, named after William H. Baldwin Jr., a longtime board of trustees member and a great benefactor to the school. This colony was comprised of eighteen hundred acres of land that had been purchased by William G. Wilcox, another member of the board of trustees, and other friends of the school.[61] The land was about nine miles from Tuskegee Institute. It was purchased to be resold to graduates and former students who wanted to be farmers but found it difficult to purchase land, animals, and implements. Selected applicants were given an opportunity to purchase farms in tracts of land averaging forty acres and granted a generous period to pay for it. The colony sold the land at an average price of fifteen dollars per acre. "If there [was] no house on the land the company [would] put up a $300.00 house so planned as to permit the addition of rooms and improvements as rapidly as the purchaser [was] able to pay for them; the cost to be added to the initial cost of the land."[62] For Washington, this was not only racial cooperation, but also a means of combating the abuses of the mortgage system, which often led to debt peonage; selected applicants were given an opportunity not only to be self-sufficient farmers, but entrepreneurs as well.

For displaying unity, obtaining business success, and overcoming adversity, Washington upheld Jews as a group for African Americans to emulate. He saw them as having been in a position similar to that of African Americans but as having elevated themselves through their business and industrial sense.[63] In his speeches and writings on the subject, Washington noted that the Jews had clung together through adverse situations, particularly in Europe. "They had a certain amount of unity, pride, and love of race; and, as the years go on, they will be more and more influential in this country, a country where they were once despised, and looked upon with scorn and derision."[64] He argued further that it was because Jews had faith in themselves that they succeeded. "Unless the Negro learns more and more to imitate the Jews in these matters, to have faith in himself, he cannot expect to have any degree of success."[65]

Faith, to Washington, had several meanings. There was religious faith, which was an integral component of his entrepreneurial philosophy. When Washington first opened Tuskegee Institute, many Macon County clergymen advised their congregations not to send their children to Washington's "ungodly" school. To them, Washington did not appear to be promoting strong religious faith. Washington emphatically expressed in his second autobiography, *Up From Slavery*, that he thought many African Americans he observed in the South sought the ministry to avoid arduous labor and that many of them were ill-suited to such a calling.[66] This attitude may have been further expressed in Washington's unrecorded speeches. However, Washington seemed to have been religious and appreciative of the emotionalism evident in many African-American religious services, although available evidence is inconclusive. Nevertheless, to improve the ministry, he started a Bible training curriculum at his school, the Phelps Hall Bible Training School.[67] A nondenominational chapel existed on campus as well. Regarding the intersection of business and religion, Washington taught that African Americans spent too much time focusing strictly on the hereafter. He thought that the afterlife deserved attention, but that more emphasis was needed on the present world and practical, everyday affairs. "The Negro," Washington declared, "needs to be taught that more of the religion that manifests itself in his happiness in the prayer-meeting should be made more practical in the performance of his daily task. The man who owns a home and is in the possession of the elements by which he is sure of making a daily living has a great aid to a moral and religious life."[68] In Washington's view, this financial security would be a major step in laying a material foundation that his race could build upon.

Washington was completely aware that he espoused a materialist business philosophy, and he stressed that he would recommend it to any group at the same stage of economic development as African Americans during the post-Reconstruction and Jim Crow eras.[69] However, reflecting back on his school days at Hampton Institute, Washington felt and articulated that there was one thing greater than material wealth, and that was character.[70] To Washington, character was something that was not inherited, but developed, usually through struggle. Unlike the robber barons of his era who believed strictly in economic "survival of the fittest," Washington thought it the duty of the privileged to manifest character by helping those less fortunate. The formation of this idea probably was influenced by the subordinate position Washington saw his race in and the constant oppression they endured. Thus, as principal of Tuskegee Institute for thirty-four years and as a national leader, Washington patterned his life according to this idea, promoting honesty as an important characteristic for African-American entrepreneurs.

In conjunction with this charitable philosophy, Washington proposed that captains of industry were needed to lead the masses of African Americans to economic freedom and, ultimately, equality with their white neighbors.[71] He expressed this idea after being made cognizant of the fact that many of the masses wanted to improve their condition but were unaware of how to do so. It is ironic that, close to the time that Washington proposed this idea, W.E.B. Du Bois had promoted the notion of the "Talented Tenth," an argument which posited that African Americans needed to provide higher education to the brightest ten percent of their race so that those individuals could lead the rest to real freedom and equality.[72] In 1889, at the Atlanta University Conference on the Negro in Business, Du Bois proposed in a formal resolution that merchants should be the best-trained young men to be found.[73] While Du Bois' plan was elitist,[74] in that only the best and brightest were to be given access to higher education, Washington's plan asked that individuals pull themselves up and then lead the masses from within, as he had done for the masses of people surrounding Tuskegee Institute, in Macon County, in the state of Alabama, and eventually throughout the nation.

Washington also thought that these captains of industry, by example and precept, should convey to the masses of African Americans that they must develop a "pioneering spirit,"[75] that is, the will to take business and financial risks. To get ahead, he felt that such was necessary. He tried to push his people, especially the educated ones, beyond being mere laborers who generally would be paid a steady wage or salary. He knew that real economic wealth was based on business ownership—someone implementing a plan to supply a demand. Consequently, he advocated that African Americans venture into all realms of lawful economic activity.

Washington held that by being economically self-sufficient African Americans would develop a sense of security—including property and personal protection, the right to a trial by jury, and, in essence, true practical American citizenship.[76] The individuals who were valuable to their communities would experience unhampered rights. An expanded professional class could be supported, and future generations would have a base from which to begin. Hence, in Washington's view, a group making itself economically viable ensured its natural and constitutional rights. To succeed, Washington felt that individuals should cast down their buckets where they were and begin to build up material foundations in their communities and beyond.

Taken together, these components constitute Washington's entrepreneurial philosophy, which was his plan for obtaining real freedom, empowerment, and equality for his people. He wanted African Americans to embrace his values and beliefs concerning business creation and development and to implement these beliefs and values once they were acquired. In essence, he pushed African Americans to acquire "entrepreneurial mindsets" and "entrepreneurial practices," becoming pioneers unafraid to go out and create something out of nothing. He realized that in America workers were either owners of the means of production or wage earners. He wanted a significant majority of African Americans to be owners of the means of production because he realized that such citizens profoundly affected policy in America. "It is in business and industry," Washington wrote, "that I see the brightest and most hopeful phases of the race situation to-day."[77] He also noted, "The Negro in this country must become, in a more potent sense, a producer of wealth as well as a consumer. He must become more of a business man, must enter all avenues of industry."[78]

Summary and Analysis

Washington's entrepreneurial philosophy was unique. It was not just a late-nineteenth and early twentieth-century form of Spencerianism or a Horatio Alger success formula.[79] Some elements of these principles existed in Washington's entrepreneurial philosophy, but his was far more distinct—it was a race-uplift strategy, consisting of practical and moral components.

Signs of progress and continuity were evident in Washington's entrepreneurial philosophy despite what has been considered his limited education. I conducted a content analysis of Washington's annual addresses before the NNBL for the years 1900, 1903, 1904, 1905, 1906, 1908, 1909, 1912, 1913, 1914, and 1915, which represent 11 of the 16 years that Washington was league president. These addresses were selected due to their availability, as those for the years 1901, 1902, 1907, 1910, and 1911 could not be obtained. From this analysis, patterns became evident. Washington's speeches from 1900 to 1909 displayed consistency in presentation as well as content. Themes such as finding a niche, the color-blindness of the market, and racial unity were stated explicitly or implicitly. Washington seldom deviated from the subject of business and how economic development would help his race. In the address of 1906, Washington began to introduce statistics to support his claims, such as the dollar amount of taxable property owned by African Americans in Georgia and the total area of unused and unoccupied land in the South.[80] Moreover, his addresses tended to be short and simple. Those from 1912 to 1915 were longer, increasingly philosophical, and possessed even more statistics. In the earlier periods, Washington's addresses had been shorter because he believed in relevancy and simplicity. He believed it was a waste of time to overburden an audience with rhetoric. According to Washington, he did not speak for the sake of it, but to convey an important message. In the later periods, it appears that he had grown more philosophical concerning business as a means of gaining real freedom and societal power. For example, quoting Shakespeare, Washington noted: "There is a tide in the affairs of men, which taken at the flood leads on to fortune." Omitted was, "All the rest of their lives is bound in shallows and miseries."[81] What Washington meant by this was that African-American men and women had to lay an economic foundation for their race's future success. If they neglected this important duty, doom would surely occur. Despite his growing philosophical tendencies, Washington continued to be factual. With the hiring of Monroe N. Work in 1908 as head of Tuskegee Institute's division of research and records, Washington became equipped even more heavily with statistical facts,[82] and he used them extensively. Audience members from the state in which the league was holding its annual meeting, upon hearing Washington cite statistic after statistic, were known to say that Washington knew more about their state than they did. Furthermore, contrary to his early policy,[83] Washington did not always focus strictly on business issues. As a national leader, he also briefly discussed other matters relevant to his race, such as voting, lynching, and constitutional rights, but he always came back to the subject of business development.

In his addresses of 1908 and 1909, Washington articulated that to be successful in business, individuals or groups had to live morally upright lives,[84] which reflected his belief that material gain was only a means to an end, not the ultimate goal. To him, there were higher dimensions of life, and morality was one of them. Spirituality was, in Washington's view, another of life's higher aims.

The most dominant themes found in the eleven addresses analyzed were: 1) establishing a material foundation and its positive effects; 2) emphasizing opportunities rather than grievances; 3) the South as the best geographical location for African-American advancement; 4) being indispensable to one's community; 5) paying the price for business success; 6) the color-blind results of merit. The theme of establishing a material foundation and its positive results was discussed in seventy-three percent of Washington's addresses, from his first in 1900 to his last in 1915. (Washington's last address was philosophical, simple, and to the point, consisting of a statement of where African Americans were economically and projections of where they should be in the near future. It could be considered his last economic statement to his people, because he died a few months afterward.) Sixty-four percent of his addresses stressed emphasizing opportunities rather than grievances. This was one theme that Washington related both to business and other issues. Thirty-six percent of the addresses mentioned that the South was the best environment for African-American upward mobility, although this percentage does not truly reflect the number of times that Washington expressed this idea. (It is also evident in his addresses that do not pertain strictly to business development.) Paying the price of business success and making oneself indispensable to one's community were both evident in about thirty-four percent of the addresses, while the issue of the market being color-blind to merit was raised in about twenty-seven percent of the addresses.

Finally, it should be mentioned that all of the themes discussed throughout this chapter were evident in one or more of Washington's addresses, including finding a niche, opportunities at one's doorstep, beginning business in a small way and growing large, being competitive, always striving to do more, strength arising from struggle, being persistent in business, and results leading to recognition. Strong, explicit themes concerning real freedom and group cohesiveness were also expressed in Washington's addresses beginning in 1908. Washington promoted ideas such as doing for oneself and one's race, the race gaining confidence as a result of business success, and unity—especially when it came to business ventures and economic success.

As conveyed in chapters 1 and 2, Booker T. Washington's business ideas did not occur in a vacuum, but were shaped and influenced by a multitude of factors. He saw and experienced the condition of his people in slavery, Reconstruction, and the nadir, and as a leader and shrewd strategist, he proposed an uplift strategy he considered proactive, emphasizing duties over rights and meeting the challenges of the nadir, a traumatic era in African-American life and history. Washington's group-advancement strategy did not promote "settling for" or "accommodating to" injustice, as has been argued. Instead, it placed greater emphasis on economic development because Washington believed that everything necessary for African-American life and survival would flow naturally from a solid economic foundation.

To better understand Washington's entrepreneurial ideas and their impact, it is important to investigate how he implemented them. Therefore, in the next three chapters, we shall examine how Washington promoted and implemented many of them by analyzing his role in the Negro Farmers' Conference, the NNBL, and on the very campus of Tuskegee Institute. Washington, who was a realist familiar with the folkways and mores of the South, believed that real action had a greater, longer-lasting impact than flowery speeches or eloquent writings. Action, perhaps, was the most important component of his entrepreneurial philosophy because, in his view, "an ounce of application is worth a ton of abstraction" and actions manifested results.

4

The Negro Farmers' Conference

Helping Those Near and Far

Background

Beginning in the early 1970s and taking his lead from August Meier,[1] historian Louis Harlan, after studying many of Washington's papers in the Library of Congress, began to write of a private or behind-the-scenes Booker T. Washington that many scholars had been unaware of.[2] This private Washington was the diametrical opposite of his public image, which has been perpetuated throughout American history. He was more aggressive, even militant at times. The private Washington, for example, worked diligently toward ending unequal facilities on public transportation, disfranchisement, and peonage measures, investing not only his limited time but also his money.[3] Like Meier and Harlan, other scholars began to take a second look at Washington and agreed that he often displayed two distinct behaviors, particularly when responding to controversial issues during the nadir of African-American history.[4]

These scholars' assessments of Washington are correct. He was a man trying to keep his growing school afloat in a setting where individuals were vigilant of, critical of, and even hostile toward African-American education. His head was in the lion's mouth as his public actions were constantly scrutinized. Furthermore, he was undoubtedly aware that, at times, unfavorable compromises had to be made until his people grew to economic strength and thereby became a force to be reckoned with. This helps to explain the discrepancy that existed between his public and private behaviors; especially concerning emotionally charged issues of his day such as lynching, voting, segregation, the convict-lease system, and debt peonage. In examining how

Washington promoted and implemented his entrepreneurial ideas, however, no inconsistency is to be found between his public and private behavior when focusing on the Negro Farmers' Conference.

The Negro Farmers' Conference

The Negro Farmers' Conference functioned as an "improvement association" that strove to influence African-American farmers in Macon County, Alabama, and beyond. On one level it encouraged farmers to get out of debt, stay free of debt, and purchase land to move toward independence. This is perhaps the level that scholars and laypersons are most readily aware of. On another and perhaps more sophisticated level, Washington and the Negro Farmers' Conference encouraged farmers to be more than just landowning, self-sufficient farmers—to be entrepreneurs. In other words, Washington's ultimate goal for African-American farmers was that they engage in agriculturally grounded businesses, which fits into his overall philosophy of using enterprise as a strategy for obtaining real freedom and societal influence.

When students came to Booker T. Washington and asked him for advice concerning which trade they should pursue while at Tuskegee Institute, he told them, both privately and publicly, that they should learn a trade that would be of value to the community where they would reside.[5] According to Washington, this was applicable education that would not only provide Tuskegee Institute students with a means to make a livelihood if they did not become teachers, but would also put them in a position to make themselves indispensable assets to their respective communities. As noted earlier, Washington saw opportunities at his students' doorsteps; he wanted them to also see those opportunities and seize them.

Washington would utilize this concept of applicable education himself. When he first came to Tuskegee and doubtlessly for the majority of the time that he lived in Macon County, Washington saw rampant poverty and ignorance.[6] He saw entire families, often consisting of eight or more members and sometimes including relatives, living in one-room shacks, sleeping upon bare earth, and lacking a sense of privacy. He saw many families sustaining themselves on a regular diet of only fat pork and corn bread or black-eyed peas and corn bread, all of which added up to an unbalanced, unhealthy, disease-prone diet. Washington also did not see many schools for African Americans in Macon County. Of the few that he did see, their school year did not last more than three and a half months, the average term being three months. Furthermore, he found many of their teachers to be incompetent.

Most importantly, however, he saw the economic effects of the nadir on the local African-American community. "With few exceptions," Washington wrote, "I found that the crops were mortgaged in the counties where I went [including Macon County], and that . . . most of the coloured farmers were in debt."[7]

Taking into consideration the poverty, ignorance, and general backwardness of the African-American people in Macon County and its surrounding districts, Washington wanted Tuskegee Institute to be of indispensable value to the surrounding communities. He wanted his school to focus on the needs of the area, to find a niche, and to provide common services for the community in an uncommon manner.[8] The major needs of the area were, first and foremost, aid in eradicating poverty and ignorance. To do this, Washington believed in focusing first on the economic or material foundation of the local African-American community, which was farming.[9]

The majority of African Americans in Macon County and the surrounding districts were farmers: wage earners on farms, sharecroppers, renters, or landowning farmers. Washington wanted these farmers to be debt-free producers who at least owned their land and farms. After all, since Reconstruction, the African-American populace still considered land ownership a basis for freedom.[10] Washington thought that being debt-free landowners and producers would allow more industrious farmers to become businesspersons—sellers of goods and lessors of land.[11]

To implement his policy of making Tuskegee Institute indispensable to the surrounding community, in 1892, eleven years after his arrival in Tuskegee, Alabama, Washington sent out seventy-five invitations welcoming local farmers, mechanics, schoolteachers, and ministers to a conference that was held at his school.[12] This gathering took place on February 23rd and was initially known as the Tuskegee Negro Conference, ultimately to be named the Tuskegee Farmers' Conference. The aim of this conference was for participants to spend a day at Tuskegee talking about their conditions and needs. From his travels throughout the country district, Washington realized the wisdom and common sense displayed by many of the so-called ignorant masses of African Americans, especially the older ex-slaves.[13] In a sharing atmosphere similar to a religious camp meeting or a revival, Washington asked these people to share their knowledge to help advance other farmers, mechanics, ministers, and schoolteachers. In short, he wanted successful workers to inform the other conference participants of how they had achieved their success. At the first conference, to Washington's surprise, over four hundred men and women, mostly farmers, came.

As the sponsor of the first Tuskegee Farmers' Conference and the principal force guiding the meeting, Washington had written inside the seventy-five invitations that at the first meeting, those individuals who desired to speak should not prepare or present a formal address. His reason for this was that he had found that when the average man or woman was asked to prepare an address, too much attention was given to rhetoric and little to the content of the speech. He wanted participants to come and talk about their conditions and needs as they would in their own homes at their firesides.[14] With this policy, Washington strove to make the conference clear, concrete, and fruitful to all participants, illiterate and lettered.

Moreover, Washington urged conference participants to emphasize their problems but to accentuate the solutions to their problems even more. As a result, the first Tuskegee Farmers' Conference and all ensuing ones were divided into two sessions. The morning session addressed problems, while the afternoon session focused on solutions. In the morning, for example, conference participants told of the limited number of African Americans in their communities who owned farms, the number who were renters, the number who lived in one-room log cabins, and the number who mortgaged their crops. In addition, the conditions of the schools and county ministry were discussed, which often proved disheartening. In terms of poverty and education, Washington sums up best the general problems discussed and the conclusions derived:

> [I]t was found that in what is known as the "Black Belt" of the South at least four-fifths of the Negro people in many counties were living in one-room cabins, on rented land, were mortgaging their crops for food on which to live, and were paying a rate of interest on those mortgages which ranges from fifteen to forty per cent per annum. The schools, in most cases, extended but three months, and were taught, as a rule, in the churches, in broken down log cabins, or in a brush arbor.[15]

In the afternoon session, conference participants expressed how community members could become landowners, free themselves from the stifling mortgage system, how ministers could improve their ministry, and how to extend the school year beyond three months. "From the first," Washington noted, "we have insisted that these conferences were to be confined, in discussion, to matters which the people themselves had in their power to remedy, rather than to matters which the nation, as a whole, or the entire race could remedy."[16] Of the saved records of the first Tuskegee Negro Conference, no direct testimonies concerning solutions have been published.[17] Subsequent conference records, however, are replete with rich testimonies. For instance, during the afternoon proceedings of the twelfth conference, in responding to how homeowners got their land and homes and to motivate others to do the same, one conference participant proudly proclaimed:

> I got mine by workin' hard an' livin' close. I did'n buy nothin' I did'n nat'ally need, an' I did'n buy half dat I did need. I married er 'oman whose father give her er cow an' we lived er long time on nothin' but milk an' bread. I made twelve bales of cotton to de mule las' year. My neighbors is beginnin' to buy land now.[18]

"Another farmer, who own[ed] two hundred acres of land, a seven-room dwelling, fifty-seven cattle, and eleven horses and colts, stated that he got his [land] by staying out of debt."[19]

At the end of the first Tuskegee Farmers' Conference (and all ensuing conferences), a series of resolutions or declarations were adopted. These resolutions served as a guide for those African-American workers, especially farmers, who wanted to advance. They could take these resolutions home, study them, and act upon them. The 1892 resolutions promoted such goals as better education, an upright ministry, the purchasing and cultivation of land, the avoidance of debt and the mortgage system, the discouragement of emigration agents, the improved treatment of women, and abstention from criminal activity.[20]

The first Tuskegee Farmers' Conference was so successful that Washington decided to make it an annual affair.[21] By 1894, he had extended the length of the conference to two days.[22] The first day was for the farmers, while the second day was for teachers who worked in educational institutions for African Americans throughout the South. Other professionals, such as ministers and businessmen, were also invited to participate. The second-day conference became known as the Workers' Conference. The teachers and other professionals generally discussed how they could best help the farmers and improve their own professions. Furthermore, as a result of the continuous growth of the meetings, the Workers' Conference devoted a portion of its meetings to issues involving women. This action established the Women's Conference as an annual part of the Workers' Conference agenda.

Each ensuing Tuskegee Conference attracted an increasing number of participants up until 1915, the last year that Booker T. Washington would live to attend these conferences. The 1893 conference attracted eight hundred participants.²³ The 1894 and 1895 conferences attracted over a thousand participants each, while by 1898 the attendance exceeded two thousand participants almost every year thereafter.²⁴

The increasing attendance at the conferences, particularly at the Farmers' Conference, still did not satisfy Washington. He knew that his conferences were only reaching a limited number of his people, many of whom only came out of habit. There were so many more that needed to be reached so that they could be educated on how to improve their condition. The nadir's effects had taken a toll on most of them. For example, at the first conference, when Washington asked the participants, "How many of you own your homes and land?" only twenty-three hands went up.²⁵ Moreover, Washington knew that Tuskegee Institute would also be evaluated based on its ability to spread the messages taught at the Farmers' Conference not only throughout Macon County, but the entire South as well.

Thus, through Washington's persuasion, in 1896, George Washington Carver, a graduate of Iowa State's Agricultural College, accepted a faculty post at Tuskegee Institute.²⁶ In coming to Tuskegee, he wanted to do the greatest good for the greatest possible number of his people;²⁷ helping his people was one of his life goals.²⁸ (Incidentally, a road in Ames, Iowa, where George Washington Carver attended college, is named after him, as is a building on the Iowa State University campus. The author observed this building while employed at Iowa State University.) Shortly after arriving in Tuskegee, Carver—like Washington, Charles W. Greene (a Hampton Institute graduate and Tuskegee Institute farm manager), and others before him—wasted little time in taking buggy rides throughout the countryside to study the condition of the farmers, whom Washington considered the bone and sinew of his race. Carver would concur with Washington that much hard work was needed to help elevate the masses of African-American farmers from their dismal condition.

Washington, keeping Carver in mind, was successful in persuading members of the 1896 Alabama State Legislature to pass a bill that helped create the Tuskegee Experimental Station.²⁹ This bill included an annual appropriation for the institute from the state. Carver, an up-and-coming, noteworthy scientist and head of the Tuskegee Institute Agricultural Department, was given charge of this project. As one of his many duties Carver experimented with anything involving agriculture that he thought would be of benefit to farmers, and he invited and encouraged them to witness his results.³⁰ In addition, he published many of his findings in quarterly bulletins that were distributed to both African-American and white farmers, as well as any others that showed an interest.[31]

Still unsatisfied with the effects of the Farmers' Conference and the experimental station, in 1897 Washington helped form the Farmers' Institute and made Charles Greene the director. Farmers near and far were invited to come to Tuskegee Institute once a month to hear lectures from agricultural faculty members, and they were encouraged to discuss their farming problems with the faculty as well as their peers. They heard lectures and discussed such issues as crop rotation, deep plowing, the correct preparation of corn and cotton, use of slack months following the harvest period, and the influence of women in the home.[32] The Farmers' Institute attracted from twenty-five to seventy-five farmers who came from Macon and adjoining counties.[33]

Based on the results of the Farmers' Institute, a short course was created in 1904, and it was developed in each ensuing year.[34] This was also a result of the widespread influence of Washington. Farmers and their entire families were invited to come daily for two weeks in January to Tuskegee Institute for five or six hours to take short courses involving farming and household care. January was considered a good month to offer these short courses because it was immediately after the harvesting period, which was a slack time for farmers. These short courses were practical and taught in an informal manner. No roll was taken, and farmers could come and go as they pleased. At the first meeting, it was with difficulty that eleven old men were convinced to participate. The second year, with an increased effort, seventeen individuals participated.[35] The third year, with continued effort, seventy people participated, and the fourth year, with still greater efforts and patience, four hundred and seventy persons participated.[36] Consequently, by 1909, 960 individuals were enrolled in the short course, and Washington's vision of reaching and educating more farmers was being fulfilled.[37]

Carver, George R. Bridgeforth, and other agricultural faculty members of Tuskegee Institute instructed short-course participants. "Courses were given for men and boys in farming, live stock raising, dairying, and poultry-raising. For the women and girls, there were poultry-raising, dairying, sewing, and cooking."[38] This was indeed a school for the entire family.

Washington continued his efforts after the above extension activities, all the ideas of which had their origin in the Farmers' Conference. Growing out of the Farmers' Institute and probably Tuskegee Institute's graduation ceremonies, fairs and parades were held on the Tuskegee Institute campus to display the results of the experimental station or lessons taught to farmers by the Tuskegee agricultural faculty.[39] Farmers would bring, for example, some of their best livestock, crop yields, or canning samples to display. In 1905 a newspaper for farmers called *The Messenger* was created.[40] It was a four-page weekly devoted exclusively to the affairs of African-American farmers in Macon County. More specifically, their farms, schools, churches, and social affairs were the primary concerns. "If a farmer plow[ed] his land in accordance with the best methods, or whitewashe[d] his dwelling and outhouses, or kill[ed] an unusually heavy hog, or cultivate[d] vegetables enough for his own consumption, or raise[d] chickens enough for himself and for market, he [was] sure of mention in *The Messenger*."[41] Due to financial difficulties, however, *The Messenger* ceased publication in 1913. In its stead, a new paper was founded in 1914, *The Negro Farmer*. Unlike *The Messenger*, it was a national newspaper and was published every other week.[42] It was published from the Tuskegee Institute Post Office up until shortly after Washington's death. Both *The Messenger* and *The Negro Farmer* were distributed to local farmers.

One of the most ambitious projects organized by Washington that also had its origin in the Farmers' Conference and had broad ramifications throughout Macon County and the entire South was the Moveable School. From his and his faculty's tours throughout the country district, Washington was convinced that there were still many farmers who had not been exposed to the ideas of the Farmers' Conference. Despite Tuskegee Institute's extension work, ignorance was still pervasive in the surrounding counties. Consequently, in 1904 Washington concluded that Tuskegee Institute had to take its modern agricultural methods to the backcountry farmers' very doorsteps. How this would be done, he was not sure, but he discussed it with Carver. Carver agreed with Washington's aim, and both men considered how this objective could be achieved. In a relatively short time, Carver offered Washington a drawing of an agricultural wagon that would ultimately be used to carry an agricultural agent and modern farming tools to backcountry farmers.[43] Specifically, Carver conceived this agricultural wagon as a one- or two-horse drawn wagon made to open toward its middle. It would carry a small milk separator, a churn, and a complete outfit for making butter, as well as large charts on soil building, orchards, stock raising, and all operations pertaining to the farm.[44] Being a practical man, Washington thought it would be valuable if Tuskegee Institute's agricultural faculty could actually show the backcountry farmers new and better farming techniques. For that reason he stressed application, saying that, "Instead of telling the farmer what to do, show him how to do it and he will never forget it."[45] With a plan of action, Washington went north to pursue philanthropic assistance for the Moveable School project.

On May 24, 1906, Washington's plan was launched. A friend of Tuskegee Institute, Morris K. Jesup of New York, gave funds for a harness, mules, and the construction of a wagon.[46] Because of this gift, the wagon that Carver had drawn became known as the Jesup Wagon, and Tuskegee Institute students made the wagon and harness in their industrial shops. George R. Bridgeforth became the first farm agent and performed well, which kept him in Washington's good grace. Due to his numerous responsibilities, however, particularly since he was the new director of the agricultural department, replacing Carver, and due to Washington's desire to have someone concentrate wholly on being a farm agent, Bridgeforth was relieved of this duty. Washington, with Bridgeforth and Carver's assistance, searched for a replacement as well as the funds to keep the Jesup Wagon operative.[47]

Washington was successful in both endeavors. The individual chosen to replace Bridgeforth was Thomas Monroe Campbell, a Georgian and a 1906 graduate of the Tuskegee Institute Agricultural Department. Both Bridgeforth and Carver supported Campbell's appointment, which was unusual since they were often at odds with one another.[48] For funds, Washington consulted Dr. Seaman Knapp, a special agent responsible for Farmers' Cooperative Demonstration Work for the United States Department of Agriculture. After a visit to Tuskegee Institute in which he spoke to Washington, Bridgeforth, and Carver and observed some results of Carver's experimental station, Dr. Knapp discarded his earlier doubts about hiring African Americans as farm agents for the United States.[49] He then negotiated an arrangement with Washington for sharing the operational expenses of the Jesup Wagon.[50] Campbell, as the federal government's first African-American farm agent, would receive one dollar annually in salary and ten dollars for expenses, serving to make him a federal employee. Furthermore, he would receive a supplemental salary amounting to $840—$500 from the General Education Board and $340 from Tuskegee Institute—and an additional operating-expense payment of $250 from the General Education Board and a commitment from Tuskegee Institute to cover additional expenses incurred beyond the $250. After November 12, 1906, Thomas Monroe Campbell began his extension work of carrying knowledge to the farmer. Washington dubbed Campbell's important work "the Farmers' College on Wheels."[51]

When the Farmers' College on Wheels was begun in the summer of 1906, Bridgeforth reached over two thousand farmers a month. After replacing

Bridgeforth and working exclusively on the same scheme, Campbell reached even more farmers, taking the Farmers' Conference teachings, via demonstrations, to the very doors of the backcountry farmers in Macon County and beyond.[52] Though the Farmers' Conference messages were tailored for the African-American farmer, white farmers were receptive as well, and a number willingly attended many of the demonstrations.[53] Several white, large farm owners were impressed and invited Campbell to come to their farms to enlighten their tenants.[54]

Campbell made a career out of being an extension agent for Tuskegee Institute and the federal government, retaining his post until February 28, 1953, well after Washington's death. The passage of the Smith-Lever Act in 1914 helped extend his career, for under the Smith-Lever Act, the federal government began to promote and support rural extension work through land-grant colleges such as Tuskegee Institute, Hampton Institute, and Auburn University.[55] The Alabama Polytechnic Institute at Auburn was made responsible for the agricultural extension work in Alabama. Fortunately, during the era of the nadir, the extension work for African-American farmers was expanded, although it was still small in comparison to that provided to whites. Campbell was first made a district manager as a result of the hiring of more African-American farm agents, then a Southern regional manager due to even further expansion. Thus, the passage of the Smith-Lever Act helped to spread the Farmers' Conference messages and further implement Washington's policy of taking the school to the farmer.[56]

The success of the Farmers' College on Wheels and, in essence, the Farmers' Conference and all of its extension work has elicited a range of responses from scholars. For example, Monroe Work, Booker T. Washington's resourceful research director, thought that the work of the Farmers' Conference was successful because it offered scientific knowledge to farmers and grew to become national in scope, initiating and promoting local farmer conferences throughout the South.[57] Moreover, he attributed to the Farmers' Conference and other extension work the increase of land ownership and systematic farming among African Americans in Macon County and surrounding districts.[58] Allen Jones, a scholar who has done extensive research on the Farmers' Conference, wrote that it was difficult to determine to what degree the annual Farmers' Conference emancipated the African-American farmer.[59] He did, however, emphasize that the number of African-American farmers in the South increased from 732,362 in 1900 to 915,595 in 1920, with the value of their farmland increasing from $69,636,420 to $522,178,137 within the same period.[60] Louis Harlan, Booker T. Washington's most distinguished biographer, doubted if the Farmers' Conference brought about much African-American self-help, escape from the crop mortgage system, farm purchasing, or improvement of rural churches and schools.[61] More recently, Karen Ferguson, an assistant professor of history at Simon Fraser University in Burnaby, British Columbia, argued that the effects of the nadir negated any widespread benefits of the Farmers' Conference and its extension work, regarding almost all of the efforts of Tuskegee Institute workers as fruitless.[62] How effective Washington's efforts were in helping backcountry farmers is an important historical question, especially for determining the success or failure of his farm extension programs. Yet, due to the improved appearance (judging by health and clothing, for example) of Tuskegee conference participants over the years, the increase in the number of area landowners, the wide distribution of *The Messenger* and *The Negro Farmer*, the increase in the number of schoolhouses, the expansion of local farmer conferences throughout the entire South, and the demonstrations provided by first George Bridgeforth and then Thomas Campbell to thousands of farmers yearly, it is difficult to believe that Washington's extension work did not have a broad-ranging effect on sections of the South, regardless of the adverse consequences of the nadir.[63] At a minimum, African Americans were better off with Washington's programs than they would have been without them. Moreover, the issue important for understanding Washington is not the unresolvable question of the Negro Farmers' Conference's literal impact, but rather what its role within Washington's broader approach and strategy was, and how it helped his entrepreneurial philosophy strive to effect real freedom, empowerment, and equality.

Hence, despite certain disparities pointed out in scholars' evaluations of Tuskegee Institute's farmer extension programs, the messages of the Farmers' Conference regarding how African-American farmers could obtain economic independence and become entrepreneurs were consistent.[64] Moreover, after applying Anselm Strauss's coding technique, a form of content analysis, to many of Washington's speeches and writings on the Farmers' Conference as well as to those of other contemporary authors who attended the conferences, three themes were discovered that consistently stood out in regard to African-American farmers gaining economic independence and becoming entrepreneurs.[65] These were "getting out of debt and staying clear of it," "becoming landowners," and "making land productive." These three themes served as a simple, step-by-step strategy for farmers to become debt-free businesspersons or at least self-reliant farmers.

Since most of the African-American farmers in Macon County and the surrounding districts were in debt, as mentioned earlier, Washington allowed and encouraged the few farmers who completely owned land to share the story of how they obtained it. With Washington conducting events and offering advice, these testimonies motivated other farmers to work toward obtaining land, not only to help themselves and their families, but also to place them in a position to come back to the next Farmers' Conference with a favorable report to share. Landowning farmers told indebted ones that if they had made bad bargains, they should be aware of them and their consequences and act accordingly. Then they and Washington offered advice and strategies on how to get out of debt and remain debt-free.

Farmers' Conference participants were first told to always avoid mortgaging their crops.[66] According to Washington, conference participants were known to mortgage their crops, usually for things they could go without or grow themselves.[67] For example, farmers often bought expensive goods such as clocks, pianos, buggies, sewing machines, or store-bought fruits and vegetables but lived on rented land and were obligated to mortgage their crops in order to live another year. Buying only what was necessary and sacrificing to get ahead were promoted by the Farmers' Conference.

Second, conference participants were advised to grow gardens and raise livestock in addition to a staple crop of cotton so that they could feed themselves and their families year-round, even be in a position to sell some surplus if they chose.[68] Concerning gardens, they were encouraged to grow them during the slack farming periods and then can their vegetables and fruits.[69] As noted earlier, when Washington first began to explore Macon County, he observed the fact that African-American farmers grew mainly cotton, usually up to their very doorsteps, and neglected growing a wide range of other crops needed to sustain themselves.[70] This folly compelled them to purchase these essential items, often at exorbitant prices.

As a fund generator for paying off debt and staying clear of it, Washington told African-American farmers at many of the conferences to raise pigs and hogs because they could always be sold to generate income.[71] Because he considered this message worthwhile, he had it published.[72] Some white-owned newspapers concurred with Washington's message and published it in their papers for a generally white clientele.[73] Following Washington's lead, George Washington Carver offered useful debt-freeing strategies to farmers.[74]

Farmers were advised to work six days a week rather than two or three. Furthermore, it was recommended that they only go to town to get needed items and not loiter, especially on Saturdays. They were advised to take more to town to sell than they planned to buy. This advice for avoiding debt was sound, and going to town but not loitering on Saturdays was probably another means by which rural farmers remained in contact with friends and associates, other than their weekly church services. To discourage African-American women from loitering in Tuskegee on Saturdays, taking her cue from her husband Booker T. Washington, Margaret Murray Washington held women's meetings on Saturdays in downtown Tuskegee. These meetings were usually well attended, as Mrs. Washington concentrated on moral and domestic issues.[75]

After African-American farmers had gotten themselves out of debt, the next step in the Farmers' Conference's plan was obtaining economic independence. How was this to be achieved? By purchasing land. Washington and the other conference participants were well aware of the difficulties that often existed when it came to purchasing land. For instance, many white farmers wanted to retain their African-American tenant farmers at all cost. As noted earlier, African Americans also had to contend with the practice of whitecapping.[76] Nevertheless, Washington's constant plea to white Southerners subsequent to his Atlanta Exposition address was that they give African Americans a fair chance, because in holding African Americans down, Washington reasoned, they were only inhibiting themselves and the progress of the South.[77]

Washington and other conference speakers told farmers to buy land, starting small with a few acres and expanding over time. In addition, they counseled conference participants not to go into debt buying land that they could not afford or mortgage land that they did possess to buy other land. This practice often caused African-American farmers to lose not only the newly purchased land, but also the land that they originally owned. The issue of obtaining land was a dominant theme discussed throughout the entire Farmers' Conference meetings from 1892 to 1915, the year of Washington's death, and even after. Moreover, it was always placed in the Farmers' Conference resolutions.[78]

Once land was obtained, Washington and other speakers emphasized to farmers that they make all of their land productive, meaning that they should first produce crops to sustain themselves and their families and then their excess crops, staple crops, and livestock could be sold.[79] This was the entrepreneurial aspect of Washington's message to rural farmers. Washington considered farmers "businessmen"[80] if they had accumulated many acres of land and were renting some of it as well as producing large quantities of crops or livestock for markets. Moreover, he was pleased when he was able to motivate farmers to free themselves of the shackles of tenant farming and become self-sufficient farmers. He was even more pleased when some of those farmers grew to be businesspersons.

In every issue of *The Negro Farmer*, a journal edited by Isaac Fisher, a former Tuskegee Institute student, countless stories of farmer-entrepreneurs were published. These stories served as examples for farmers to emulate. Washington claimed that he had no control over this journal, but a reading shows that his influence was pervasive. In a column titled "Winner From the Soil," accounts of farmers who adhered to the advice of the Farmers' Conference, by owning their land and being producers of goods for the market, were featured.[81] For example, a man by the name of Jonas W. Thomas had bought many acres of land and became a landlord.[82] Another named Deal Jackson was presented because it was said that he was the first person to produce and sell a bale of cotton in the markets of Georgia every year for ten years.[83] Henry Kirklin of Columbia, Missouri, had grown an extensive garden and had sold most of his crops on the market for a substantial profit, and Joseph R. Smith was a farmer who lived near Oklahoma City, Oklahoma, and grew Spanish peanuts for a profit.[84]

All the persons above exemplified the views of Washington and other speakers at the Farmers' Conference, but the story of the "Potato King" was a favorite of Washington's, as it showed his concept of making land productive. Junius G. Groves, born a slave in Green County, Kentucky, in 1850, was the so-called Potato King.[85] In 1879, due to the effects of the nadir, Groves and other African Americans migrated to Kansas in search of a better life. Such a significant number of them migrated to Kansas that historians have identified their movement as the Kansas Exodus. Groves found it difficult to find work because at that time the labor supply far exceeded demand. To get work, Groves was forced to take a job as a farm wage worker earning forty cents a day, thirty-five cents below the market rate for a farmhand. Nonetheless, Groves worked hard for three months until his employer saw his value and increased his wages to the market rate. Groves, according to Washington, soon after met his future wife and married her.

Groves and his wife began their union as sharecroppers with little or no money.[86] The contract that they made with a local planter was that they be lent nine acres of land to cultivate, a team of animals, seeds, and tools in return for two-thirds of their profits on the harvested crops. At year's end, the Groveses realized net earnings of one hundred and twenty-five dollars. They took their earnings and reinvested the bulk of them into farming, investing fifty dollars in a lot in Kansas City, twenty-five in a milk cow, and fifty in the next year's crop. The next year, the planter struck a similar arrangement but increased their land to twenty acres. The Groveses again worked hard that year and all ensuing years, realizing continuous profits until they were finally able to purchase more of their own land. They purchased eighty acres of some of the most fertile land in Kansas, near Edwardsville, and they eventually purchased five adjoining farms until they possessed a large, plantation-style farm of their own.[87]

According to Washington, as large farm owners, the Groveses now ran a profitable business enterprise. They grew and harvested a multitude of crops. For example, "In the apple orchard there [were] seven thousand trees, six years old, from which [one] year four carloads of apples were gathered. There [were] eighteen hundred trees in the peach orchard, seven hundred in the pear orchard, and two hundred and fifty in the cherry orchard."[88] They also grew apricots and grapes in abundance.[89] All these crops were taken to the market and sold for a profit. Furthermore, the Groveses were now employers as well, especially during peak harvesting periods. During these busy times, they were known to have hired up to fifty farm wage earners, both African Americans and whites, anyone who wanted to work.[90]

For his and his wife's hard work and because he grew, harvested, and marketed a great number of white potatoes, Junius Groves was called the Potato King. In one year alone, he and his wife produced on their farm 721,500 bushels of white potatoes, averaging 245 bushels to the acre.[91] As reports showed, according to Washington, this was 121,500 bushels more than any other individual grower in the world had, at that time, produced.[92] Finally, in concluding Washington's example of Junius Groves, who advanced from slavery to wage earner to tenant farmer to landowner and finally to entrepreneur, he credited hard work, thriftiness, and his wife for helping him to be a success. Unquestionably the Groveses' case epitomized Washington's and other Farmers' Conference speakers' advice to farmers concerning self-help and economic independence, which was: stay clear of debt, become landowners, and make land productive.[93]

More research will probably be conducted into whether or not the Farmers' Conference and its extension work had a significant impact on farmers of Macon County as well as throughout the entire South. This historical debate will most likely continue. Washington, however, must be given credit for his immense efforts to improve the lot of the masses of African-American farmers in the South, regardless of how many of them were emigrating.[94] He wanted the Negro Farmers' Conference to serve as an improvement association, encouraging African-American farmers to achieve higher objectives, ultimately to be entrepreneurs. According to Emmett J. Scott, Washington focused extensively on farming uplift strategies because at the time the majority of African Americans were, in fact, farmers.[95] He saw their condition and wanted to improve it, as he was aware that improvement in the parts improves the whole. Washington would display this same effort and zeal in organizing and managing the NNBL, consistently furthering his uplift strategy privately and publicly.

5

The National Negro Business League

A History and Analysis

The NNBL was another forum in which Booker T. Washington espoused his entrepreneurial ideas and, as in his statements during the Negro Farmers' Conference, there was no inconsistency between his public and private articulations of his entrepreneurial ideas. As noted in chapter 1, Washington's entrepreneurial ideas were crafted to suit the age in which he lived, comprising a strategy to counteract the effects of the nadir and, most importantly, a crucial program for the upward mobility of his people. Furthermore, Washington's advocacy of African-American business development in the NNBL is what has made him known to scholars and laypersons as a champion of entrepreneurial development.[1] This chapter will validate these assertions.

More specifically, by analyzing the NNBL from 1900 to 1915, this chapter further demonstrates how Booker T. Washington implemented and promoted his entrepreneurial philosophy as a strategy for real freedom, empowerment, and equality, not only making him a champion of African-American business development, but also institutionalizing his entrepreneurial philosophy. The NNBL was the medium through which Washington hoped his economic message would reach the greatest number of people. Moreover, this chapter further maintains and substantiates Washington's vision of African-American entrepreneurs operating in the open market, which complemented his belief that to become really free and respected, African Americans had to make themselves indispensable assets in their respective communities, both to other African Americans and whites. As an endnote and perhaps most importantly, unlike other analyses of the NNBL, by reviewing the history of the NNBL and analyzing it this chapter offers other plausible interpretations for a number of significant events that occurred.

A History of the National Negro Business League

In 1900 Washington founded the NNBL.[2] As a national leader, Washington consistently received numerous invitations to speak throughout the country. En route to many of his engagements, he had the rare opportunity to observe many African Americans single-handedly engaged in business ventures. According to Washington, "the number of successful business men and women of the Negro race that I was continually coming in contact with during my travels throughout the country was a source of surprise and pleasure to me. My observations in this regard led me . . . to believe that the time had come for bringing together the leading and most successful colored men and women in the country who were engaged in business."[3] Washington felt that if he could have these businesspersons meet and interact with one another, they would be further encouraged and inspire others in their respective locales to undertake entrepreneurial ventures. Moreover, during the winter of 1900, Washington, T. Thomas Fortune, the owner and editor of *The New York Age*,[4] the leading African-American paper of the day, Emmett J. Scott, and other friends discussed strategies for bringing together African-American entrepreneurs and for promoting business development among African Americans.[5]

These men agreed that a meeting should be held in Boston, Massachusetts, on Thursday and Friday, August 23rd and 24th. They viewed these dates as a good time for a meeting because it was considered a slack period for businesspersons as well as Washington, who had a demanding executive role at Tuskegee Institute. Moreover, during the summer of 1900, steamship lines and railroads offered reduced rates to Boston.[6] To bring the meeting to fruition and promote business development, a list of African-American businesspersons that resided throughout the country was compiled and a circular was generated inviting them to come to Boston for the first meeting. The requirement for actively participating was that an individual "be engaged in business." Washington's goal for the first meeting (and all ensuing ones) was to allow businesspersons to gain knowledge and encouragement from one another and to motivate the delegates to establish local leagues among African Americans in their respective communities.[7] Being a practical man, as aforementioned, Washington would take pride in this because he felt that African Americans actually engaged in business ventures expressing their experience would be more helpful than theoretical advice. Elaborating upon the intent of the first meeting, Washington wrote:

It is very important that every line of business that any Negro man or woman is engaged in be represented. This meeting will present a great opportunity for us to show the world what progress we have made in business lines since our freedom. This organization is not in opposition to any other now in existence but is expected to do a distinct work that no other organization, now in existence, can do as well.[8]

Some scholars argue that the idea of the NNBL originated in the mind of the great scholar W.E.B. Du Bois, not Washington's.[9] Even Du Bois bluntly stated this and in a later publication alluded to it.[10] These scholars argue that at the 1899 Atlanta University Conference concerning Du Bois' study "The Negro in Business," Resolution Six-c called for the promotion of African-American businessmen's leagues. This, of course, took place before Washington launched his first organizational meeting in 1900. More specifically, in the words of the conference participants, "The organization in every town and hamlet where colored people dwell, of Negro Business Men's Leagues, and the gradual federation from these of state and national organizations [should be promoted]."[11] Furthermore, to strengthen their case, these scholars mention that later in 1899, Du Bois became the director of the Afro-American Council's Negro Business Bureau and undertook the responsibility of organizing local business leagues. Du Bois, portrayed as a scholar of humble means, consented to being the director provided that the council would make postage funds available for his use.[12] Several months later, scholars point out that Washington's friend, T. Thomas Fortune, killed the appropriation, preventing Du Bois from carrying out his job, and then, in 1900, Emmett J. Scott, Washington's faithful secretary, became the new director of the Afro-American Council's Negro Business Bureau, since Du Bois was not reelected. This argument supports Louis Harlan's Tuskegee Machine Thesis.[13] It is conceivable, but it is far from conclusive. The meaning of these events is probably more complex than these scholars are willing to concede.

The following issues weaken the argument of those who claim that the idea of the NNBL had its origins in the mind of W.E.B. Du Bois. First of all, Fortune's overt reason for helping to kill a much-needed appropriation is not apparent. Some justifiable reason had to have been given to Du Bois and the other Afro-American Council members, especially those outspoken ones loyal to Du Bois, such as Ida B. Wells-Barnett. How else, after all, was Du Bois to perform his duty of organizing local leagues? Such an incident provided justifiable grounds for resigning. Du Bois did not, however, resign, but was voted out of his position. Second, at the time that Washington was organizing the NNBL, Du Bois made no claim that Washington was expropriating his idea and undercutting the work of the Afro-American Council. Ida B. Wells-Barnett did make this charge,[14] but to confront his critics, Washington attended the Afro-American Council meeting held in 1900. All the while, Washington and Du Bois appear to have been maintaining an amicable relationship. In 1899 Washington twice offered Du Bois a job at Tuskegee Institute.[15] The second offer stipulated that Du Bois would conduct sociological studies involving the people of the Gulf states, including the country districts, smaller towns, and cities, and teach one course. In April of 1900, Du Bois respectfully declined these offers, but this still did not tarnish his relationship with Washington.[16] For in July of 1901, Washington invited Du Bois to camp with him in West Virginia. Du Bois responded that he would be delighted to accept Washington's invitation.[17] Furthermore, in compiling his list of businesspersons that would be invited to the first meeting of the NNBL, Washington asked Du Bois for his list of businessmen,[18] and Du Bois agreed to send it.[19] This should not be interpreted as unusual. Washington, like many others, initially considered Du Bois an authority on historical and sociological issues and willingly quoted not only from the businessmen's list, but also from other scholarly works by Du Bois.[20] Du Bois, on the other hand, during these doubtful periods of tension, more than once visited the Farmers' Conference held annually at Tuskegee Institute,[21] and in 1902, he proposed gathering data on the conference participants for Washington's and the other participants' use.[22] Moreover, in 1902 he even asked Washington to speak at the Atlanta University Conference on Negro artisans, to which Washington consented.[23] The Boston Riot of 1903 and Du Bois' famous critical essay,[24] "Of Mr. Booker T. Washington and Others,"[25] would help alter their apparently affable relationship.[26]

Third, throughout the period from 1899 to 1903 and after, Washington never conceded that the NNBL was originally Du Bois' idea. If Du Bois, in Washington's mind, was truly the author of this important idea, it is strange that Washington did not give him some semblance of credit, at least initially, especially since at earlier times Washington almost acted as a big brother to Du Bois.[27] And to his discredit, Du Bois never challenged Washington's claim until he openly opposed many of Washington's leadership stances and was instrumental in forming and developing the Niagara Movement.[28] Furthermore, as August Meier has so thoroughly documented, following Reconstruction and the advent of the nadir, individuals high and low were advocating self-help and entrepreneurial development for the survival and progression of African Americans, including Du Bois' hero, Alexander Crummell.[29] Accordingly, the promotion of business development as a liberation and empowerment strategy did not occur in a vacuum. Thus, it is conceivable and debatable that Washington, like Du Bois, reacted independently and creatively according to the zeitgeist.

Nevertheless, the first NNBL meeting successfully took place in Boston, with four hundred delegates in attendance. "They came from thirty-four states, from Mississippi to Maine, from Virginia, and from California, thus justifying the word 'National' in the new organization's title."[30] The purpose of the first meeting was to elect officers, hear testimonies from successful businesspersons, and to establish local leagues throughout the country. Booker T. Washington was elected president, Giles B. Jackson, vice president, T. Thomas Fortune, chairman of the executive committee, E. A. Johnson, compiler, Gilbert C. Harris, treasurer, and E. E. Cooper, secretary.[31] As the organizer of the first NNBL meeting and newly elected president, Washington asked those delegates that were listed on the agenda as presenting papers or addresses that they be short and compact, unrestrained, and spoken plainly and openly without regard for mere grammatical forms.[32] By the time of the second meeting of the NNBL, Washington would have it established that delegates were to speak for no more than twenty minutes plus five more to answer questions from other delegates.[33] If any speaker was not straightforward concerning how they achieved their business success, Washington and other delegates would ask them questions that would compel them to get back on track. Washington did not want speakers to present exercises in elocution or loftily pontificate, just give a brief summary of their business successes in plain, direct, simple language that anyone could understand. Furthermore, Washington asked the delegates that they not introduce political discussions into the meetings or emphasize the negative events that were occurring. Instead, he requested that they concentrate on positive issues and emphasize their opportunities over their grievances.[34] The implementation of this policy was in accord with Washington's public stance against open involvement in politics, and it was a carryover from the manner in which he administrated the Tuskegee Farmers' Conference. Washington and his aides worked diligently to ensure that this policy was enforced, sometimes to the consternation of a few delegates.[35] Washington reasoned that there were plenty of organizations that dealt with the political status of African Americans, and that he wanted the NNBL to be strictly an economically uplifting organization that emphasized duties rather than political rights—duties of introspection, self-help, and frugality.

At the end of the first meeting, similar to the Negro Farmers' Conference, a series of resolutions and recommendations were drawn up. In part, the resolutions gave the NNBL its name, stated its objective, established membership requirements, and defined the specific officers that the league would have, its meeting time, and the procedure whereby resolutions could ultimately be debated on the floor among delegates.[36] Moreover, Washington and the members of the NNBL Committee on Regulations and Rules recommended that local leagues be established throughout the nation and that delegates be sent to the annual meeting.[37] They further recommended that local leagues keep in contact with the national organization, hold monthly meetings, if practical, and that their meetings be free of complicated and useless parliamentary machinery. They finally recommended that parliamentary and technical discussions be avoided, as far as possible, with a view toward concentrating time and strength on the real objectives of the organization.[38] A stenographer recorded these resolutions and recommendations, along with the proceedings of the NNBL. This information was to eventually be distributed to NNBL delegates. In his closing remarks, Washington stated:

> My friends, I must not detain you longer, but I must make a single request, and that is that you take the spirit of this meeting into your homes, to your immediate localities; that you take the resolutions which you will find printed and distributed, plenty of them here, to your homes; that you take the sprit of this meeting, the suggestions that the committee have put in print, and that in each community you try to plant the spirit to form an organization that will result in the employment of the colored people where you live.[39]

Washington was so pleased with the success and enthusiasm displayed during the first meeting that he sent his secretary a telegram which stated, in part, that the "meeting was an overwhelming success beyond expectations."[40]

Following the first meeting in Boston and attempting to promote business development,[41] the NNBL met annually in various cities throughout the nation. For example, in 1901 the second annual convention was held in Chicago, and Oscar DePriest, who would be elected to Congress in 1928 as the first Northern African American to win a seat, was an integral part of the local league that sponsored the Chicago meeting.[42] In 1902 the third annual gathering was held in Richmond, Virginia;[43] in 1903 the fourth annual meeting was held in Nashville, Tennessee.[44] In 1904 the fifth annual gathering was held in Indianapolis, Indiana.[45] In 1905 the sixth annual meeting was held in

New York City,[46] and so on. According to Washington, each successive meeting tended to outdo the previous one. These annual conventions continued even after Washington's death. The second edition of Washington's book, *The Negro in Business*, indicates that the NNBL was still in existence as late as 1992.[47] The 1915 meeting, which was again held in Boston, Massachusetts, would be the last annual gathering that Washington would attend. Almost as though Washington knew that his address would be his last before the league, he not only delivered an effective address, but also thanked his aides for all the assistance that they had rendered him over the years.[48] After this sixteenth annual meeting, he nearly collapsed from physical exhaustion. He died three months later.

From 1900 to 1915, the NNBL meetings became the greatest occasion for Washington to espouse his entrepreneurial ideas. Following the pattern established at the first meeting, Washington usually spoke twice each meeting. He would give opening remarks, usually after the invocation. These opening remarks were generally comments welcoming the delegates who had come from places near and far, and Washington would thank the local league that was responsible for sponsoring the annual meeting and the related social outings. Toward the end of the conference, Washington would give his annual address. A larger audience, consisting of the usual NNBL delegates as well as nondelegates who had come just to hear Washington speak, would usually gather for this speech. In these addresses, Washington promoted his entrepreneurial ideas and values, telling delegates and nondelegates to get practical education, to find an economic niche, to start small in business and grow large, to pay the price of business success, to put the attention of religious faith into their business activities, to learn all they could within their occupations and never become complacent, to not be afraid to take risks, and to pioneer businesses (as is explained in chapter 3).

A Boston reporter who witnessed Washington's first annual address, heard the propounding of his business ideas, and experienced the other NNBL proceedings indicated that the majority of the league delegates' speeches could be interpreted as "sheer platitudes."[49] Although not completely true, there is some validity in this observation. Common prototypes, such as delegates who rose from meager beginnings to middle-class status, or sayings involving the color-blindness of the market, for example, were often presented. But perhaps after reflecting on the epoch, the Boston reporter added, "the Negro race [is] in need of platitudes."[50] These platitudes, in all probability, helped to counter the discouraging influences of the nadir. Moreover, the NNBL delegates who were on the schedule as speakers often presented narratives that not only had an uplifting benefit, but had an educational value as well, as is reflected in the following:

> The struggle of the black man in this country is everywhere much the same. He must go out, as it were, and dig out of nothing something. He must close his eyes to opposition and let work and perseverance be the key-note of his ambition. The success that is built from the ground with one's own hand is lasting and sacred, but things thrown upon us generally go as they come. All of us must work without ceasing along our chosen lines, for that is the only key that will unlock the door of opportunity.[51]

Moreover, common themes such as starting small and expanding, being persistent and frugal, paying attention to small details, carrying out a contract and meeting all obligations, staying abreast of modern methods, keeping businesses clean and inviting, practicing morality in business, and always satisfying customers were apparent in most of the speeches.

The addresses of the NNBL delegates and the impression they generated were not without criticism. Sometimes it appeared as though some businesspersons were boasting when they spoke of their accomplishments and what they owned, while at other times it seemed that some of their declarations were fictitious. After attending the second annual conference in Chicago, Minnie R. Barbour, a woman who contributed articles on race to several African-American newspapers, wrote: "Thus for three days these Business Men blew their own horns, made and carried their own bouquets, each trying to blow louder than the other."[52] Barbour even doubted the authenticity of some of their testimonies. Even though she was not a member of the NNBL, her words carried some validity. Nannie H. Burroughs, who was a life member of the NNBL, years later wrote Washington a letter similar in content to Barbour's article.[53] She wrote that for some time she had been skeptical of many of the testimonies of several of the delegates, feeling that a number of them had given misleading information. This practice, she thought, not only had a bad effect on other delegates that knew and lived among these unreliable ones, but would also make the philanthropic whites feel that because African Americans were doing so well, they should carry more of the financial burden of uplifting themselves. Washington, who for years was aware of this issue, agreed with Burroughs and asked her to speak to the delegates at the 1914 NNBL convention in Oklahoma.[54] Burroughs, however, was unable to attend. In attempting to counter these behaviors, especially after the first meeting, and in view of his experiences in administrating the Farmers' Conference, Washington, according to Emmett J. Scott, made it a habit to fact-check unusual claims.[55] When delegates appeared to be exaggerating or embellishing, Washington and others usually got them back on course by asking questions.

Regardless of these occurrences, Washington strove to help make the NNBL a positive organization that encouraged entrepreneurial development among African Americans, emphasizing opportunities over grievances.[56] He did not want petty disagreements or allegations to destroy the NNBL; his vision was that the league be a constructive assembly rather than a destructive organization. Attorney E. Brown, for example, wanted Washington to question the authenticity of the Metropolitan Mercantile and Realty Company at the 1906 Atlanta meeting of the NNBL, claiming that the company was guilty of defrauding ignorant African Americans.[57] Though Washington did not doubt Brown's claim, he refused to consider such an issue on the floor of the NNBL meeting. This, of course, disappointed Brown, who in turn wrote Washington a letter expressing his frustration and bewilderment and questioning Washington's leadership.[58] Unfortunately, what Brown did not understand was that Washington wanted opportunities highlighted—at least in a public setting—and not issues or events that would create animosity between members, which could prohibit the NNBL from fulfilling its purpose.

As the NNBL became better known throughout the country, it grew by leaps and bounds. By 1906, it was reported that four hundred local leagues were in existence,[59] mostly in the South where there were larger concentrations of African Americans. With the league's increasing popularity, the administrative work of keeping the NNBL operative increased tremendously as well, causing the league to become more structured. With Washington's growing responsibilities managing and raising funds for Tuskegee Institute, as well as being a major leader of his race, he relied more on his secretary, Emmett J. Scott, to respond to routine requests and issues involving the league. Thus, Scott unofficially became the corresponding secretary of the NNBL. And, as the NNBL grew, Washington became reluctant to make decisions concerning the organization without first consulting its executive committee.[60]

Furthermore, between 1903 and 1906, two significant events occurred. First, around 1903, Fred R. Moore, who was the editor of *The Colored American Magazine* and whose business ideas were similar to Washington's (although at times nationalistic),[61] was made the national organizer for the

NNBL.⁶² Second, the NNBL became incorporated in the state of New York on January 10, 1906, which meant that the league could legally issue certificates of membership to local leagues for a fee of five dollars.⁶³ Taking out a five-dollar certificate, according to Moore, ensured that local leagues would not only be identified with the NNBL, but would also receive literature on how other African-American businesses around the nation were doing as well as helpful advice on running their own.⁶⁴ Besides the legal scope of the incorporation and the new literature and advice offered, the five-dollar fee was an attempt by the league to raise badly needed funds for its operations. To raise further funds, in 1904 the NNBL charged two dollars annually per person for its membership fee and twenty-five dollars for a lifetime membership. Nevertheless, the money generated from these charges was not enough to keep the league financially afloat. It was continuously in debt, even after the death of Washington.⁶⁵ For a time, even Andrew Carnegie contributed operating funds to the NNBL, but this still did not alter its beleaguered financial condition.⁶⁶

Regardless of the financial status of the NNBL, Moore was hired as national organizer, his job being to help ensure that local leagues were being organized throughout the nation and monitor the local leagues already operative. Realizing the importance of having a national organizer to help promote business development, Washington and the Executive Committee of the NNBL agreed to pay Moore an annual salary.⁶⁷ Moore was paid fourteen hundred dollars, with the stipulation that he would work full time at helping to organize, reorganize, and encourage the maintenance of existing local leagues, as well as submit weekly reports.⁶⁸ Moore would eventually learn that his assignment was not only inspiring, but time-consuming, taxing, and at times, disturbing and annoying.

In conducting the NNBL's directive and ultimately fulfilling Washington's goal of promoting business development, Moore traveled throughout the country, North and South. He visited such cities as New York, Philadelphia, Baltimore, Boston, Worcester, Springfield, Washington, D.C., Alexandria, Virginia, Albany, Georgia, Hartford, Connecticut, and New Bedford, Massachusetts. In New Bedford, he encountered individuals who were antagonistic toward Booker T. Washington's leadership and opposed to a local league being organized in their midst.⁶⁹ Agitated but undaunted, Moore worked on.⁷⁰ He traveled to such remote areas as East Spencer, New York, where he met George W. Cook, a brick manufacturer and secretary of the local business league of Ithaca, New York; he continued to Scranton, Pennsylvania, Meriden, Connecticut, and Bristol, Tennessee. He submitted reports of his travels to Washington, who in turn submitted them to the executive committee.[71]

It is difficult to determine with assuredness how active the local leagues were during Washington's lifetime. The available evidence is meager for assessing the local leagues over the entire sixteen years that Washington was president of the national body. Washington, of course, wanted the local leagues to be very active, meeting at least once a month,[72] as well as promoting business development in their respective locales.[73] Many local leagues, however, were probably organized only on paper and reorganized in August of each year so as to send delegates to the annual convention.[74] Regardless, the local leagues were well aware of Washington's directive—to promote business development in their respective communities—because many appear to have responded affirmatively to it.[75]

Moreover, in terms of the number of active local leagues, as could be expected, there was fluctuation over the years. For instance, in 1909, *The Tuskegee Student*, a publication of Tuskegee Institute, reported that 500 local leagues were scattered throughout the country, which marked an increase of 100 from the 1906 figure,[76] while for the years 1914–15, Monroe N. Work reported 295 chartered leagues.[77] How reliable these figures are is debatable,[78] but the NNBL by 1915 probably had close to three hundred local leagues, which were generally identified by the fact that they had been chartered. Furthermore, according to Theodore W. Jones, an active local league and NNBL executive board member in Chicago, those leagues in the South that existed around higher concentrations of African Americans were more active than most others, especially when compared to those in the North or in remote areas.[79] Jones was not the only one to have made that assessment. As an indication of their progress, the Mississippi NNBL delegates, led by Charles Banks, had their reports dominate the Thursday sessions of the 1909 annual gathering.[80]

Washington, however, was very concerned about whether the local leagues were active. As a result, he insisted on receiving weekly reports from Moore. In one letter, he made Moore aware that he still had not received information requested on a previous day; he then asked Moore to let him know how many letters were sent out of his office within the last six months, how many members belonged to the local league of Greater New York, Brooklyn, and so forth, how often they met, and what activities they were undertaking.[81] In his annoyance over still not having received the weekly reports, Washington wrote to Moore: "I hope that you are bearing in mind that I have not received your weekly report for last week and the week before last. I wish you would please let me have the reports regularly as I am anxious to put them in the hands of the Executive Committee so that they might see what you are doing."[82] In the same letter, Washington told Moore to go back to Philadelphia to help strengthen the local league there, reported to be in weak condition.[83] Nine days later, Washington still had not received his reports from Moore. He sent Moore yet another letter and finally received an encouraging report eleven days later.[84]

After 1906, the business league correspondence between Washington and Moore dwindled as Moore's assignments were reduced. Finally, in 1907, the national organizer's position was temporarily abolished and replaced by state organizers managed by Emmett J. Scott.[85] This effort was generally unsuccessful. In 1909 Charles Moore of North Carolina was appointed national organizer, serving disjointed terms.[86] In 1913 Ralph W. Tyler, a journalist and politician, was given the position.[87] In attempting to organize and reorganize local leagues in West Virginia and some Northern locales north of the Ohio River, Tyler sent Washington a report identifying inactive local leagues in West Virginia that had not met in years. Tyler advised Washington that it would be a good policy for the NNBL to reorganize many of its inactive local leagues in the North before establishing new ones. His reasoning was that the reestablished leagues could serve as examples rather than disappointments for the newly created ones, as well as demonstrating the effectiveness of the national body.[88] In 1915, by the time of the Sixteenth Annual Convention of the NNBL, Charles H. Moore, former English professor at North Carolina A & M College, was again the national organizer.[89] In his final annual address before NNBL delegates, Washington thanked Moore and other aides, also praising Moore for being devoted and active in his national organizing activities.[90]

An Analysis of the National Negro Business League

A common historical interpretation of Washington's entrepreneurial philosophy has developed and endured for at least fifty years. In essence, this interpretation argues that Washington was promoting the development of a separate African-American economy; in other words, that he was advising and directing African-American entrepreneurs to cater only to the African-American market.[91] From a business perspective, this would be considered an unwise, profit-limiting directive. This assessment of Washington's business outlook and market strategy is based largely on the following statements that he made in a 1905 article in *Charities* magazine which posed the question, "why should African-American business men go south?"[92] Washington wrote:

> But where the great masses of the Negro population are, there are the best opportunities for Negro business men. Experience has shown, I believe, even in the North, that the largest opportunities for the Negro in business are in providing for those needs of other members of his race, which the white business man, either through neglect, or lack of knowledge, has failed or been unable to provide. The Negro knows the members of his own race. He knows the Negro people of his neighborhood, in their church, and in their family life, and is able to discriminate in his dealings with them. This superiority in the matter of credits is in itself a business advantage, of which competition cannot easily deprive the Negro, and one which, with the extension of the modern methods of business, is likely to become of increasing importance.[93]

It is imperative that this interpretation of Washington's entrepreneurial philosophy be discarded because it misrepresents his business outlook. More specifically, in Washington's 1905 statement he did not recommend that African-American entrepreneurs conduct business exclusively or even chiefly in the African-American market, thereby promoting a separate economy. And, most importantly, he did not intend such a narrow practice to be implemented. Washington was well aware of the importance of conducting business in the open market. In fact, the promotion and execution of open commerce was an indispensable aspect of his real freedom and empowerment strategy. Washington felt that there was "no color in business."[94]

What Washington did mean by these assertions was that African-American entrepreneurs, due to their intimate knowledge of the needs and wants of African Americans, possessed a distinct advantage over most white businesspersons, who generally neglected the African-American market. In Washington's opinion, African-American entrepreneurs possessed a golden opportunity to dominate their market, which they should do before strong competition emerged. Doing so, Washington thought, would aid their advancement in the industrial, financial, and commercial world. Washington's statements, in essence, reflected the importance of dominating a familiar market as well as unfamiliar ones.

There is an abundance of evidence to support these assertions. First, in his numerous writings and speeches throughout the years, when Washington presented case studies on successful African-American entrepreneurs, especially involving Southerners, a common theme is found, which is that a significant number of these entrepreneurs catered to a mixed clientele.[95] Lewis Adams and Dr. Cornelius Dorsette, discussed in chapter 2, serve as examples. Second, in his 1912 address before the NNBL, Washington advised African-American farmers to grow enough crops to meet the rising demand of markets, which he saw as responsive to merit and not race. Hence, Washington proclaimed:

> This year our country will probably produce 3,125,000,000 bushels of corn, 695,443,000 bushels of wheat, 1,136,700,000 bushels of oats, 338,800,000 bushels of potatoes and 16,000,000 bales of cotton. In this tremendous production here again is no color line. We want to see to it that as a race we not only produce our share, but that we hold on to our share of the wealth that grows out of the manufacturing of trading in, and transporting these commodities. Activity in these directions will bring to us influence and usefulness that no political party can give us or take from us. Before it is too late, I want my race to lay hold on the primary sources of wealth and civilization.[96]

Thirdly, regarding African-American entrepreneurs, Washington consistently let it be known that in the South, where the vast majority of African Americans lived, they were not dependent on the African-American market alone. For example, in 1907, Washington wrote: "I have been repeatedly informed by Negro merchants in the South that they have as many white patrons as black; and the cordial business relations which are almost universal between the races in the South proves, as I have elsewhere said, that there is little race prejudice in the American dollar."[97] Furthermore, in his 1913 address before the NNBL, Washington declared:

> Remember, as I have said, that we have a race of ten million with whom to do business and in the South especially our commercial activity is not confined to our race. In a Southern city when I was spending a half hour in a Negro bank, I noted that one-fourth of the people who came in to do business with the bank were white people. Young men, young women, there are openings in this great country of ours for Negroes to establish and maintain many additional and various kinds of business concerns.[98]

In further discounting the separate-economy thesis, besides the examples of Washington's writings and speeches, his real freedom and empowerment strategy for African Americans can be deployed. Undoubtedly, accepting the separate-economy thesis would not only trivialize Washington's leadership program, but it would also, most importantly, distort the true meaning of his objective of having African-American entrepreneurs be perceived by their individual communities as indispensable, particularly by those white members who were in positions to effect societal change.[99] From his early encounters with Tuskegee entrepreneur Lewis Adams, as noted in chapter 2, and his observation of the influence Adams had over the entire Tuskegee community, Washington reasoned that if African Americans could be persuaded on a mass scale to go into business and grow to be indispensable to their respective communities by offering quality goods and services, this would serve as a major step toward solving the race problem.[100] The advancement of an individual entrepreneur was, in Washington's view, an advancement for the entire race. "Friction between the races," Washington further noted, "will pass away as the black man, by reason or his skill, intelligence, and character, can produce something that the white man wants or respects in the commercial world."[101]

Furthermore, Washington's role in creating and developing Tuskegee Institute served to reinforce what he had learned by observing Adams. He saw and understood, for instance, that as Tuskegee Institute's economic relationship with the surrounding community expanded, particularly with whites, it began to be viewed as an indispensable, revenue-generating aspect of the community, much needed for the stability of the local economy.[102] Consequently, what Washington saw and experienced became the core of his strategy for how African Americans would advance and truly gain their rights. Hence, contrary to what has been argued, conducting business chiefly in a segregated market was not the strategy espoused by Washington or a vision that he held. Unfortunately, critics misread Washington's entrepreneurial philosophy probably because they do not fully appreciate its complexity or effects, which were not as narrow as they claim. This, indeed, confirms the need for a broader understanding of the intricacy of Washington's entrepreneurial philosophy, as underscored in chapter 3.

Additionally, critics want to have it both ways. In the great debate between Washington and Du Bois, Washington is seen as too attentive to white society, too accommodating, and at worst, as an Uncle Tom. Conversely, critics argue that he promoted withdrawing from white society and economy, indulging in a fantasy of self-sufficiency and self-enclosure within a black parallel economy. To see Washington as holding both positions is difficult, since they pull in opposite directions. Neither of these interpretations really fit Washington. Circumstances made him a shrewd strategist who operated as a skillful technician, dealing as best he could with the very real problems he and his people confronted.

Notwithstanding spurious critiques of Washington and therefore the NNBL as well, the league was not flawless. As mentioned earlier, the NNBL did not sustain itself financially year after year. For an organization that at one point had up to six hundred local leagues and somewhere between five and forty thousand active members (and perhaps even more unofficial ones), this financial weakness must be attributed to a grave error.[103] Moreover, for an organization to espouse self-help and racial solidarity yet rely on a reluctant Andrew Carnegie to furnish much-needed operational funds was not only hypocritical, but also sent an unhealthy message about ideas and praxis.[104]

In addition to the one-time charter fee, the annual membership fee, the lifetime membership fee, and the selling of NNBL paraphernalia such as badges and buttons at annual meetings, other self-help efforts to generate operational funds would perhaps have helped, especially since information published on NNBL delegates tended to portray them not only as successful, but prosperous.[105] The NNBL records at the Tuskegee University Archives are replete with letters from Washington and Scott that reflect their concern over the financial status of the NNBL, which should have reflected prosperity.[106] These financial concerns would be an issue with the NNBL even after Washington's death.

The NNBL would also have been strengthened if it had offered at its meetings more discussions by experts on the mechanics of operating a modern, successful business; for instance, the use of advertising techniques, the value of proper bookkeeping and accounting methods, awareness of personnel and management issues, business law, and the psychological value of a business's appearance and upkeep. For an astute and attentive listener, all of these lessons and more could have been derived from the testimonies of the delegates who presented at the annual meetings, expressing their business ups and downs and ultimately successes. For the average delegate, however, more concrete lessons on business mechanics would likely have been extremely helpful.

As an example, at the 1907 NNBL annual meeting in Topeka, Kansas, William Carter, a bookkeeper and assistant accountant at Tuskegee Institute who was also instrumental in improving the institute's financial operations, presented an address titled, "The Accountant as a Factor in Business."[107] In his presentation, Carter offered valuable lessons in bookkeeping, how accounting advanced from bookkeeping, the value of accounting, its increasing utility as businesses expanded, and the value of accounting for banks (especially important since the number of African-American banks was increasing during Washington's NNBL presidency). More addresses of this caliber—straightforward and plain in the manner that Washington would have demanded—would have helped. At least Nannie H. Burroughs, who had questioned the validity of some of the testimonies of NNBL delegates, thought so, for in a 1915 letter to Emmett J. Scott, she wrote:

> Most of our enterprises have written all around and about these words: "Negroes run this shop." Can't you get a few experts to talk to us on, How to Lift the Standard, How to Run Ideal Stores, How to Advertise? O, please let us strike a new note. I am tired of hearing Negro Millionaires tell of their wealth and influence.[108]

Burroughs's observations and comments were timely and, of course, long overdue. But besides Burroughs's advice, the NNBL, during Washington's presidency, could have benefited greatly from an NNBL business venture, something that the entire nation could have taken note of. Washington was aware of this idea because he received letters from league members suggesting the need for the implementation of such a strategy. Charles Banks, for instance, in a letter dated May 23, 1906, wrote to Washington:

> I have also been thinking that the time is at hand when the N.N.B.L. should put some business project before the country that will command national attention, and at the same time be fathered by our organization. While it is true that the stimulation and encouragement gathered in our annual meetings are of inestimable value, yet I am inclined to think that we will have to make some new departures, as an organization to keep things going upward.[109]

Another league member, like Banks, suggested that an abundance of land be purchased in the West for real estate purposes, that land be procured in the South in order to produce and sell timber, that a coal mine be purchased, and that a department store be bought.[110] These potential ventures were not only to be league-directed, but act as a source of employment for the African-American masses. Despite these suggestions, the new direction that Banks and others envisioned would be taken only after Washington's death.[111]

Still, the NNBL had more positive dimensions than negative ones. First, Washington should be commended for establishing an organization whose purpose was to promote entrepreneurial development among African Americans, particularly since scholars have argued that one reason for the failure of African-American businesses during the nadir was the absence of a business tradition.[112] Rather than being content with this situation and concluding that no businesses could be successful, Washington set out not only to increase the number of African-American entrepreneurs, but also to dispel the myth that a business tradition was prerequisite for business success.

Second, with respect to the NNBL, Washington was aware of the structural limitations prevailing in the United States such as racism and particularly segregation; as aforementioned, he wanted always to emphasize opportunities rather than injustices perpetrated against his race.[113] This was the main reason why he did not want the NNBL to be a political organization. Thus, NNBL delegates, in responding to Washington's leadership directive, expressed how they had seized opportunities in their midst and capitalized on them. Their testimonies were to serve as an inspiration to themselves and others. Scholars,[114] however, have argued that Washington did not consider structural issues or evaluate the status of African-American businesses while promoting the NNBL's objectives. But it should be pointed out that he was well aware of the structural issues as well as the status of African-American businesses. Instead of being discouraged by what he knew, however, he designed his organization to be constructive and progressive, even in the face of an overwhelming number of barriers.

Third, the very existence of the NNBL helped initiate the creation of the National Negro Funeral Directors' Association, the National Negro Press Association, the National Negro Bar Association, the National Negro Bankers Association, and the National Association of Negro Insurance Men.[115] All of these organizations were affiliated with the NNBL, promoted its aim, and had members active in it. As an example, Charles C. Spaulding—who lived in Durham, North Carolina, headed the North Carolina Mutual Insurance Company, and was inspired by Booker T. Washington—was not only an active member of the NNBL, but also an active member of the National Association of Negro Insurance Men.[116]

Fourth, evidence indicates that some local leagues were involved in community issues involving race progress in addition to promoting business development. The Montgomery, Alabama, local league is a case in point.[117] This league adhered to Washington's directive of promoting business development. Its members first met once a month, then, as they grew, weekly. It also sent agents out into the local community to promote business development and maintain existing businesses. Moreover, when the Montgomery City Council changed the cemetery entrance rules to require African Americans to enter from the rear, the local league met with the city council and convinced them to reverse their decision. Furthermore, when a new school was needed to accommodate the African-American population, the local league again met the proper authorities, informing them that a new school for whites had just been built with school tax funds but nothing similar had been done for African Americans. Since the school board had nearly exhausted its funds, the local league offered to raise money to purchase the land for the proposed school, provided that the school board purchased the building. This arrangement was satisfactory to both parties and was accordingly instituted. The local league of Richmond, Virginia, concerned over the disenfranchisement movement taking place in the state and partially attempting to counteract it, asked Washington to speak before a mixed audience which was to include the governor and state legislatures.[118] Washington acceded to the request and delivered an address which was well received.

Apparently, Guideline Number Three of the NNBL's pamphlet "Hints and Helps for Local Negro Business Leagues" was instrumental "in fostering an interest in civic affairs, such as sanitation, clean yards, cultivating pride, in making attractive in appearance the home districts [of African Americans], and in other ways, showing an interest in everything that makes for a better community life."[119] The meaning of these statements is ambiguous, especially considering that the NNBL was officially a nonpolitical organization. If Washington had any input, did this relate to politics, or just the aesthetics of local communities? Although we do not have a conclusive answer, the local leagues probably responded to the pressing needs of their communities regardless of any nonpolitical mandates from Washington, helping their communities in any way that they could.

Fifth, at a time when domestic values served as a leadership force in the lives of American women, especially those of the middle class, the NNBL, during Washington's leadership, was always encouraging female entrepreneurs.[120] They joined the NNBL and often formed separate women's business leagues that worked in conjunction with the national body. When Washington called for the assembly of the NNBL in 1900, he wanted positive responses from women as well.[121] He recognized that their advancement was a critical component needed for the progress of his race. In traveling throughout the country he also saw women engaged in business ventures, performing hard and often unsung labors.[122] Like the men, he wanted them to come to the Boston meeting (and all ensuing gatherings) and not only share their experiences, but also fraternize with fellow businesspersons.

Women were always an integral part of the NNBL, even though Washington rarely mentioned them in his book, *The Negro in Business*, as a driving force behind entrepreneurial ventures. Despite this, however, as mentioned earlier in regard to Nannie H. Burroughs, their advice and suggestions were generally respected. Thus, ever since the first meeting of the NNBL, one or more women were usually placed on the agenda as speakers. The criterion for membership was not gender, but whether an individual was engaged in a business venture. For instance, at the first meeting, Mrs. A. M. Smith, Mrs. A. Thornton, and Mrs. Casneau spoke.[123] At the second gathering, Albreta [sic] M. Smith, Dora A. Miller, and Emma L. Pitts offered addresses,[124] and this inclusion of female speakers was continued at other meetings.

The types of businesses that female members of the NNBL were involved in were usually those associated with roles commonly designated for women in the early twentieth century, such as restaurant owners, caterers, milliners, dressmakers, manicurists, and hairstylists.[125] There were, however, women operating in fields then atypical for their sex, such as doctors, pharmacists, and even a banker.[126] Regardless of their line of work, all moral and honest labor performed by these women was considered noble by the NNBL,[127] which preached Washington's doctrine of finding an economic niche, performing better than anyone else,[128] and expanding.

Perhaps the most famous female member of the NNBL was Sarah Breedlove Walker, better known by her commercial name, Madame C. J. Walker.[129] Walker ultimately became a millionaire by developing a hair-products business which successfully sold merchandise throughout the United States and abroad.[130] Historians have implied that Washington behaved in a sexist manner toward Walker when she attended the 1912 NNBL annual meeting. Walker, according to these historians, was invited to speak by Washington. Before speaking, however, Walker had to wait while speaker after speaker presented their address, and after being continuously ignored, she finally stood up and aggressively began delivering her own testimony, first exclaiming, "Surely you are not going to shut the door in my face. I feel that I am in a business that is a credit to the womanhood of our race."[131] After she had gained and maintained the attention of league members, she further commented, "I went into a business that is despised, that is criticized and talked about by everybody—the business of growing hair. They did not believe that such a thing could be done, but I have proven beyond the question of a doubt that I do grow hair!"[132] Because her story was so impressive, she was made a keynote speaker at the next annual gathering.[133] Whether Washington was being sexist is difficult to determine, but judging by the correspondence exchanged between him and Walker, they appear to have had a respectful working relationship.[134]

Nonetheless, as insinuated by Walker's remarks, men dominated the NNBL.[135] They made up the majority of the membership, the majority of delegates attending the annual meetings, and the lion's share of those presenting papers or addresses. Men were also predominant in the leadership roles. This pattern was a product of the times and was in line with the standards of the Victorian era that many blacks and whites, especially elites, followed. Nevertheless, the recorded testimonies of male league members reveal that successful male entrepreneurs generally paid homage to their wives for not only being partners in their undertakings, but also for being crucial to their very success.[136] At the end of an address, when a male delegate would be asked who contributed toward his success, it was not unusual for him to say that it was his wife.[137] Some even said that if it had not been for their wives, they would have failed or given up.[138] John Wanamaker, a successful white storeowner, was asked by Washington to address the NNBL. After seeing female delegates at the 1905 New York NNBL gathering, he complimented the male delegates for incorporating women into their organization as well as their business lives.[139]

Sixth and finally, as with its inclusion of women, if we are to evaluate the NNBL as a promoter of African-American businesses during Washington's lifetime, it must be judged successful in spite of its flaws. The fact that the NNBL met annually and had numerous local leagues, many of which were active, is proof in and of itself that the league fulfilled its mission.[140] Still more evidence of its success is to be found by analyzing the growth of African-American businesses during Washington's lifetime. Table 8 below illustrates the growth of African-American businesses from 1863 to 1913.

Table 8. Growth of African-American businesses from 1863 to 1913 (in 1,000's of owners and operators)

Year	Total African-American businesses	Numerical change over preceding date	Percentage change over preceding date
1863	2	(x)	(x)
1873	4	2	100
1883	10	6	150
1893	17	7	70
1903	25	8	47
1913	40	15	60

Source: Jessie C. Smith and Carrell P. Horton, *Historical Statistics of Black America: Agriculture to Labor & Employment* (New York: Gale Research, 1995), p. 282.

A steady growth is evident from 1863 on, with the most significant growth occurring between the years 1903 and 1913, when the NNBL was at its peak.[141] There was an increase of fifteen thousand businesses—a sixty percent growth. Moreover, an NNBL statistical report comparing the years 1900 and 1924 revealed a similar pattern, indicating that in 1900, 20,000 African-American businesses existed, while in 1924, 65,000 existed, which reflected an increase of 45,000, a 225 percentage point increase.[142] Although table 8 does not prove conclusively that the NNBL was entirely responsible for this significant growth, it is beyond a doubt that its presence had a significant influence on this growth, especially as indicated during the period from 1903 to 1913.[143]

Some scholars have stressed that the growth of African-American businesses was meager in comparison to that in white-owned-and-operated businesses during the same period.[144] They further point out that African-American businesses were, without exception, small and insignificant to the greater American economy. These scholars are correct in their assessments; however, the entrepreneurial growth reflected above is an accomplishment, especially considering the depths from which many of these business operators arose. Many of them, like Washington, had been enslaved and arose against difficult odds that often served as structural barriers to success. The effects of the nadir were pervasive and rapidly worsening. Furthermore, most of them arose in the absence of a business tradition, which was limited if not completely suppressed by slavery, and thus they operated generally on a trial and error, hit and miss basis. Washington, who was an evolutionist,[145] made it his policy not to compare the economic growth of white businesses, in general, with those of African Americans.[146] He reasoned that African-American businesses had to be judged on their own merit and that business success, no matter how infinitesimal, was success and should be judged as such. He envisioned that in time the African-American entrepreneur, through no artificial forcing but simply with hard, persistent work, would be on par with white American businessmen, contributing to the well-being of the American economy.[147]

It was Washington's dream and aim to ensure that African Americans were a vital part of the American economy and ultimately of society in general, which, in his mind, would bring about true freedom and real American citizenship as prescribed by the United States Constitution.[148] Washington espoused his economic ideas of self-help and making oneself indispensable to one's community both publicly and privately, with the NNBL serving as a major national forum for the advocacy of these ideas.

When analyzing Washington on a micro level, as executive of Tuskegee Institute, which will be covered in the next chapter, it becomes clear that he exhibited the same consistent behavior, espousing and implementing his business ideas to obtain real freedom and empowerment for his race.

6

Fundraising, Management, and Industrial Education

Booker T. Washington as a Business Executive and Promoter of the Tuskegee Spirit

Long before establishing either the Negro Farmers' Conference at Tuskegee Institute or the NNBL, Booker T. Washington conducted himself as an executive and was a driving force behind maintaining Tuskegee Institute's very existence.[1] His role at Tuskegee Institute was much more than that of merely a school administrator. He helped establish a facility where Tuskegee Institute could hold its initial classes and helped provide the first land on which the school would be built. After class sessions in the early days, he led his students to the fields to clear land so crops could be planted and harvested for the subsistence of all, thereby instituting the first study-work routine at Tuskegee Institute. When more funds were needed to maintain Washington's growing school, he and Olivia Davidson, the first female principal of Tuskegee Institute and the woman who later became Washington's wife, traveled around the country to campaign for much-needed philanthropic funds.[2]

On a more important level, as is the case with the Tuskegee Farmers' Conference and the NNBL, there were no inconsistencies between his entrepreneurial philosophy and his practices at Tuskegee Institute. On campus, Washington wanted his message of self-help imparted to his students so that they could continue fighting for real freedom and empowerment. Washington, as head of Tuskegee Institute, managed his school in a meticulous manner to ensure that his leadership objective was being fulfilled. Students were educated, and when they left Tuskegee Institute, especially the graduates, it was expected that they would exemplify the Tuskegee spirit by not only becoming indispensable assets to their respective communities, but also by willingly reaching out to help others. After all, according to Washington and as underscored in chapter 2, economic racial progress was considered essential to advance African Americans.

To ensure that his students would be educated and thereby manifest the Tuskegee spirit, Washington, both as a businessman and fund-raiser, sold the idea of industrial education to prospective donors. The rapid growth of Tuskegee Institute shows that he was successful. Moreover, regardless of the views any donors might have held about industrial education for African Americans, Washington sought to use that education, along with several other of his uplift methods, to help rescue the masses of African Americans from relegation to the lower echelons of the social structure. And so, in this chapter, Washington's fund-raising and revenue-generating activities, his managerial practices, and his promotion of industrial education will to be analyzed. More specifically, we shall examine Washington's role as an executive, focusing on how he implemented many of his business ideas and continued to promote his entrepreneurial philosophy on campus as a strategy for real freedom and empowerment.

Fund-raising & Revenue-generating Activities

As a founder and head of Tuskegee Institute, Washington quickly became aware that the two thousand dollar appropriation from the state of Alabama would not be enough to meet the growing demands of an expanding school. When Tuskegee Institute opened on July 4, 1881, Washington admitted thirty students, half of them male and half female, mainly from Macon County, Alabama. Many others wanted to be admitted, but due to a lack of facilities and a teaching staff of only one, these potential students were regrettably turned away.[3]

Six weeks after Tuskegee Institute opened, Olivia Davidson, who had graduated from Hampton Institute in 1879 and completed a two-year program at Framingham Institute in Massachusetts, became a teacher there.[4] She worked hand-in-hand with Washington to establish an educational foundation for the school as well as a material base of land and buildings.[5] Davidson had been exposed to the aforementioned Hampton model of education, and according to Washington, she believed in it. She had also studied a liberal arts curriculum at Framingham Institute. Upon joining the Tuskegee Institute faculty, she immediately contributed to the early pedagogical methods of the school, sharing the heavy teaching load with Washington.[6]

As the eagerness of students for education at Tuskegee Institute steadily increased—and with it the need for on-campus housing, particularly for female students—the press for additional funds also grew. With this new challenge, fund-raising and revenue-generating skills became a necessity, for school fees and student labor were insufficient to cover operating costs. According to Washington, Davidson first responded to this challenge, and he learned greatly from her.[7] She went among both the African-American and white citizens of Macon County to solicit funds, as well as pies, cakes, and other items that could be sold at Tuskegee Institute fund-raising festivals. When this was not enough, she headed north to speak at churches and other social gatherings, informing Northerners of the Tuskegee Institute's mission and financial needs. Her efforts were fruitful. Indeed, during the early days, she and Washington traveled together, dividing up prospective territories and collecting funds.[8] Washington praised Davidson, who died in 1889, in his first two autobiographies.[9] In his second one Washington wrote, "No single individual did more toward laying the foundations of the Tuskegee Institute so as to insure the successful work that has been done there than Olivia A. Davidson."[10]

In regard to fund-raising, General Armstrong, like Davidson, was a person from whom Washington learned. When plans were being drawn for Alabama Hall, Tuskegee Institute's second building, General Armstrong invited Washington to travel to Northern locales with him to raise funds, but for Tuskegee, not Hampton Institute.[11] This act further impressed Washington and increased his respect and admiration for General Armstrong. He realized that Armstrong was aware that when people gave funds for African-American education they did not mean for it to be concentrated in one place, such as Hampton Institute. Accompanied by a quartet of singers, a method similar to a practice begun at Fisk University,[12] they embarked on their fund-raising trip. General Armstrong informed Washington that when he appealed to audiences for funds, he should give them an idea for every word he uttered. According to Washington, he applied this advice not only to his fund-raising addresses, but to his other public speeches as well.[13] From these early influences and experiences, Washington's fund-raising knowledge and skills improved significantly, and he ultimately became a master fund-raiser who was sought for advice in the matter.

As mentioned in chapter 2, Washington learned from experience that he could get the best results from fund-raising efforts by employing a system of operation,[14] a technique he had initially learned from Viola Ruffner. Washington first, in a dignified manner and without begging, would present the needs of Tuskegee Institute and explain how helping to fulfill them, in any manner, large or small, would not only help the South, but the entire nation.[15]

African Americans who heard this message did not have to be convinced of its validity, because their efforts to gain an education following slavery were enormous, and this made them receptive to any legitimate efforts for educational advancement.[16] For whites, on the other hand, particularly those donors capable of giving large sums, the dignified manner in which Washington presented Tuskegee Institute's financial needs no doubt served to be more convincing, especially in view of the numerous requests that they received daily for funds. Moreover, in his campaign for funds, Washington always highlighted what Tuskegee Institute and its students were doing to help themselves, and he would end his remarks by stressing what a little extra assistance from donors could help accomplish.[17] Self-help, the dignity of labor, and the Protestant work ethic were his themes, and he effectively employed the language of the mainstream business environment on prospective donors. These activities would eventually aid in making Tuskegee Institute the best-funded African-American school of Washington's day.

Secondly, if Washington had a list of potential donors to consult in a specific region or a series of addresses to present in that same region, he made it his practice to do the full job, whether he procured funds there or not. He did not want to be neglectful because he was well aware that any individual to whom he had spoken personally or who had heard his public address, whether or not they initially gave, could potentially contribute in the future. Consequently, he saw it as extremely important to establish such contacts.

Thirdly, in a businesslike fashion, as mentioned in chapter 3, Washington tried to stretch every dollar that his school was given, especially those from wealthy donors. Perhaps reflecting on the lessons he learned from William Baldwin, he reasoned that if these people were wise and shrewd enough to earn such large amounts of income, they would also be wise in giving some of it away if they chose to do so.[18] Therefore, he appealed to their intelligence,[19] trying to be prudent with every dollar that they contributed to the advancement of Tuskegee Institute and attempting to make each dollar purchase two dollars' worth of materials or services.

Fourth, in marketing Tuskegee Institute and trying to place the students that it produced, Washington was insistent that everything about the institute be clean, orderly, and wholesome. This applied to everything connected with it, including the buildings, the grounds, the equipment, the animals, the faculty, the staff, and the students. Washington correctly reckoned that the institute would be better supported if its appearance was pleasing to anyone who chose to look.[20] After viewing Tuskegee Institute, most visitors were extremely impressed.[21]

Fifth, Washington adhered to the wishes of donors. If they gave the institute restricted funds, he disposed of them as they stipulated. For instance, some funds were given specifically for the general operating expenses of the school, while others were given specifically for scholarship purposes, for the construction of buildings, the purchasing of equipment, the endowment fund, and a central power and heating plant. Washington, an astute businessman, was quick to let donors know how their money was being used and how it had helped the school to help itself by publishing *The Southern Letter*, a four-page monthly paper which contained brief reports of Tuskegee Institute's progress, *The Tuskegee Student*, which was an alumni newsletter, the annual principal's and treasurer's report, and by directly corresponding with donors.[22]

Finally, Washington and other Tuskegee Institute fund-raisers would often be accompanied by the "Tuskegee Quartet,"[23] who, like the Fisk Jubilee Singers and the Hampton Singers, would serenade prospective donors with folk songs and plantation melodies; they were an instant success and were often called back for encores. In fact, when Washington, shortly after Andrew Carnegie gave the institute's endowment six hundred thousand dollars in U.S. Steel bonds, requested more funds from him for an organ to put in the Tuskegee Chapel, Carnegie suggested Washington do without it because, he said, the Tuskegee singers would sound much better without instrumental accompaniment.[24]

Tuskegee Institute's gifts from donors increased steadily over the years, as did the audiences that came to hear the Tuskegee Quartet. During the first year of the school's existence, Washington and Davidson managed to collect $855.83 to supplement the $2,000 appropriation from the state of Alabama.[25] At the end of the 1900 fiscal year, eleven years after Davidson's untimely death at the age of thirty-five, $236,163.40 had been collected, plus $152,232.49 for a year-old endowment fund.[26] By 1915, the year of Washington's death, $379,704.83 had been collected, and the endowment fund had increased to $1,970,214.17.[27] Nevertheless, the steady increase in donor funds was never enough to meet the ever-increasing expenses of Washington's expanding school. Washington, in attempting to meet these obligations, generally spent "two-thirds of his time, strength, and resourcefulness merely in endeavoring to raise money."[28] However, he considered it noble work because Tuskegee Institute was helping to instill in his students the mindset of being pioneers who would contribute to the well-being of their respective communities.

Washington's last successful fund-raising campaign was completed in

1915.[29] In addition to funds for Tuskegee Institute's yearly operating expenses, he and the Tuskegee Institute Board of Trustees had been engaged in efforts to raise two hundred and forty-five thousand dollars for a central power and heating plant. Washington, like successful corporate executives of his day, created a campaign wherein five school representatives canvassed strategic territories throughout the nation—north, south, east, and the new territories out west, which were beginning to present gifts to Tuskegee Institute.[30] To prove their authenticity, the representatives carried a personal letter of introduction written and signed by Washington. Each day these representatives sent Washington a telegram to let him know how much they had collected for the day. The next morning he would send a reply telegram letting them know how much had been collected in total so that they all would know how far they had progressed towards achieving the overall goal. By June of 1915, all but four or five thousand of the two hundred and forty-five thousand dollars he had sought had been raised. To relieve Washington of further worry, the trustees made up the difference, giving Tuskegee Institute its first central power and heating plant.

Fund-raising was not the only method by which Tuskegee Institute obtained money. In harmony with Washington's endeavor to make the institute indispensable to the surrounding community, the institute provided a number of goods and services to Macon County and surrounding areas. For instance, they sold bricks, buggies, shoes, clothes, furniture, farm animals and produce, mattresses, cabinets, tinware, houses and land, and offered such services as professional printing, tailoring, woodcutting, wheelmaking, tinsmithing, harness-making, painting, and blacksmithing.[31] These profit-generating industries, according to Washington, first developed out of Tuskegee Institute's need to survive and sustain itself rather than simply for the sake of teaching a trade.[32] Furthermore, although these industries were profitable, in comparison to the funds obtained from donors, they contributed less toward the income needed to meet the annual expenses of Tuskegee Institute. Nevertheless, according to Washington, they taught the students trades, the philosophy of work, the dignity of labor, the doctrine of self-help, and knowledge that could help them to sustain themselves if they decided not to become strictly teachers.[33]

Managerial Practices

Besides generating funds, Washington managed Tuskegee Institute rigorously, similar to an established professional manager. He thoroughly knew the operations of the campus because he experienced its development from a little shanty to a multimillion-dollar institution. As Louis Harlan has written, Washington was indeed master of the Tuskegee campus.[34] When Washington was on campus, he would rise early in the morning, usually before others had awakened, and meticulously make his rounds.[35] A stenographer would often accompany him so that he could dictate letters as he made his tours, observing what was wrong and what was right. He would examine everything that his sharp senses could detect: unfenced animals, paper scraps on the grounds, faded fences, dirty areas, unpleasant odors, and unhooked gates. As faculty, staff, and students awakened and the campus routines began, Washington would often consult students to see if they were satisfied with all aspects of the institution, and if they were not, he wanted to hear their complaints,[36] often to the displeasure of some teachers. Then, as class session began, Washington would go in and out of classrooms to ensure that instructors were using the correlative method of teaching—that is, relating lessons to real-life situations.[37] If this practice was not being adhered to, the instructor or instructors in error would be reprimanded for not following school policies,[38] and if they persisted, after a warning, they generally would be let go.[39]

As Tuskegee Institute experienced rapid growth, especially after the Atlanta Exposition address, Washington was compelled to be away from campus six months a year, largely for fund-raising purposes. Nonetheless, by this time he had an effective management system in place. The board of trustees helped to manage and direct the school. As the principal and cofounder of Tuskegee Institute, Washington served as chief executive. An executive council also existed and was comprised of the principal, treasurer, secretary, general superintendent of industries, director of mechanical industries, director of the department of research and the experimental station, commandant, business agent, chief accountant, director of the agricultural department, registrar, medical director, dean of the women's department, director of women's industries, chaplain, director of the extension department, superintendent of buildings and grounds, dean of the Phelps Hall Bible Training School, and director of the academic department.[40] The individuals in charge of each of these divisions had authority over them and answered to Washington, whose adage was not to do anything that someone else could do just as well.[41]

Like the professional managers of the Progressive era,[42] Washington created a hierarchical system of management and required all subordinates to comply with it. Those that did not would be sure to be reprimanded or let go.

Numerous letters exist showing how Washington reprimanded employees for not deferring to their supervisor.[43] Moreover, when Washington drafted a letter complaining about some subordinate, it was not uncommon for him to send a copy to the supervisor of the individual in error.[44]

When Washington was away from campus, the treasurer, Warren Logan, who was also a Hampton Institute graduate, served as the chief executive-in-residence (or acting principal),[45] and when Washington and Logan were both absent, the duty would usually fall on the shoulders of Emmett J. Scott. Logan had been at Tuskegee Institute virtually since its beginning, whereas Scott came after Washington's 1895 Atlanta Exposition address.[46] This, perhaps, had something to do with Washington's choice of executive-in-residence when he was away.[47]

Besides Logan and Scott, John H. Washington, Booker T. Washington's elder brother, also exercised great influence during Washington's absence. He too was a Hampton Institute graduate that had been with Tuskegee Institute almost since its beginning. Commencing his career as a business agent, he soon was promoted to superintendent of industries. Like Logan and Scott, Washington considered his brother a vital leader-in-residence who was not only an important manager of the school, but a pillar of strength and wisdom as well.[48] Washington would acknowledge his deep respect for all three men in a codicil to his will.[49]

Moreover, whether Washington was on campus or not, he requested daily reports of the activities at Tuskegee Institute. For example, he would demand a report on the number of gifts and pledges received, the expenses incurred for the day, the number of students who were expelled or dropped out of the school, the names of teachers who had not attended the daily chapel service, the number of bricks produced, and the number of eggs hatched.[50] Washington was also insistent on receiving these reports on a timely and daily basis; if he did not, a reprimand was sure to be received by those deemed accountable. When he was away, regardless of where he was, he wanted these reports sent so that he could stay abreast of what was occurring at home, away from his ever-watchful eyes.

From the daily reports and the influence of William Baldwin it appears that Washington became ever more of a stickler about thriftiness, curbing expenses,[51] and maintaining Tuskegee Institute's good credit rating with merchants. It was not uncommon at Washington's Sunday-evening chapel talks for him to remind students that Tuskegee Institute was their school and that they should do all they could to help maintain it and keep expenses down, recommending such measures as not accepting food that they did not intend to eat, turning out lights when not in use, not throwing trash on the school grounds, and not defacing or destroying school property.[52]

Moreover, since total annual gifts and revenue often were less than Tuskegee Institute's total annual expenses, Washington, who began at Tuskegee as a schoolteacher, grew to be a financial manager as well.[53] Baldwin and Daniel C. Smith helped Washington to understand more clearly how slight financial laxity and errors could lead to major fiscal problems.[54] For this reason, Washington studied the American economy more closely and projected the effects of its cyclical patterns on Tuskegee Institute's fundraising and revenue-generating activities. For instance, during the Spanish-American War as well as at the beginning of World War I, he foresaw that the annual receipts from gifts would decrease,[55] and he, in turn, directed Logan to establish a committee whose purpose it was to find ways to curb expenses and implement the findings.[56] Washington stayed abreast of the committee's work and continuously reminded Logan to find ways to reduce financial carelessness and curb expenses. When Logan or his staff, for instance, had not paid certain bills on time and Washington found out about it, he reprimanded Logan for the negligence of his office and for potentially damaging Tuskegee Institute's good credit rating, expressing to him further that, "as I have said before, this is the kind of thing that hurts us."[57]

In accord with Washington's urging of frugality among faculty, staff, and students, as an executive and educator he worked toward establishing a savings department on campus, primarily to teach students how to save. Washington felt that all country schools should have a savings department for promoting saving and investing.[58] To avoid being perceived as competing with local banks, which had been financially supportive of Tuskegee Institute, after consulting his board of trustees and Charles W. Hare, a local Tuskegee lawyer, Washington established in 1902 "The Savings Department of the Tuskegee Institute" in lieu of a savings bank.[59] This savings department existed for many years, though the amount in savings accounts was relatively small. For example, during the last quarter of fiscal year 1914–15, $4,712.63 was recorded as the aggregate sum of savings,[60] while during the next quarter this figure decreased to $1,335.73,[61] which probably reflected the use of funds during the holiday period. Although student deposits were generally small, some not averaging more than ten cents per deposit,[62] Washington was pleased that the students were practicing the principle of frugality, beginning small and hopefully growing large, and acquiring a habit that would serve them well once they left Tuskegee Institute.

The Tuskegee Building and Loan Association (TBLA) and the Dizer Fund, like the savings department, were two other initiatives launched as a result of Washington's leadership philosophy and executive skills. Washington was continuously trying to create African-American landowners that might grow to be entrepreneurs like Junius G. Groves. The TBLA, which was formed in 1895,[63] was administered like the Baldwin Farms project,[64] except that its clientele was not limited wholly to Tuskegee Institute alumni. Any faculty, staff, alumni, or community member who was willing to purchase shares of stock and pay low monthly dues was entitled to be a member.[65] In return, members received dividends, and those with sufficient collateral had the exclusive privilege of borrowing funds at a reasonable rate to purchase real estate, make payments on land, pay off encumbrances, or for other purposes.[66]

The TBLA was a cooperative venture which was also established to counteract such practices as debt peonage during the nadir. The funds generated from stock sales and monthly dues created an aggregate pool of money from which members could draw. For the year 1901, for instance, thirteen loans were made, amounting to $2,260.[67] In 1902 the total funds loaned since the inception of the TBLA amounted to $14,775, with nothing lost due to bad loans.[68] During the Great Depression, the TBLA was still in existence. According to John H. Palmer, a TBLA member and the registrar of Tuskegee Institute, these small funds helped many members become property owners.[69]

In about 1892, the Dizer Fund, whose purpose was similar to that of the TBLA, was established to help African Americans buy property.[70] A gentleman and his wife that resided in Boston, who did not care to have their names made public, donated funds for this project,[71] adding to their initial appropriation over time. Funds were to be loaned in sums of fifty to three hundred dollars at an eight percent interest rate, with preference given to Tuskegee Institute students or graduates. The donors also specified that the Tuskegee Institute Board of Trustees could use the interest from the Dizer Fund in any manner that it deemed best for the benefit of the Institution.[72] Unfortunately, some fund recipients, due to their failure to pay back their loans, lost their property. Washington, who was ever cognizant of the fact that the donors were studying the progress of this fund and would base future appropriations on its success, impressed upon his treasurer to not only manage the fund in a strict, businesslike manner, but also to aggressively search for new, potentially reliable clients.[73]

Promotion of Industrial Education

Washington raised funds, generated revenue, and managed his school in a strict, businesslike fashion to fulfill the Tuskegee mission,[74] which was to educate as many willing souls as possible so that they could go out into the world and be assets to their communities, thereby uplifting their race.[75] When students arrived at Tuskegee Institute for the first time, they quickly learned the routine of the school. They awoke, had their classes, worked, and retired all at specific times.[76] The purpose of this was to instill a system of discipline and curb all forms of idleness; Washington and his aides inspected the students to make sure they kept up with their duties. When he first implemented this policy, Washington wrote back to Hampton Institute, "I require all to keep their clothes neat and clean, and their hair combed every morning, and the boys keep their boots cleaned.... To see that this is done I have a morning inspection, as we did at Hampton."[77] He also made the boys drill in a military fashion.[78]

Furthermore, during Washington's leadership, two types of students existed at Tuskegee Institute, day students and night students.[79] The day students, who were able to pay their school fees, attended school half a week and worked on the farm or in some trade department the other half. The night students, who were unable to pay any of their school fees, worked days, often doing strenuous work, and went to school for a few hours at night. Washington particularly admired the efforts of the night school students, who were willing to work for up to ten hours a day for an education. In working days, night students accumulated financial credit in their account so that in a year or two they could afford to attend day school and thereby more speedily complete their education. Another reason that Washington was fond of night school was that he had been a night school instructor at Hampton Institute and remembered the earnestness of his students.[80]

According to Roscoe Conkling Bruce, head of the academic department at Tuskegee Institute and a fellow admirer of the night school students, at the height of Tuskegee Institute, during Washington's lifetime, thirty-six trades were taught.[81] Brick-making, for example, was started first as a result of the need for buildings and due to the high cost of importing bricks. To fulfill other needs of the school, carpentry was started next, followed by printing, mattress- and cabinet-making, wheel-making, tinsmithing, harness-making, and shoemaking.[82] The fulfillment of these needs not only met the requirements of the school, but also advanced students' knowledge of farming or a trade. To supplement the teaching of agriculture and trades, academic courses were also taught, including sciences, mathematics, English, geography, and history.[83] Of course, as previously noted, the academic course work had to be correlated with the agricultural and trade work, and Washington constantly scrutinized the academic department to ensure that this was occurring.

Besides the education received in barns, fields, and industries, perhaps the capstone of students' education at Tuskegee Institute was Washington's Sunday-evening lecture at the school chapel, which was similar to the Sunday-evening address given to students by General Armstrong at Hampton Institute. These lectures were important because they reiterated and reinforced the mission of the school and Washington's educational and economic hopes for his students.[84] He spoke to his students on such topics as helping others, influencing by example, the virtue of simplicity, doing one's best, not being discouraged, the importance of being reliable, getting on in the world, individual responsibility, and substance versus shadow.[85] Among other things, these lectures served to further disseminate Washington's entrepreneurial philosophy. For instance, in a lecture titled "Down to Mother Earth," Washington said, in part:

> What I have tried to say to you to-night about agricultural life may be said with equal emphasis about city occupations. Show me the race that leads in work, in wood and in metal, in the building of houses and factories, and in the constructing and operating of machinery, and I will show you the race that in the long run molds public thought, that controls government, that leads in commerce, in the sciences, in the arts and in the professions.
>
> What we should do in all our schools is to turn out fewer job-seekers and more job-makers. Any one can seek a job, but it requires a person of rare ability to create a job.[86]

In another lecture titled, "What is to be Our Future?," Washington stated:

> You will find that people will look to us more and more for tangible results. Not only here, but all over the country, our race is going to be called on to answer the question: "What can the race really accomplish?" It is perfectly well understood by our friends as well as by our enemies, that we can write good newspaper articles and make good addresses, that we can sing well and talk well, and all that kind of thing. All that is perfectly well understood and conceded. But the question that will be more and more forced upon us for an answer is: "Can we

work out our thoughts, can we put them into tangible shape, so that the world may see from day to day actual evidences of our intellectuality?"[87]

It was not uncommon for students to express fond memories of Washington's Sunday-evening lectures when asked years later about the things that stood out about their experience at Tuskegee Institute.[88]

One possible reason why Washington's educational program may have been perceived as memorable was because it was designed to train students to be pioneers, people who were unafraid to go off into communities, particularly in the underdeveloped South, and establish schools or businesses.[89] His curriculum also trained students to "develop a mindset of doing for themselves and others."[90] Therefore, contrary to what has been argued, Washington never trained his students to attend his school with the sole intent of seeking employment, nor did he train them to fit into a lower stratum within the social order or be neo-slaves.[91] Although entrepreneurship was promoted highly and considered necessary, if his students were employees, that was acceptable, because in Washington's mind, all honest labor was honorable.

In evaluating the impact of Washington's teachings on his students, a comprehensive study needs to be undertaken analyzing the progress of his students after they left Tuskegee. Unfortunately, such a study does not currently exist, although it would surely help put to rest the controversy over the effectiveness of industrial education.[92] Even so, upon examining many of the numerous sources on Washington, along with the occupations of some of his former students, it is clear that Washington's teachings had a significant impact on many of their lives.[93] Though scores of his students became teachers who further disseminated the Tuskegee Mission,[94] a number of others became entrepreneurs.[95] Since this book is a study of Washington's entrepreneurial ideas and practices, two examples of entrepreneurs that were directly influenced by the Tuskegee Mission will serve to underscore Washington's probable impact on his students.

Frank and Dow Reid were brothers who attended Tuskegee Institute for three years.[96] They did not graduate, but they did internalize the messages that Washington gave them during his Sunday-evening lectures—to own land, improve its condition, and become entrepreneurs.[97] The Reids lived in Dawkins, Alabama, which was about twelve miles from Tuskegee, and prior to attending Tuskegee Institute, they and their parents were among the large number of renters in Macon County. After leaving Tuskegee Institute, by working hard and practicing frugality, they eventually purchased 620 acres of land and rented 1,565 acres for a total operation of 2,185 acres. A significant portion of this land they subleased for a profit. In addition, they operated a profitable cotton gin and a general store. In following Washington's creed of being indispensable to their respective community economically and otherwise, the Reid family was instrumental in helping to maintain not only their church, but the local school as well.[98]

David L. Johnston, unlike the Reid brothers, graduated from Tuskegee Institute.[99] He was born to parents who spent their youth in slavery. Johnston, the eldest son of nine children, worked on a farm alongside his aging parents, who were tenant farmers. When he could, Johnston attempted to gain a rudimentary education from schools that were open an average of three months per year. When both his parents became ill, Johnston took it upon himself to take care of them and a number of his siblings, including his sister and her six children. Johnston, who still longed for an education, worked various jobs until he was able to obtain enough money to cover his responsibilities and enroll in the Tuskegee Institute day school. During the academic year and especially over the summers, Johnston still worked to support his family. In 1889, remarkably, Johnston earned his diploma and soon after entered the Meharry Medical College to study pharmacy. In 1896 he successfully completed his program. After being a partner in a drugstore for a short period, Johnston opened up his own successful business, the Union Drugstore, on a busy thoroughfare. Johnston, in comparing the schools he had attended, felt that at Tuskegee he had learned more useful life skills and lessons. Reflecting further, he wrote: "At Tuskegee we were taught the truism, 'If you can not find a way, make one.'"[100]

Johnston and the Reid brothers are just two examples among a multitude of students that were influenced generally by Tuskegee Institute and, specifically, by the entrepreneurial ideas and practices of Booker T. Washington, who was a taskmaster as well as an executive.[101] Washington's drive and determination in coordinating fund-generating activities, managing the growing operations of Tuskegee Institute, and promoting and implementing his philosophy of industrial education not only granted an educational opportunity for needy students such as Johnston and the Reid brothers, but also exposed them to his entrepreneurial philosophy, which many of them practiced upon leaving Tuskegee Institute. Moreover, Washington worked tirelessly toward expanding and maintaining Tuskegee Institute because he wanted the Tuskegee spirit to be instilled in his students so that they could contribute toward the well-being of their respective communities as entrepreneurs, teachers, or other types of employees. In this way they would serve as a force seeking real freedom and empowerment, ultimately significantly improving the status of African Americans and helping bring about equality.

Hence, on a micro level, Washington's entrepreneurial philosophy undoubtedly had a great influence on the Tuskegee Institute campus, as there were no inconsistencies between his ideas and practices. Tuskegee Institute was Washington's abode and was operated in a strict, businesslike manner according to his iron will, educating students to be of indispensable value to their respective communities. As a result, it was not uncommon for Tuskegee Institute students, particularly the graduates, to manifest the Tuskegee spirit wherever they went after leaving school, and to pay homage to their principal and their alma mater. On a macro level, when examining Washington's broad economic influence on African-American life and history, which is the subject of the concluding chapter, this same pattern is evident. There are numerous tributes to what was considered to be the wisdom and effectiveness of Washington's widespread entrepreneurial philosophy.

7

Washington's Broad Economic Influence on African-American Life and History

Before concluding a study on Washington's entrepreneurial ideas and practices, a scholar should attempt to deal with questions involving the historical significance of Washington's economic program and legacy. Although the African-American self-help movement, which occurred immediately before and during the nadir, did not originate with Washington,[1] he articulated and promoted ideas of self-help perhaps better than any other individual of his epoch. He certainly publicly championed business formation and development more than any other African-American, and he institutionalized his ideas with the creation and development of Tuskegee Institute, the Negro Farmers' Conference, and the NNBL.

To demonstrate the pervasiveness of Washington's entrepreneurial philosophy over time in major dimensions of African-American life and history, this chapter on one level seeks to begin examining the predominance of Washington's broad influence and to show that he is the father of the extensive promotion of twentieth-century African-American business development. On a much broader level, it seeks to explain why Washington's entrepreneurial philosophy so strongly impacted African-American life and history many years after his death, inspiring a great number of people. In this context, individuals who acknowledged that they internalized aspects of Washington's business philosophy—which helped to shape their economic outlooks—exemplify influence, as do individuals who were indirectly inspired by Washington through the influence of a mentor or leader.

This effort has not been seriously undertaken before for a number of reasons, primary among them Du Bois' famous critique of Washington. Moreover, a firm historical interpretation has existed which argues that, since Washington was supposedly promoting obsolete skills and a segregated African-American economy, his economic program was not only ill-considered, but also unusually narrow. Acceptance of this interpretation in all probability has served to convince many scholars that further research on Washington or his economic programs is futile. However, as has been consistently argued throughout this text, Washington's entrepreneurial philosophy was much broader than scholars have generally characterized it as being since it was a critical basis of his leadership program. For this reason, if we are to continue to rediscover and redefine Washington and his historical significance, it is imperative to begin to examine Washington's vast economic influence on major dimensions of African-American life and history.[2]

In support of this, perhaps no one has offered a more extensive and convincing argument concerning the predominance of Washington's entrepreneurial philosophy than Harold Cruse,[3] who in his work *Rebellion or Revolution* (1968) emphasized that everything Washington pursued was "cast in an economic mold."[4] "And it was in this fashion," wrote Cruse, "that Washington actually laid the basic economic foundation and motivation for [twentieth-century] Negro nationalism in America even though he himself was no militant nationalist."[5] Commenting further on Washington's contribution to African-American nationalism, Cruse wrote:

> Washington was the Negro bourgeois prophet par excellence, which is an important fact to keep in mind when discussing nationalism of any kind. For nationalism is usually bourgeois in its origins. It is only after bourgeois leaders express nationalist politico-economic programs and ideologies that the masses of people pick up the slogan and the ideals and support such leaders.[6]

Understanding this, it is impossible in a single chapter to underscore entirely the effects of Washington's entrepreneurial philosophy on major dimensions of African-American life and history. However, this chapter proposes to initiate this important work by focusing on three dimensions: one composed of African-American entrepreneurs, another consisting of leaders, and a final one containing members of the intelligentsia. To accomplish this, a sampling of individuals who lived throughout the nation during the twentieth century is provided for each broad dimension, and each individual epitomizes Washington's widespread influence and, more importantly, verifies that he is the father of the extensive promotion of twentieth-century African-American business development. Other dimensions and samples certainly could have been chosen and examined, and perhaps they will be covered in future studies. Nevertheless, a sampling of African-American economic practitioners or thinkers in any African-American community throughout the nation between 1900 and 1972 will yield results similar to those highlighted in this chapter. However, the samples that have been chosen herein were selected because they represent individuals who often actively and directly impacted the political, economic, and social plight of their respective communities. Moreover, some overlap exists between the three dimensions because certain individuals in one dimension engaged in other activities which would place them in an additional category. For example, successful African-American entrepreneurs have often been community leaders as well. Individuals were placed in a specific dimension based upon the career that first gained them public fame.

The Entrepreneurial Dimension

An almost endless list of entrepreneurs were inspired by Booker T. Washington's economic message of self-help, both while he lived and long after his death. Indeed, from the time of the first meeting of the NNBL in Boston to shortly after the Civil Rights Movement, any American community north, south, east, or west that had a substantial African-American population generally had a number of entrepreneurs who were significantly impacted by Washington.[7] Undoubtedly, this consistent pattern serves as evidence for the pervasiveness and enduring popularity of his views.

In Harlem, New York, Philip A. Payton Jr., a respectable member of the NNBL, in 1904 founded the Afro-American Realty Company, a firm that rented Harlem properties, mainly to African Americans.[8] Payton, besides being a successful businessman, is most remembered for opening Harlem to African-American tenants. Reputedly, one angry Harlem realtor, in attempting to get revenge on another Harlem realtor, allowed Payton to rent apartments in one of his buildings to African Americans. This event caused a white flight, thereby opening up other rental properties and ultimately all of Harlem to African Americans.[9] And, as history has shown, Harlem grew to become one of the most, if not the most, cosmopolitan African-American communities in the nation.

Payton—who was also instrumental in helping to organize the 1905 annual NNBL meeting in New York City—attributes his inspiration for organizing the Afro-American Realty Company to the ideas and work of Booker T. Washington. It was while he attended the 1902 annual NNBL meeting in Richmond, Virginia, that he gained the inspiration to form his company.[10] Furthermore, after the Afro-American Realty Company was formed, Payton brought in other NNBL members as shareholders or members of his board of directors.[11] His most popular stockholder and board member was probably Emmett J. Scott, the corresponding secretary of the NNBL and Washington's personal secretary.[12]

Dr. Ezekiel E. Nelson, who resided in Buffalo, New York, was a physician and businessman. Unlike Payton, he was not a member of the NNBL. However, "[he] recall[ed] in later years that the Black uplift themes of the Washington era had a major influence [on] his thinking,"[13] as he had strongly considered attending Tuskegee Institute.[14] Like Washington, he espoused self-help and racial solidarity as viable strategies for the economic advancement of Buffalo's African-American community.[15] Unlike Washington, he espoused cooperative economics. For four decades (from 1930 to 1970), Dr. Nelson worked with almost fanatical zeal to convince African-American residents of Buffalo that cooperative economics and racial solidarity would enable the race to escape from poverty and economic oppression. He preached that by working together, pooling their resources, and supporting cooperative enterprises, African Americans could build powerful economic institutions that would enable them to produce many of the goods and services that were needed and desired by the community. Supporting these types of business activities, he felt, would create jobs, particularly for the young, as well as ensure a higher standard of living for all involved in the cooperative ventures. And the profit generated could be reinvested into the community to establish new businesses. Thus, similar to Washington, who Dr. Nelson greatly admired and was impacted by, his adage was self-help.

In Tennessee, particularly in Nashville, as in Buffalo and New York City, Washington's influence was also pervasive.[16] James C. Napier, who was a banker by profession, a friend and associate of Washington's, and a man deeply inspired by Washington's entrepreneurial philosophy,[17] organized the first Tennessee branch of the NNBL.[18] Following this, he helped generate other branches in towns and cities throughout Tennessee, making Washington's idea of business promotion a reality.[19] Reflecting his allegiance to and respect for Washington, in a letter Napier wrote to him concerning two lectures delivered by Du Bois, Napier noted the following:

> [W.E.B. Du Bois] had a good audience at each meeting. There was a fine occasion for him to impress some fact, some practical idea upon the minds of a large number of intelligent, ambitious and progressive young people. He seemed not to have discovered this opportunity and during his three hours failed utterly to offer a single word of advice or counsel touching the practical side of the life which these young people

will soon have to face. His paramount aim seemed to be to show that he had profound learning and had made deep research. No thought of the influence he might exert in shaping the lives or activities of the hearers seems ever to have entered his mind. He simply showed *"learning."*

After it was over and Mrs. Napier and I came to compare notes we agreed that there was little or no benefit to be derived from these lectures; and that one of your speeches of an hour's length would result in greater benefit to the race and to all who might hear it than a whole month of such recitals would bring.[20]

Moreover, impressed with Napier's work and dedication, the NNBL Executive Committee agreed to hold the 1903 annual meeting in Nashville.[21] Later that year, as Washington felt overwhelmed with his responsibilities maintaining Tuskegee Institute and the NNBL and because his entrepreneurial views were so close to Napier's,[22] he asked Napier to assume the NNBL presidency.[23] Napier, in turn, respectfully declined and helped convince Washington to retain his post.[24] After Washington's death, however, Napier did become the second president of the NNBL and held that post until 1921.[25]

Like the towns and cities in Tennessee and New York State, urban locales throughout the nation, both during and after the Great Migration, contained numerous entrepreneurs who were deeply inspired by Washington's entrepreneurial philosophy.[26] Due to the growing effects of segregation, as alluded to earlier, most of them were compelled to conduct business exclusively with the African-American market as opposed to the open market that their forefathers and mothers had operated in during the nineteenth century and earlier.[27] In response to segregation, these new entrepreneurs, often to the consternation of their elders and in contrast to Washington's community indispensability idea, often promoted such nationalistic ideas as independent schools, social organizations exclusively for African Americans, "buy black" economic campaigns,[28] and the establishment of a separate economy parallel to that of white America's. These patterns are evident throughout most African-American urban studies that cover community transformations during and immediately after the Great Migration.[29]

As with the evidence available in many African-American urban studies, focusing on a few other significant entrepreneurs who were significantly inspired by Washington further serves to strengthen the argument for the pervasiveness of Washington's economic influence and the concept of him as the father of the extensive promotion of twentieth-century African-American business development. Arthur G. Gaston, Herman Russell, and John H. Johnson serve as excellent examples. All of these men, who learned from Washington's entrepreneurial philosophy, overcame obstacles and established successful and long-lasting businesses. And in accord with Washington's idea of helping the least fortunate, these men tried to contribute to the well-being of their respective communities by helping members of the underclass.

Arthur G. Gaston, who was born in 1892, three years before Washington's famous Atlanta Exposition address, wanted to attend Tuskegee Institute but was unable to.[30] Notwithstanding, Washington's entrepreneurial philosophy was deeply ingrained in him, initially through Washington's visits to the school he was able to attend—Tuggle Institute—and Gaston's reading of *Up From Slavery*, a book that deeply impacted his life.[31] *Up From Slavery* was the first book Gaston ever owned, and he read it repeatedly, absorbing Washington's business maxims.[32] His favorite idea concerned merit because it convinced him that merit was the key to business success, not color, and this gave him hope that, despite rampant racism, he could still succeed.[33] After graduating from Tuggle Institute, Gaston set out to make his mark in life.

In a short time Gaston went through a number of jobs (for example, selling subscriptions for the *Birmingham Reporter*, building railroad cars for the Tennessee Coal and Iron Company, and so forth) and grew to be dissatisfied with being a mere laborer.[34] He envisioned himself as an entrepreneur supplying his community's needs. Aware of his community's desires, Gaston began operating businesses to fulfill several of them. In 1932 he established the Booker T. Washington Burial Insurance Company, which offered life and health insurance to African-American patrons; in 1939 he opened the Booker T. Washington Business College to train individuals for business careers; in 1952 he founded the Vulcan Realty and Investment Corporation to buy, sell, and manage real estate in the growing Birmingham market; in the early 1960s he opened a motel and restaurant to accommodate African-American victims of Jim Crow laws;[35] he started the Citizens Federal Savings Bank in response to difficulty African Americans were encountering when attempting to borrow money to finance their homes and churches; and finally he constructed the A. G. Gaston Building to rent out office space.[36] Furthermore, Gaston, a longtime member of the NNBL, eventually served as its president. He was also asked to be a board member of Washington's school, Tuskegee Institute, the very school he had initially been unable to attend. Gaston, who reflected the Tuskegee spirit by sponsoring a senior-citizens home and a boys club in Birmingham, Alabama, gladly accepted the responsibility of being a Tuskegee Institute board member. In part because he had followed the teachings of Washington,[37] in 1992, on the eve of his one hundredth birthday, *Black Enterprise* magazine bestowed upon Gaston the title,[38] "Entrepreneur of the Century."[39] It was *Black Enterprise* magazine's twentieth anniversary edition, dedicated to the celebration of African-American businesses.

Herman Russell, like Arthur G. Gaston, was deeply influenced by the entrepreneurial philosophy of Booker T. Washington. When he was a mere youth, his father, a plasterer by trade who believed in Washington's philosophy of hard work and thrift, inculcated into him such values as stretching a dollar, purchasing land and holding onto it, and being self-reliant.[40] Accordingly, when Russell, who was born in 1930, graduated from high school, he attended Tuskegee Institute and studied building construction. Following his 1953 graduation, Russell returned to Atlanta, Georgia, his hometown.

Imbued even more with Washington's entrepreneurial philosophy, Russell set out to become a successful entrepreneur, starting small and expanding. After the death of his father, he first took over his father's valuable plastering business and expanded it. Soon thereafter, he started constructing duplexes, followed by the construction of four-hundred- and five-hundred-unit complexes. Eventually, after proving that his company's work was superb, he won larger jobs that entailed more responsibility. For example, as a subcontractor, he helped build the Equitable Life Assurance Building, which is one of the tallest buildings in downtown Atlanta. He earned the contract to build the Martin Luther King Jr. Community Center and participated in a joint venture helping to build the Metro Atlanta Rapid Transit System (MARTA). Russell, who believes in Washington's adage of helping those in need, frequently worked to provide jobs for indigent African Americans.[41]

John H. Johnson—who founded and developed *Ebony* magazine, and who, like Gaston, did not attend Tuskegee Institute but like Russell became affiliated with it—became a Tuskegee Institute board member in 1954.[42] (Given the success of *Ebony* magazine and Johnson's other businesses,[43] many readers might wonder why Johnson himself was not named entrepreneur of the century. This is probably because Gaston not only had a series of successful businesses, but was an entrepreneur much longer than Johnson was.)

Johnson, who managed his publishing company in an autocratic manner,[44] similar to the way Booker T. Washington managed Tuskegee Institute, was deeply influenced by Washington's entrepreneurial philosophy and felt his business success exemplified it, especially Washington's following statement: "One farm bought, one house built . . . one man who is the largest taxpayer or has the largest bank account, one school or church maintained, one factory running successfully... one patient cured by a Negro doctor, one sermon well preached, one office well filled—these will tell more in our [African American's] favor than all the abstract eloquence that can be summoned to plead our cause."[45] Moreover, Johnson treasured the fact that his wife's grandfather was a close friend of Washington's, and of the many books that he read reflecting the self-help principle, *Up From Slavery*—Washington's second and most famous autobiography—was among the best for him.[46] He later echoed Washington's words, "cast down your buckets where you are," in advising African-American and white entrepreneurs seeking economic opportunities in the United States.[47]

Payton, Napier, Dr. Nelson, Gaston, Russell, and Johnson are a few of the numerous notable entrepreneurs who were significantly impacted by Washington's entrepreneurial philosophy. All of these businessmen operated their businesses at various times throughout the twentieth century, mainly in different locales. This strengthens the argument that Washington's entrepreneurial philosophy not only broadly influenced the economic dimension of African-American life and history, but ultimately made Washington the father of the extensive promotion of twentieth-century African-American business development.[48] Moreover, unlike the foregoing notable entrepreneurs that were economically influenced by Washington, most entrepreneurs that Washington motivated are not well known,[49] as reflected by the multitude of unknown entrepreneurs that participated in the annual Tuskegee Farmers' Conference, the NNBL meetings, and attended Tuskegee Institute. Yet entrepreneurs were not the only group inspired by Washington's economic message.

Leadership Dimension

African-American leaders were also highly inspired by Washington's economic message, particularly those who felt, like Washington, that the only legitimate option for their people's upward progression was by self-help efforts, an outlook that has resonated strongly in American history mainly at times when race relations were at a low point. Maggie Lena Walker (1867–1934), a contemporary of Washington, serves as an excellent example of this notion.[50] She, like Washington, believed that the only sure help was self-help,[51] and she promoted this principle to her race in general but especially to women, who she saw as copartners of men.[52] Thus, in the Order of Saint Luke, a benevolent religious society that Walker joined at the age of fourteen,[53] she rose through its ranks,[54] and by her early adult years Walker became an acknowledged local community leader of Richmond, Virginia. In this role she promoted efforts to end segregation, lynching, Jim Crow railroad cars, and unequal education for African Americans.[55] Moreover, as her sense of duty increased, Walker became an even more active community leader. For instance, she became a board member of the Urban League, a sponsor of the Boy Scouts, a supporter of the YMCA, and an active member of the Negro Organization Society, the Virginia Interracial Commission, and the NAACP.[56]

One reason why Washington noticed Walker is because, in 1903, through the Order of Saint Luke, she formed and headed a bank, the Saint Luke's Penny Savings Bank.[57] Washington indirectly took some credit for this as well as for the creation of other African-American-owned-and-operated banks that were formed throughout the nation soon after August 23–24 of 1900, the period when the NNBL first met. Washington,[58] as well as several of his cohorts,[59] emphasized that it was the influence of the NNBL that sparked and accelerated such entrepreneurial activities as Walker's bank. Furthermore, before acknowledging her in his books,[60] Washington congratulated her upon her success and honored her by asking her to speak about banking before the NNBL, to which she consented.[61]

Washington's activities certainly impacted Walker. To what extent is unclear, mainly because many of the primary-source documents by and about Walker are unavailable to researchers and Walker, unlike Washington, never really kept an extensive paper trail of her activities.[62] Nonetheless, it is known that Walker deeply respected Washington and his work,[63] and she was a proud lifetime member of the NNBL.[64] A number of times she urged Washington to come and speak before the Richmond community, to which he eventually assented.[65] And when the Richmond local business league's activities had waned, she was one of the chief individuals who promoted its presence and revitalization.[66] Furthermore, like Washington, she promoted landowning and implemented this idea by helping African Americans gain loans through her bank.[67]

As with Walker, Washington inspired Marcus Garvey, who was born in 1887 in Saint Ann's Bay, Jamaica. Garvey lived his formative years in Jamaica, then a British colony. At a very young age he was a natural leader of men. Desiring to see other countries and find employment, he traveled throughout the West Indies, South America, and parts of Europe. On these journeys Garvey was aware that wherever he went, people of African descent were on the bottom echelons of society. With this in mind, while in London, he came across Washington's second autobiography, *Up From Slavery*, and eagerly read it. Concerning the profound impression it made upon him and how it helped him to determine his life's mission, Garvey later wrote:

> I read "Up From Slavery," by Booker T. Washington, and then my doom—if I may so call it—of being a race leader dawned upon me in London after I had traveled through almost half of Europe.
>
> I asked: "Where is the black man's Government?" "Where is his King and his kingdom?" "Where is his President, his country, and his ambassador, his army, his navy, his men of big affairs?" I could not find them, and then I declared, "I will help to make them."[68]

Shortly after being exposed to Washington's ideas, Garvey hurriedly returned to Jamaica and formed his organization, the Universal Negro Improvement Association (UNIA), actively corresponding with Washington to seek approval and advice.[69] While in Jamaica, one of the first projects that the UNIA proposed was the creation of an industrial school similar to the Tuskegee Institute,[70] as noted by the *Daily Chronicle*, a Jamaican newspaper:

> The Universal Negro Improvement Association is about taking up and putting through a scheme to establish in Jamaica a large industrial farm and institution on the same plan as the Tuskegee Normal and Industrial Institute of which Dr. Booker T. Washington is head. The object of the farm and institute will be to provide work for the unemployed and to provide the opportunity of training young coloured men and women for a better place in the moral, social, industrial and educational life of the country. Young men and women are to have the opportunity of learning a vocation and to gain a sound moral, literary and industrial training so that when they leave the institution they may by example and leadership help to change and improve the moral and industrial condition of the country.[71]

This proposal, however, would be short-lived, because Garvey, who initially had intended just to visit the United States to study the plight of African Americans, would ultimately make Harlem his headquarters. In any event, through their correspondence, Washington offered encouragement to Garvey.[72]

Around 1914, Garvey desired to make a trip to the United States. Besides studying the plight of African Americans, he wanted to visit Booker T. Washington. Garvey finally came to the United States in 1916, but by then, as Garvey had learned while in Jamaica, Washington had died. Nevertheless, to pay homage to Washington, Garvey visited Tuskegee Institute and was very impressed with the school and especially George W. Carver, whom he saw as not only a renowned scientist and a credit to his race, but also as a man who lived and carried himself in a humble manner, being friendly to all.[73]

Garvey, who was a separatist (unlike Washington), promoted business ideas that paralleled those of Washington's. For example, like Washington, he espoused ideas from the Protestant ethic such as self-reliance and individual responsibility.[74] Furthermore, like Washington, he thought that establishing an economic foundation should be an African American's first priority,[75] and he believed that a good character was an essential ingredient not only as a sign of civilization, but also as a means of upward mobility.[76] Concerning self-reliance, Tony Martin, a biographer of Garvey, noted:

> The most important area for the exercise of independent effort was economic. Garvey believed, like Washington before him, that economics was primary. Successful political action could only be found on an independent economic base. "After a people have established successfully a firm industrial foundation," he wrote, "they naturally turn to politics and society, but not first to society and politics, because the two latter cannot exist without the former."[77]

Garvey, who believed in undertaking capitalist ventures in the United States (and in other countries, including the continent of Africa, so long as a significant amount of the proceeds were to be used to build a "United States of Africa"), established the Negro Factories Corporation and the Black Star Steamship Line, naming one of his ships the *Booker T. Washington*.[78] The Black Star Steamship Line was part of an intricate plan to purchase, through the sale of stock, a chain of ships that would carry a number of African Americans back to Africa, and the Negro Factories Corporation was established with the intention of developing black businesses throughout the world, generally where a significant number of blacks lived. Thus, although the leadership approaches of Washington and Garvey differed,[79] Garvey acknowledged this difference and nonetheless admired Washington and his work, learned from him, and considered him a true aristocrat of his race sprung up from the masses.

Elijah Muhammad, who was the leader of the Nation of Islam from 1933 to 1975, was also influenced by Washington's entrepreneurial philosophy, but this influence mainly was effected indirectly through his exposure to Garveyism.[80] Upon arriving in Detroit during the 1920s, Muhammad joined the UNIA along with many other Southern migrants.[81] There he learned many things,[82] including the entrepreneurial philosophy of Garvey,[83] which not only had been significantly impacted by Washington, but also paralleled Washington's. After becoming a leader, Muhammad, like Garvey, taught his followers that, in addition to separation, only hard work, frugality, and self-sufficiency could achieve economic stability and ultimately real freedom. Unlike Washington and Garvey, he felt that Islam was the true religion of African Americans and that the spreading of it could not only unify them, but also improve their economic predicament as well. Concerning this, Muhammad wrote:

> It is a great job trying to change the so-called Negroes from the ways of their slave masters and to unite them. It may take much suffering but I say that it CAN be done. Islam will unite us all. I know Christianity can't unite us; instead, it divides us. That is what it was intended to do, to divide us. The religion of Islam makes one think in terms of self and one's own kind. Thus, this kind of thinking produces an industrious people who are self-independent.[84]

Muhammad's economic program was similar to that of Washington's, as Harold Cruse has so eloquently written, "[it] was nothing but a form of Booker T. Washington's economic self-help, black unity, bourgeois hard work, law-abiding, vocational training, stay-out-of-the-civil-rights-struggle agitation, . . . etc., etc., morality. The only difference was that Elijah Muhammad added the potent factor of the Muslim religion to a race, economic, and social philosophy of which the first prophet was none other than Booker T. Washington."[85] Cruse is correct, because in Muhammad's book, *Message To The Blackman in America*, where he explains his economic plan, business ideas similar to Washington's are evident.[86] For example, he emphasized values of the Protestant work ethic,[87] especially the virtue in hard work, discipline, self-reliance, saving, and spending only when necessary. Like Washington before him, he also stressed purchasing land for farming and resource extraction, as well as group work ventures. Moreover, Muhammad's students, particularly Malcolm X,[88] and Louis Farrakhan,[89] promoted his entrepreneurial outlook, just as Washington's students had spread his.

The Intelligentsia Dimension

As with the African-American leaders and entrepreneurs, the intelligentsia—that is, the thinkers and scholars—began, soon after the death of Washington, to reflect deeply upon Washington's leadership strategy and legacy. Although Washington lost the great debate to W.E.B. Du Bois, many of the intelligentsia have wondered whether Washington was not, in fact, right. And the concern raised by this issue heightened when the intelligentsia reflected more on the past and current status of African Americans and compared it to that of other groups. Accordingly, this description applies to a large number of individuals.[90] However, focusing on five members of the intelligentsia who wrote during different decades should suffice to convey the continuous presence and pervasiveness of Washington's entrepreneurial ideas in African-American life and history until the early 1970s, as well as to support the idea that Washington is the father of the extensive promotion of twentieth-century African-American business development.

On December 9, 1915, in East Orange, New Jersey, at a memorial service honoring Washington and his legacy, W.T.B. Williams, a Harvard graduate and Southern educational worker, gave an address titled, "Booker T. Washington: An Appreciation."[91] In this address, Williams first noted that many people regarded Washington as the greatest African-American of his time, if not of all time, as well as one of the greatest Southern men of any race.[92] Williams thereafter elaborated on Washington's vision, his societal contributions, and his legacy.

Concerning Washington's entrepreneurial philosophy, Williams underscored that "Washington was among the first to visualize the coming remarkable material development of the South."[93] And, according to Williams, when Washington saw the economic opportunities available in the South, he promoted them to his people, encouraging them to take advantage of these opportunities and develop economic niches by doing common tasks in an uncommon manner.[94] Moreover, Williams noted that Washington left an institution—Tuskegee Institute—to carry on his mission and extend his legacy.

Williams' address was given about three weeks after the death of Washington, and one could legitimately argue that this does not really show the longstanding pervasiveness of Washington's entrepreneurial philosophy. But that it has indeed been pervasive is evident, because among the intelligentsia a pattern does exist of publicly revisiting and reviving Washington and his ideas by arguing that he offered a viable economic uplift program. Therefore, Williams' remarks immediately following Washington's death contributed to the beginnings of such a pattern, and for this reason need to be considered.

In 1940, for example, Henry Jerkins, a contributor to *Opportunity*, a periodical published by the National Urban League, wrote that the problem concerning economic adjustment for African Americans was still acute. Moreover, he stressed that Washington's solution was still effective, as it had brought economic independence to thousands who had tried it and found it workable.[95] Nineteen years later, in revisiting and reflecting upon Washington, Chuck Stone, writing for the *New York Age*, presented a series of ideas concerning Washington's entrepreneurial philosophy and legacy. A few are listed below:

(1) The wise words of Booker T. Washington which were completely misunderstood and misrepresented are truer 65 years later than they were on that history-filled day [the day of Washington's Atlanta Exposition address].[96]
(2) Through the years Negroes have never understood the most elementary facts about the American economy [as Washington tried to teach them]. Either you are a producer and manager or a worker. To be a part of the power structure of America, you must control money. This, the Negro has never done.[97]
(3) Perhaps if a few more Negroes in 1895 had understood the real meaning of Booker T. Washington's message, the whole structure of America's biracial society would have been different today. Had more Negroes busied themselves with the need to become owners of industry, the "race problem" in its most serious light would have offered a brighter hue.[98]

Randall E. Brock, writing about Washington in a 1992 article for the magazine *Crisis*, emphasized that with over a third of the African-American community in dire poverty and with the American economy in transition, Washington's economic strategy, divorced from its political prescriptions, was still valid.[99] Concurring with Brock in a 1997 essay, John Sibley Butler (after reflecting on Washington's entrepreneurial philosophy and the then-current economic status of African Americans) argued that Washington was right because he understood the relationship between business enterprise, education, and the success of future generations.[100]

This list could go on almost indefinitely because Washington's entrepreneurial philosophy was so far-reaching. He broadly influenced African-American life and history, as is made evident by the cases of the aforementioned individuals selected from among African-American entrepreneurs, leaders, and members of the intelligentsia. This recurring attention given to Washington's entrepreneurial ideas reflects the continuous search by members of the African-American community for strategies and solutions that would gain them practical first-class citizenship, economic power, and societal influence. Past uplift activities (for example, a resurgence of African-

American political power during the presidency of Franklin D. Roosevelt, the Civil Rights Movement, the election of Barak Obama to the U.S. presidency, and so forth), although extremely helpful, have not completed the job. It also reflects the realization that higher levels of self-help efforts are still needed and that Washington's economic program was and perhaps still is viable, as alluded to below by political analyst Earl Ofari Hutchinson:

> The new civil rights revolution of today is about economic development. How is that different from what Booker T. Washington was advocating a century ago? Whether or not we are where we should be or want to be with economic development in the black community, there has always been a strong emphasis throughout on business and entrepreneurship as well as on education. These themes started with Booker T. Washington.[101]

Conclusion

Booker T. Washington, a Shrewd Strategist

This book calls for a reconstruction of the manner in which Booker T. Washington is written and taught of, emphasizing that understanding his entrepreneurial philosophy is essential to understanding him since it was the crucial component of all his uplift programs. Washington's entrepreneurial philosophy was shaped and molded by political, economic, and social forces that dominated during Reconstruction, the nadir of African-American history, and by key events and individuals who served to either enhance his budding business philosophy or expand it once it had been established. Moreover, Washington's entrepreneurial philosophy was formed by his observation of the effects of the economic relationship between Tuskegee Institute and Macon County, Alabama, and the surrounding area. Through the goods and services it offered, Washington saw Tuskegee Institute become valued as an indispensable asset to the local area. He eventually reasoned that if African Americans everywhere could grow to be of such indispensable value to their surrounding communities, both to African-Americans and whites, the race problem would eventually solve itself in a natural and unforced manner. Consequently, Washington consistently advocated this strategy both publicly and privately, emphasizing duties over rights.

In attempting to classify Washington's entrepreneurial philosophy and conception of duties, it becomes clear that Washington's entrepreneurial philosophy was a hybrid. It was neither purely capitalistic nor purely socialistic, but contained elements of both ideologies. Washington advocated capitalistic ideas such as private enterprise, taking risks, capturing the African-American market, competing in and capturing significant shares of the open market, and developing economic niches, all of which coincided with the views of industrialists of his day. Simultaneously, he advocated a group uplift program. He espoused such ideas as supporting worthy African-American ventures, creating captains of industry, contributing toward community development, developing high character—which he considered more important than material wealth—and helping those least fortunate. Washington, as a shrewd technician, operated as best he could in the political, economic, and social setting in which he found himself and his people, privileging the group over the individual.

In addition to the argument above, my book has emphasized areas in which little, if any, substantial work has been done. It has argued, for example, that Washington was an entrepreneur, judging this by the way in which he initiated and orchestrated Tuskegee Institute's selling of goods and services to the local market, as well as how he raised funds for, maintained, and operated the school. This book has taken great pains to reconstruct and spell out Washington's entrepreneurial philosophy on the basis of his speeches and writings, tracing his economic progress and comparing and contrasting stages of his development. In terms of the setting in which Washington operated, the segregated environment was not only underscored, but also the general economic environment and the specific economic setting of Macon County, Alabama, and the state of Alabama. Lastly, a discourse on the magnitude of Washington's economic influence on African-American life and history was initiated, examining his effect both while he lived and after his death.

In his analysis of Washington's economic program, which Washington believed could serve as a strategy for helping to end white racism, W.E.B. Du Bois was right. Washington did place the sole responsibility on the shoulders of African Americans for rectifying their oppressive condition. Provided that the law was applied equally and justly to both African Americans and whites, Washington said that African Americans should be solely responsible for their own uplift. This, of course, was a tremendous burden to place upon a people who were not responsible for their condition, which stemmed from the results of slavery, Reconstruction, and the nadir of African-American history. Of course, the various levels of government and society rightfully should have contributed toward altering the plight of African Americans. However, in 1895, in the heart of the rural South, how long would Washington have lasted if he had stated that the South, the federal government, or both should be held accountable for the plight of African Americans? Not long. On the other hand, Washington was an optimistic realist who may have felt that the South, the federal government, and even the nation were responsible, yet he operated judiciously, finding opportunities in endless disadvantages and persuading African Americans that they could uplift themselves through their own efforts.

In Washington's mind the other options that he could have advocated were not viable alternatives. He could have, for instance, advocated that African Americans seek out economic opportunities in Northern settings, but he felt that if they left the South en masse, problems would arise unless they had something to offer the communities they entered. The numerous urban race riots in the North offer some credibility to Washington's thought process. Emigrating from the United States and making a life in another country was another option. Several of Washington's contemporaries espoused this position, but Washington noted that most of them rarely followed their own advice. Moreover, like Frederick Douglass before him, Washington felt that his people had invested their blood, sweat, and lives into making America what it was and therefore had rightly earned a stake in it. Promoting violence for retaliation in kind was another option, but Washington felt that it was best for America to try to heal and improve race relationships, and like many whites, he felt that African Americans should take part in the "helping-healing process." Furthermore, he stated that those who advocated violent means for African Americans to improve their plight ought to suffer the results of their mad advice alongside their followers. Protesting vigorously for political and civil rights, which was believed by many to be the key to establishing an economic foundation, was another option. Many of Washington's most vehement critics promoted such a strategy and were angered and frustrated that Washington did not overtly do the same. However, most of these critics lived in cities or in the North where brutal retaliation for such protesting was not an imminent threat as it was in the rural South where Washington and most African Americans lived. Du Bois, for example, lived in Atlanta during most of the time that Washington was a national leader. He would eventually move to New York City and finally to Ghana, West Africa. Ida Wells-Barnett lived in Memphis, Tennessee, but was run out of that city for courageously protesting a local lynching. She moved to Chicago and established her base there. William Monroe Trotter, perhaps the most consistent and embittered Washington critic, grew up in a Boston suburb and eventually resided in Boston.

Moreover, like his contemporary critics, scholars (for example, W.E.B. Du Bois, Abrahm L. Harris, Sterling D. Spero, and C. Vann Woodward) have roundly criticized Washington's promotion of industrial education as if it were an end instead of a means to an end. These scholars have argued that Washington was promoting skills at his school that were rapidly becoming obsolete due to technological advancements during the Industrial Revolution. Many of those skills, however, were still relevant even after Washington's day.[1] These scholars failed to grasp that the most important issue in the entrepreneurial philosophy that Washington tried to instill in his people was the *producer mindset*—that is, not settling for being "mere laborers and consumers." Washington understood that the owners of the means of production were the real molders of American society and, like the industrialists of his day, he understood and advocated that African Americans find a niche, start small, build a foundation, expand, and help others. Consequently, he promoted any type of education that could show African Americans "how to be entrepreneurs or how to make an honest, independent living." He did this on the Tuskegee Institute campus, at the Negro Farmers' Conference, and at the NNBL meetings, all of which consisted of a diverse group of entrepreneurs who paid homage to Washington while he lived and certainly after he died, as Washington's ultimate aim was to contribute toward African Americans participating in the mainstream of American society.

Unfortunately, Washington's entrepreneurial philosophy did not bring about the results that he envisioned, for several reasons. First, like Americans in general and because of the effects of the nadir, African Americans were constantly migrating to cities and Northern locales, which partially went against Washington's leadership program for advancement. Furthermore, African Americans did not strive to be entrepreneurs on the level that Washington had hoped they would. Most remained in the laboring class or were relegated to the position of farm wage earners, tenants, renters, or domestic, unskilled workers. Those African Americans who became entrepreneurs were generally compelled to conduct business exclusively within the African-American market, mainly as a result of the effects of de facto and de jure segregation, which limited their potential profits and their capacity to hire within an expanding African-American labor pool. This structural racism was unaffected by the pleas put forth in Washington's Atlanta Exposition address.

With de facto and de jure segregation strengthening and permeating all areas of society, especially after the first Great Migration, Washington's entrepreneurial philosophy became even more difficult to practice. Whites and African Americans were being pushed into distinct societies and their interaction was rapidly decreasing. Washington's entrepreneurial philosophy was based on the premise that African Americans and whites, if necessary, could be as separate as the fingers of the hand except in matters relating to mutual progress. Washington was not promoting social equality with whites. However, for mutual progress, he was promoting an entrepreneurial-consumer relationship, in which African Americans would be businesspersons as well as whites, meaning that they could enter communities and undertake activities beneficial to both races. Furthermore, Washington was promoting interdependency between the races so that African Americans would not be dependent on whites for so many of their needs and wants.

Additionally, it was difficult for Washington's "indispensable-asset" strategy to work as it had in the case of Tuskegee Institute. Whites were fleeing from neighborhoods where African Americans were taking up residence and would no longer live in communities where they could observe African Americans who were indispensable assets; whites and African Americans would become more alienated and isolated from one another. This played a significant role in weakening Washington's approach, especially after his death.

Nevertheless, Washington's entrepreneurial philosophy still permeated many African-American communities and inspired individuals to become entrepreneurs through hard, persistent work. This is evident in any African-American community studies covering predominately the period from 1900 to about 1972 or in a sampling of African-American enterprises during that period. This is true throughout all sections of the country. Moreover, the long life of Washington's organization, the NNBL, speaks for itself.

Thus, having considered the effects of segregation on Washington's real freedom and empowerment strategy, and in concluding this book on Washington's entrepreneurial ideas and practices, a few remarks concerning the lessons this work attempts to convey and the future research it hopes to inspire are certainly in order. First, it is imperative to not accept uncritically hegemonic views of this or any historical figure, for Washington's business philosophy was more intricate than scholars have generally thought. Secondly, it is important to examine complex historical figures such as Washington from a number of different perspectives (for example, as businessman, executive, revenue generator, and so on) instead of just writing him off as an accommodationist who promoted industrial education and controlled the powerful Tuskegee machine. At present, the secondary literature generally portrays this hegemonic image of Washington, often vastly clashing with primary-source data. Historians such as myself and others are asking different questions of primary sources and thereby uncovering more involved or different aspects of Washington. Concerning future studies, more research should generally be done focusing on Washington's economic activities. After all, all of Washington's uplift programs involved economics. Specifically, more research should be done on his students—whom he motivated to undertake entrepreneurial paths—those who graduated and those who did not. This would likely further reveal the pervasiveness of his entrepreneurial ideas. In his second autobiography, Washington noted that his school had administered surveys to its former students. More research should be done regarding the economic similarities between Du Bois and Washington, because so much attention has been given only to their differences. It was only after philanthropists (for example, Andrew Carnegie, John D. Rockefeller Sr., and so on) heavily supported Washington's educational philosophy, almost to the exclusion of African-American liberal arts colleges and universities, that an overt split emerged between Washington and Du Bois. Du Bois did not have a problem with training the masses of Southern African Americans in industrial skills, so long as the Talented Tenth were trained in liberal arts colleges and universities. More research should be undertaken on all the general themes covered in this book, especially regarding the entrepreneurs, leaders, and members of the intelligentsia that Washington's philosophies influenced. All of these areas could be explored further and would aid in removing the layers of obscurity surrounding the true Booker T. Washington.

Washington was not the uncourageous Uncle Tom that history has often portrayed him as. Analyzing him from a business perspective makes this even clearer. Instead, he was a man who was quite aware of his perilous surroundings, the stage of development at which his people were, and what he thought it would take to advance and truly free them. Because of the general apathy and hatred in the nation toward African Americans following slavery and Reconstruction, Washington—who was aware that enemies surrounded him and his people in great numbers—knew that he had to operate judiciously in order to help his people. Rather than overtly protesting for civil and political rights, which Washington knew firsthand would largely inflame racial hatred, he told his people to go out and make themselves indispensible assets to their respective communities. This, according to Washington, would not only eventually serve to ensure all of their rights, but it would help to end white racism as well.

This study finds its justification in the fact that no one to date has attempted to reconstruct Washington's entrepreneurial philosophy, particularly from his speeches and writings, and deeply analyze it. Moreover, his economic influence was pervasive; so much so, in fact, that no legitimate

African-American business history can be written that does not make some reference to Washington—who was a champion of African-American entrepreneurial development and the father of the extensive promotion of twentieth-century African-American business development. There is yet more work to be done on Washington, and my study can serve as a foundation for it.

Notes

Introduction

1. The terms "entrepreneurial ideas" and "business ideas" will be used interchangeably because in this book they both have the same meaning. The same applies to "entrepreneurial philosophy" and "business philosophy."

Chapter 1. The Setting that Shaped Booker T. Washington's Entrepreneurial Philosophy

1. Logan, *The Betrayal of the Negro, from Rutherford B. Hayes to Woodrow Wilson*, 11.
2. Washington, *The Future of the American Negro*, 11–15; Washington, *Up From Slavery*, 60 & 134.
3. Washington, *The Future of the American Negro*, 11–12.
4. Ibid.
5. Ibid., 12.
6. Washington viewed African Americans' recently gained political power during Reconstruction as artificial because, in his mind, it was maintained by the Union Army and had not been earned by African Americans developing an economic base and making themselves an economic force throughout the South.
7. Washington, *Up From Slavery*, 56–57.
8. By comprehensive I mean an in-depth study extensively covering the violence perpetrated against African Americans throughout all the Southern states during Reconstruction.
9. Smith, *Black Voices From Reconstruction, 1865–1877*, 122–131.
10. Foner, *Reconstruction: America's Unfinished Revolution, 1863–1877*, 575–87.
11. Mathews, *Booker T. Washington: Educator and Interracial Interpreter*, 4.
12. Woodward, *Origins of the New South 1877–1913*, 216.
13. Work, *Negro Year Book and Annual Encyclopedia of the Negro 1912*, 90.
14. "Colored Indignation: The Effects of the Supreme Court Decision," in *African American History in the Press*, Volume II: 1870–1899, eds. Ellavich and Estell, 1027.
15. Harlan, "The Secret Life of Booker T. Washington," 393–416.

16. Washington, "A Speech Before the National Education Association," (speech, National Education Association, Madison, Wisconsin, July 16, 1884), in HBTWPV2, 347.

17. Washington, "The Atlanta Exposition Address," (address, Atlanta Exposition, Atlanta, Georgia, September 18, 1895), Tuskegee University Archives, 9.

18. McLaughlin, "Mississippi and the Negro Question," 829.

19. Anonymous, "Disfranchising the Negro," 385.

20. Ibid.

21. Ibid.

22. Franklin and Moss, *From Slavery to Freedom: A History of African Americans*, 7th ed., 259.

23. Woodward, *Origins of the New South 1877–1913*, 322.

24. Work, *Negro Year Book and Annual Encyclopedia of the Negro 1912*, 67; Logan and Cohen, *The American Negro: Old World Background and New World Experience*, 136–40; Quarles, *The Negro in the Making of America*, 172.

25. Woodward, *Origins of the New South 1877–1913*, 342–43.

26. Ibid., 343.

27. Franklin, *Reconstruction After the Civil War*, 82–83.

28. Thrasher, "The Alabama Constitutional Convention," 437.

29. Ibid., 439. This statement is from General J. B. Graham of Talladega, chairman of the Alabama Committee on Education.

30. Smith, "Is the Negro Disfranchised?," 1048.

31. Ibid.

32. Anonymous, "The Alabama Decision," 346. One convention delegate was recorded as saying: "This is a white man's country, and I believe that not a single white man should be disfranchised, and I am opposed to the enfranchisement of any negro in the State of Alabama, let it be *Booker Washington or any one else*." [Italicization is original to the text.]

33. Bond, "Negro Education: A Debate in the Alabama Constitutional Convention of 1901," 57–59.

34. Thrasher, "The Alabama Constitutional Convention," 439.

35. Washington, *Up From Slavery*, 237.

36. Henry Cabot Lodge and Terence V. Powderly, "The Federal Election Bill," 257–73.

37. George Washington Campbell to Booker T. Washington, Tuskegee, Alabama, July 16, 1890, in HBTWPV3, 66–67.

38. Work, *Negro Year Book and Annual Encyclopedia of the Negro 1912*, 65.

39. Tourge, *The Invisible Empire*, 15.

40. Bernstein, "Plessy V. Ferguson: Conservative Sociological Jurisprudence," 197.

41. Washington, "Who Is Permanently Hurt," *Our Day*, Tuskegee, Alabama, June 1896, in HBTWPV4, 186–87.

42. Washington to Charles Allmond Wickersham, Tuskegee, Alabama, January 17, 1910, in HBTWPV10, 265.

43. Washington to the Interstate Commerce Commission, March 25, 1906, (BTWPLC), Microfilm: Container 19, Shelf no. 18, 185, Reel no. 16; Washington to Charles Allmond Wickersham, Tuskegee, Alabama, November 29, 1905, in HBTWPV8, 452-53.

44. Adams to NNBL delegates, memorandum, Box 28, Folder 217, The National Negro Business League, BTWCTU, 1.

45. Washington to Cyrus F. Adams, August 13, 1906, Box 28, Folder 217, The National Negro Business League, BTWCTU, 1.

46. Ibid.

47. Washington to Charles Allmond Wickersham, Tuskegee, Alabama, November 25, 1914, in HBTWPV13, 185-86.

48. The term "freedpeople" refers to former slaves who lived during Reconstruction and the nadir. Its meaning is the same as that of "freedmen," but it is a gender-neutral term.

49. Litwack, *Been in the Storm so Long: The Aftermath of Slavery*, 401-402.

50. U.S. Bureau of the Census, *Negro Population, 1790-1915*, 572.

51. Ibid., 571.

52. Washington, "The Negro as a Farmer," 175-81.

53. U.S. Bureau of the Census, *Negro Population, 1790-1915*, 526-27.

54. Mandle, *The Roots of Black Poverty*, 23.

55. Meier and Rudwick, *From Plantation to Ghetto*, 217-22.

56. Wright, "The Economic Condition of Negroes in the North, Tendencies Downward: Third Paper: Poverty Among Northern Negroes," 707.

57. Ibid.

58. Logan, *The Betrayal of the Negro: From Rutherford B. Hayes to Woodrow Wilson*, 152-57.

59. The first Great Migration refers to that period in United States history when hundreds of thousands of African Americans migrated out of the South during World War I.

60. See chapters 2 & 4 of John Sibley Butler's work, *Entrepreneurship and Self-Help Among Black Americans: A Reconsideration of Race and Economics;* also chapters 2 through 6 of Juliet E. K. Walker's work, *The History of Black Business in America: Capitalism, Race, Entrepreneurship*.

61. W.E.B. Du Bois, *The Atlanta University Publications: no. 4*, 29-39.

62. Ibid., 6.

63. "Data Sheet on the National Negro Business League Meeting which took place in Richmond, Virginia on August 25, 26, & 27 of 1902," Box 33, Folder 230: The National Negro Business League, BTWCTU, 3; Frazier, *Black Bourgeoisie*, 50.

64. Du Bois, *The Atlanta University Publications: no. 4*, 19.

65. Butler, *Entrepreneurship and Self-Help Among Black Americans: A Reconsideration of Race and Economics*, 71-77.

66. In essence, Economic Detour Theory, as explained by Butler, advances three basic postulates. The first is that the institution of segregation, de jure in the South

and de facto in the North, represented a governmental program. As such, it involved the interference of government in the normal operations of the marketplace. The next component of the theory argues that African Americans, due to institutional racism, were the only group to which the policy of segregation was applied. They were forced to operate only within a segregated African-American market. Other ethnic groups were not restricted to developing a market among their own people; they were permitted to sell their goods and services to whomever they pleased. This, of course, enhanced their potential for success and, ultimately, profits. Similarly, it has been shown to be true that, throughout history, when African-American business enterprises developed a clientele outside of their community they were more likely to be successful. The third element of the theory stresses that foreign groups, who had not engaged in service to the United States, were not subjected to segregation. When they got off the boats that brought them to the shores of America, they enjoyed all the rights and privileges of citizenship within a relatively short time.

67. U.S. Bureau of the Census, *Negro Population, 1790–1915*, 91–92.

68. Ibid., 512.

69. Ibid., 517 & 521.

70. Ibid., 588.

71. Ibid., 587 & 607.

72. "Report of a Special State Commission on Agricultural Education at Tuskegee Institute," in HBTWPV13, 102. The Alabama State Commission's report, in part, noted: "There are 1,000,000 negro wage hands working on farms in the State of Alabama. Negroes operate 42% of the farmlands of the State. There are 93,000 negro tenant farmers in the State who cultivate a total of 3,600,000 acres. There are 17,000 negro farmers in the State who own and operate a total of 1,500,000 acres."

73. U.S. Bureau of the Census, *Negro Population, 1790–1915*, 607.

74. Hibbard, "Tenancy in the Southern States," 486. The Black Belt refers to those mineral-rich sections of the Deep South that slaveholders migrated to en masse during the era of the cotton gin to grow cotton. It also refers to that region of the South that had a high concentration of African Americans compared to whites.

75. U.S. Bureau of the Census, *Negro Population, 1790–1915*, 517.

76. Ibid., 521.

77. Washington, *Up From Slavery*, 72–78.

78. U.S. Bureau of the Census, *Negro Population, 1790–1915*, 798.

79. Washington, *Up From Slavery*, 73.

80. U.S. Bureau of the Census, *Negro Population, 1790–1915*, 767.

81. Edwards, "Classes of Negro Farmers in Macon County, Alabama: First Paper, Wage-Earners," 459.

82. Ibid., 461.

83. Edwards, "Classes of Negro Farmers in Macon County, Alabama: Second Paper, Share-Croppers," 534.

84. See these other works by Edwards: "Classes of Negro Farmers in Macon County, Alabama: Third Paper, Renters," 559–61; "Classes of Negro Farmers in Macon County,

Alabama: Third Paper, Landowners," 635–38; and "Classes of Negro Farmers in Macon County, Alabama: Fifth Paper, Landowners," 672–75.

85. Edwards, "Classes of Negro Farmers in Macon County, Alabama: Third Paper, Renters," 559.

86. Ibid., 559–61.

87. Ibid., 559.

88. Ibid.

89. Washington, "Delivered Before the Boston Unitarian Club 1888," (speech, Boston Unitarian Club, Boston, Massachusetts, 1888), Box 113, Folder Unnamed, BTW-CTU, 9; Washington, *Up From Slavery*, 77; Washington to George Washington Cable, in HBTWPV3, 7–9.

90. Brewer, "Poor Whites and Negroes in the South Since the Civil War," 27–28.

91. More specifically, according to John M. Mecklin, a scholar who taught at Lafayette College, "The 'color line' is the result of this effort of the ruling group to make the black constantly aware of his subordinate status and actually to restrict him to it in the absence of legal means for so doing." See page 347 of Mecklin's work, "The Philosophy of the Color Line," 343–57.

92. Anonymous, "A Southern Domestic Worker Speaks," in *A Documentary History of The Negro People in the United States, 1910–1932*, ed. Aptheker, 50.

93. Ibid.

94. Ayers, *The Promise of the New South: Life After Reconstruction*, 132.

95. Harlan, *Booker T. Washington: The Making of a Black Leader, 1856–1901*, 216–17.

96. Stewart, *Portia: The Life of Portia Washington Pittman, the Daughter of Booker T. Washington*, 28.

97. Washington to John Harvey Kellogg, Tuskegee, Alabama, October 4, 1915, in HBTWPV13, 376–77. See the description of Alfred Tuckerman and his comments on the way that white Northerners viewed African Americans in HBTWPV12, 186.

98. Grimshaw, "Lawlessness and Violence in America and Their Special Manifestations in Changing Negro-White Relationships," 64.

99. Tolnay and Beck, *A Festival of Violence: An Analysis of Southern Lynchings, 1882–1930*, 18–19.

100. "A Negro Moved to Montgomery for Safe Keeping," 2; "A Lynching Carnival expected and the Victim to be a Negro," 1.

101. Wells-Barnett, *On Lynchings, Southern Horrors, A Red Record, Mob Rule in New Orleans*, 65 & 58–70.

102. Ware, "The Atlanta Riots," *Outlook* 84: 562; Grimshaw, "Lawlessness and Violence in America and Their Special Manifestations in Changing Negro-White Relationships," 64.

103. Zangrando, *The NAACP Crusade Against Lynching, 1909–1950*, 6–7; Work, *Negro Year Book and Annual Encyclopedia of the Negro 1912*, 148–49; Work, *Negro Year Book and Annual Encyclopedia of the Negro 1913*, 237–38.

104. Zangrando, *The NAACP Crusade Against Lynching, 1909–1950*, 5–7.

105. Tolnay and Beck, *A Festival of Violence: An Analysis of Southern Lynchings, 1882-1930*, 33.

106. Ibid., 34.

107. Mathews, *Booker T. Washington: Educator and Interracial Interpreter*, 208; Spencer, *Booker T. Washington and the Negro's Place in American Life*, 192-93.

108. Mathews, *Booker T. Washington: Educator and Interracial Interpreter*, 208.

109. Ibid.

110. Tolnay and Beck, *A Festival of Violence: An Analysis of Southern Lynchings, 1882-1930*, 38.

111. Jackson, "Booker T. Washington's Tour of the Sunshine State, March 1912," 275-76.

112. Washington, "A Protest against Lynching," Tuskegee, Alabama, February 22, 1904, in HBTWPV7, 447-48.

113. Chesnutt to Booker T. Washington, Cleveland, Ohio, October, 19, 1908, in HBTWPV9, 662-63; Harlan, *Booker T. Washington: The Wizard of Tuskegee, 1901-1915*, 264.

114. Chesnutt to Booker T. Washington," Cleveland, Ohio, October, 19, 1908, in HBTWPV9, 662.

115. Restrictive covenants and gentlemen's agreements were arrangements between landlords not to rent their property to African Americans in order to keep them out of certain neighborhoods. This practice occurred extensively during the nadir.

116. Gerber, *Black Ohio and the Color Line 1860-1915*, 254-57; Franklin and Moss, *From Slavery to Freedom: A History of African Americans*, 8th ed., 348.

117. Crouthamel, "Springfield Race Riot of 1908," 164-81.

118. D'orso, *Rosewood: Like Judgment Day*, 2-13; Dye, "Rosewood, Florida: The Destruction of an African American Community," 605-22. The Rosewood, Florida, massacre began in January of 1923.

119. Washington, "A Statement on Lynching," (statement, NNBL convention, Baltimore, Maryland, August 19, 1908), in HBTWPV9, 612-13.

120. Rosengarten, *All God's Dangers: The Life of Nate Shaw*, 109.

121. Samuel Chapman Armstrong to Dudley Allen Sargent, Hampton, Virginia, May 5, 1887, in HBTWPV2, 347.

122. Washington, "Part of Address of Booker T. Washington before Alabama State Negro Business League," (address, Alabama State Negro Business League, February 18, 1910), Box 33, Folder 230, The National Negro Business League, BTWCTU, 1.

123. Washington to Emmett Jay Scott, Crawford House, Boston, Massachusetts, November 23, 1900, in HBTWPV5, 678.

124. Washington to James Sullivan Clarkson, Tuskegee, Alabama, September 16, 1902, in HBTWPV6, 515-16 & 526.

125. Zangrando, *The NAACP Crusade Against Lynching, 1909-1950*, 5.

126. Tolnay and Beck, *A Festival of Violence: An Analysis of Southern Lynchings, 1882-1930*, 37.

127. Baker, *Following the Color Line*, 176.

128. "Angry Miners Lynch Negro," *Montgomery Advertiser*, October 13, 1910, in *100 Years of Lynchings*, ed. Ralph Ginzburg, 72.

129. Ibid., 59.

130. Washington, *Up From Slavery*, 74.

131. Washington, "Delivered before the Boston Unitarian Club," (speech, Boston Unitarian Club, Boston, Massachusetts), Box 113, Unnamed Folder, BTWCTU, 2.

132. Harlan, *Booker T. Washington: The Making of a Black Leader, 1856–1901*, 143.

133. Washington, "A Speech before the Unitarian National Conference," (speech, Unitarian National Conference, Saratoga, New York, September 21, 1886), in HBTWPV2, 309.

134. Washington, *Up From Slavery*, 74–75.

135. Johnson, "Tuskegee, A Typical Alabama Town," 524.

136. Ibid., 525.

137. "A News Item from the Tuskegee News," *The Tuskegee News*, Tuskegee, Alabama, June 13, 1895, in HBTWPV3, 558–61.

138. George W. Lovejoy to Booker T. Washington, Olustee Creek P.O., Pike County, Alabama, August 12, 1888, in HBTWPV2, 476–78; Harlan, *Booker T. Washington: The Making of a Black Leader*, 164–65; "A Letter Written by a Negro Causes a Commotion," 1.

139. Harlan, *Booker T. Washington: The Making of a Black Leader*, 165; Washington to the editor of the *Tuskegee Weekly News*, Tuskegee, Alabama, August 14, 1888, in HBTWPV2, 479.

Chapter 2. Key Influences that Helped to Mold and Develop Washington's Entrepreneurial Ideas

1. By a "group-advancement" philosophy, I mean possessing a more intense concern for the collective group's advancement than that of the individual's, or, in other words, possessing a strong group outlook.

2. Washington, *Up From Slavery*, 60; Washington, *The Future of the American Negro*, 52–56.

3. Washington, *Up From Slavery*, 39.

4. Ibid., 86 & 91.

5. Ibid., 52.

6. Richardson, "Early Days at Tuskegee," 333–35.

7. Scott and Stowe, *Booker T. Washington: Builder of a Civilization*, 7.

8. Washington, *Up From Slavery*, 91.

9. Ibid.

10. Ibid.

11. Ibid., 86. Miss Olivia Davidson was not only a "great worker" for Tuskegee Institute, but she eventually became Booker T. Washington's wife. When comparing Olivia Davidson to his other wives, Washington praised her the most in print.

12. Washington, "The Awakening of the Negro," 323; Washington, "Education and

Getting Down to Business," 480; Washington, "What Co-operation Can Accomplish," 660–64.

13. Washington, *The Story of My Life and Work*, 160–61.

14. Ibid., 177–86.

15. Frederick Douglass died on February 20, 1895, about seven months prior to Washington's Atlanta Exposition address. Booker T. Washington respected Douglass tremendously.

16. Washington, "Chapters From My Experience II," *The World's Work*, November 1910, (BTWPLC), Microfilm: Reel no. 415, 13,633.

17. Ibid., 13,633–634.

18. Ibid., 13,634.

19. Washington, "The Privilege of Service," 684–88.

20. Washington, *Up From Slavery*, 104.

21. Unfortunately, Washington never went into specifics about how his mother taught him lessons in truth, honor, and thrift.

22. Washington, *The Story of My Life and Work*, 62.

23. Harlan, *Booker T. Washington: The Making of a Black Leader, 1856–1901*, 40–45.

24. Ibid., 49.

25. Washington, "An Article in Everybody's Magazine," September 1902, in HBTWPV6, 531; Harlan, *The Making of a Negro Leader, 1856–1901*, 42–45.

26. Thrasher, *Tuskegee: Its Story and Its Work*, 11.

27. Ibid., 10.

28. Washington, *The Story of My Life and Work*, 50–52.

29. Ibid., 51.

30. Ibid., 52.

31. Viola Knapp Ruffner to Margaret James Murray Washington, Baltimore, Maryland, January 21, 1896, in HBTWPV4, 103; Viola Knapp Ruffner to Booker T. Washington, Charleston, South Carolina, October 30, 1897, in HBTWPV4, 333; Viola Knapp Ruffner to Booker T. Washington, Charleston, South Carolina, February 27, 1899, in HBTWPV5, 46.

32. Armstrong, *Education for Life*, 45.

33. Washington, *Up From Slavery*, 43.

34. Armstrong Talbot, *Samuel Chapman Armstrong: A Biographical Study*, 186. Edith Armstrong Talbot was the daughter of Samuel C. Armstrong.

35. "Nothing to Do!," *Southern Workman* 3: 26.

36. Ibid.

37. "Labor," 18.

38. "Negro Labor," 45.

39. Washington, "Industrial Education," Selma, Alabama, April 7, 1882, in HBTWPV2, 194.

40. Washington, "Some Results of the Armstrong Idea," (speech, Hampton Institute, Hampton, Virginia, January 31, 1909), 174.

41. In its simplest form, the Protestant work ethic is the belief in working hard for the good of the soul, promoting the idea that work builds character, especially when one engages in it without complaint. Moreover, it stresses that cleanliness is next to God.

42. Washington, *The Story of My Life and Work*, 58–59; Washington, *Up From Slavery*, 43–44.

43. "Praying and Working," 4; "Don't Put Off Work Today for Tomorrow," 2; "Success in Business," 58; "Labor," 18.

44. Samuel C. Armstrong, *Education for Life*, 19.

45. Denison, "Samuel Chapman Armstrong," 92; "Industry," 4.

46. "Things" is the actual terminology Booker T. Washington frequently used to describe nonabstract items.

47. "Practice and Theory," 75; Washington, "Some Results of the Armstrong Idea," 175–76.

48. Although Samuel Armstrong promoted the learning of trades at his school, according to Washington, when he entered Hampton Institute in 1872, industrial training was at its beginning stages, consisting of farming, carpentry, and shoemaking. Washington, "The Privilege of Service," 684; Armstrong, *Education for Life*, 20; Lyman Abbott, "General Samuel Chapman Armstrong, Educational Pioneer," in *Silhouettes of My Contemporaries*, 144.

49. Armstrong practiced this concept during his school days (1858–59) on Punahou, one of the Hawaiian Islands, according to one of his schoolmates. Emerson, "A Reminiscence of General Armstrong," 710.

50. Washington, "The Negro and the Signs of Civilization," in *African American Political Thought, 1890–1930: Washington, Du Bois, Garvey, and Randolph*, ed. Wintz, 41–43.

51. Washington, *The Negro Problem: A Series of Articles by Representative American Negroes of To-Day*, 13–18; Armstrong, *Education for Life*, 21.

52. "Buying Land," 58; "Homes for All," 2.

53. Ibid.

54. Washington, "Speech Delivered at the Old South Meeting House," (speech, Boston, Massachusetts, December 15, 1891), (BTWPLC), Microfilm: Reel no. 409, 3.

55. Ibid.

56. Washington, *My Larger Education: Being Chapters From My Experience*. On page 13, Washington said the following: "I said to myself that I would try to learn something from every man I met; make him my text-book, read him, study him, and learn something from him. So I began deliberately to try to learn from men."

57. Washington, "Some Results of the Armstrong Idea," 175–76; Moreover, from Samuel C. Armstrong's book, *Education for Life*, note these two expressions: (1) "Determination, courage, endurance, faith,—these are some of the things which flourish in the hard conditions of our night school, and experience has taught us that it is only through contact with the real things of life that these virtues can be made permanent and characteristic," p. 25. (2) "The way to strengthen the weak is constantly to test

them under favorable conditions. To change low ideas of their mutual relations into higher ones, they must be trained, not in the abstract, but in the concrete," p. 35.

58. Washington, *My Larger Education: Being Chapters From My Experience*, 19 & 207.

59. Washington, "Chapters From My Experience III," *The World's Work*, December 1910, (BTWPLC), Microfilm: Reel no. 415, 13,783–788; Washington, *Up From Slavery*, 62–64.

60. Washington, "The Survival of the Fittest," (speech, Tuskegee Institute, Tuskegee, Alabama, December 2, 1905), in HBTWPV8, 456–60.

61. Pusateri, *A History of American Business*, 201.

62. Ibid., 176.

63. See Chandler's book, *The Visible Hand: The Managerial Revolution in American Business*.

64. Baida, *Poor Richard's Legacy: American Business Values from Benjamin Franklin to Michael Milken*, 110–42.

65. Thimm, *Business Ideologies in the Reform-Progressive Era, 1880–1914*, 65; Pusateri, *A History of American Business*, 236. Perhaps it should be stated that Spencer misapplied or tried to apply Darwin's theory to society; although businessmen embraced Spencer's philosophy, it was an embarrassment to many serious scientists.

66. Washington, "The South as an Opening for a Business Career," (speech, Washington, D.C., November 20, 1891), (BTWPLC), Microfilm: Reel no. 409, 1.

67. Washington and Du Bois, *The Negro in the South*, 85–86.

68. Ayers, *The Promise of the New South: Life After Reconstruction*, 105–106.

69. Ibid., 107.

70. Ibid., 110.

71. Cason, "Alabama Goes Industrial," 163.

72. Ayers, *The Promise of the New South: Life After Reconstruction*, 110.

73. Summers, *The Gilded Age or, The Hazard of New Functions*, 33; Oates, "Industrial Development of the South," 566–67.

74. Washington, "The South as an Opening for a Business Career," (speech, Washington, D.C., November 20, 1891), (BTWPLC), Microfilm: Reel no. 409, 2. On page seven of Washington's speech, he said that over a ten-year period of living in the South he was influenced by "all classes of people as well as [economic] conditions in the South."

75. Ibid., 7.

76. Washington, "Chapters From My Experience II," *The World's Work*, (BTWPLC), Microfilm: Reel no. 415, 13633.

77. August Meier, "Negro Class Structure and Ideology in the Age of Booker T. Washington," 258–59; August Meier, *Negro Thought in America 1880–1915*, 42.

78. Washington, "Chapters From My Experience II," *The World's Work*, (BTWPLC), Microfilm: Reel no. 415, 13633; Washington, "The South as an Opening for a Business Career," 2; Washington, *Frederick Douglass*, 275–76; Washington, "Negro Disfran-

chisement and the Negro in Business," 310–11; Washington, *A New Negro for a New Century*, 379–405.

79. Wilkeson, "The Labor Problem," 2.

80. Douglass, "Great Britain's Example is High, Noble, and Grand: An Address Delivered in Rochester, New York," (address, Rochester, New York, August 6, 1885), in *The Frederick Douglass Papers: Series One, Speeches, Debates, and Interviews*, Vol. 5, 1881–95, eds. Blassingame and McKivigan, 209–10.

81. "The Negro in the South," 2.

82. "More Farmers, Journalists, Lawyers, etc., Wanted," 2.

83. "Needs of the Race," 1.

84. Ibid., 1.

85. "A Few Successful Business Colored Men," 2.

86. Meier, *Negro Thought in America 1880–1915*, 42–58; Fortune, "Gospel of Co-Operation," 1; "A Successful Business Man," 1; "Boston's Business Basis: What the Colored Competitor Must Offer," 4; Williams, *History of the Negro Race in America From 1619 to 1880*, 552.

87. Du Bois, *The Atlanta University Publications: Nos. 1, 2, 4, 8, 9, 11, 13, 14, 15, 16, 17, and 18* (New York: Arno Press & The New York Times, 1968), publication no. 4, 56.

88. Washington, *The Story of the Negro: The Rise of the Race from Slavery*, 28–29.

89. Washington, *The Story of My Life and Work*, 78–79.

90. Washington, *Up From Slavery*, 80.

91. Ibid. Wilbur F. Foster and Arthur L. Brooks were the two men with whom Lewis Adams made an arrangement.

92. Washington, *The Story of My Life and Work*, 78.

93. Washington, "A Speech before the National Educational Association," (speech, National Educational Association, Madison, Wisconsin, July 16, 1884), in HBTWPV2, 257.

94. Washington, "Chapters From My Experience III," *The World's Work*, (BTWPLC), Microfilm: Reel no. 415, 13736 & 13,783–788; Washington, *Up From Slavery*, 62–64.

95. "The Alabama Statute Establishing Tuskegee Normal School," [Montgomery, Ala., Feb. 10, 1881], in HBTWPV2, 109.

96. Washington, *The Future of the American Negro*, 52–56.

97. "The Catalog of Tuskegee Normal School," [Tuskegee, Alabama, January 1882], in HBTWPV2, 165–66; Warren Logan to Booker T. Washington, Tuskegee, Alabama, November 22, 1899, in HBTWPV3, 19–20.

98. Washington, *The Story of My Life and Work*, 87.

99. Washington to Cornelius Nathaniel Dorsette, Tuskegee, Alabama, February 28, 1883, in HBTWPV2, 219–20.

100. Ibid., 257, 448–49, & 501.

101. Ibid.

102. Washington, "The South as an Opening for a Business Career," 4–5.

103. Ibid.

104. Washington, *The Story of My Life and Work*, 72–73.

105. Washington, *Up From Slavery*, 80.

106. Washington, *The Story of My Life and Work*, 73.

107. Washington, *Up From Slavery*, 94.

108. Washington to Warren Logan, Tuskegee Institute, Tuskegee, Alabama, February 13, 1915, in HBTWPV13, 238–39.

109. Ibid.

110. Washington, *Up From Slavery*, 84–85; Washington, *The Story of My Life and Work*, 82; "Booking," 18; J. E. Davis, "Hampton at Tuskegee," 528–29.

111. Washington, *Up From Slavery*, 84–85; Washington, *The Story of My Life and Work*, 82.

112. Stewart, *Portia: The Life of Portia Washington Pittman, the Daughter of Booker T. Washington*, 18.

113. James Fowle Baldwin Marshall to Booker T. Washington, Hampton, Virginia, November 12, 1881, in HBTWPV2, 153 & 226.

114. Ibid.

115. Washington to James Fowle Baldwin Marshall, Malden, West Virginia, July 19, 1882, in HBTWPV2, 207.

116. Stewart, *Portia: The Life of Portia Washington Pittman, the Daughter of Booker T. Washington*, 18.

117. Washington, "A Speech before the Alabama State Teachers' Association," (speech, Alabama State Teachers' Association, Selma, Alabama, April 7, 1882), in HBTWP2, 191–95; Washington, "A Speech before the National Educational Association," (speech, National Educational Association, Madison, Wisconsin, July 16, 1884), in HBTWP2, 255–62; Washington, "A Speech before the Unitarian National Conference," (speech, Unitarian National Conference, Saratoga, New York, September 21, 1886), in HBTWPV2, 308–13; Washington, "A Speech before the Alabama State Teachers' Association," (speech, Alabama State Teachers' Association, Montgomery, Alabama, April 11, 1888), in HBTWPV2, 427–35; Washington, "A Speech before the Philosophian Lyceum of Lincoln University," (speech, Lincoln University, Lincoln, Pennsylvania, April 26, 1888), in HBTWPV2, 439–51; Washington, "A Speech before the Boston Unitarian Club," (speech, Boston Unitarian Club, Boston, Massachusetts, 1888), Box 113, Unnamed Folder, *BTWCTU*, 1–11; Washington, "The South as an Opening for a Business Career," 1–17.

118. Washington, *Character Building*, 81–86; Washington, *Working with the Hands*, 55–66.

119. Washington, *My Larger Education: Being Chapters from My Experience*, 19; Scott and Stowe, *Booker T. Washington: Builder of a Civilization*, 290.

120. Ibid.

121. Scott and Stowe, *Booker T. Washington: Builder of a Civilization*, 291.

122. Ibid.

123. Ibid.

124. William Baldwin Jr. to Booker T. Washington, New York, New York, January 21, 1898, (BTWPLC), Microfilm: Reel no. 392, 1.

125. Daniel Cranford Smith to Booker T. Washington, Hampton, Virginia, December 20, 1895, in HBTWPV4, 96; William Baldwin Jr. to Daniel C. Smith, New York, New York, April 7, 1898, (BTWPLC), Microfilm: Reel no. 392, 1–2.

126. William Baldwin Jr. to Booker T. Washington, New York, New York, September 27, 1898, (BTWPLC), Microfilm: Reel no. 392, 1.

127. Daniel C. Smith was Tuskegee Institute's auditor until 1912.

128. William Baldwin Jr. to Booker T. Washington, New York, New York, October 11, 1898, (BTWPLC), Microfilm: Reel no. 392, 1.

129. Daniel C. Smith to Booker T. Washington, Brooklyn, New York, July 10, 1898, (BTWPLC), Microfilm: Reel no. 392, 1–2.

130. Ibid., 2.

131. William Baldwin Jr. to Booker T. Washington, New York, New York, January 26, 1900, (BTWPLC), Microfilm: Reel no. 392, 2.

132. Washington, *My Larger Education: Being Chapters from My Experience*, 15 & 19; Scott and Stowe, *Booker T. Washington: Builder of a Civilization*, 290.

133. Washington, *Up From Slavery*, 120.

134. Ibid., 87–95.

135. Baldwin, "Extracts from Address of Mr. Wm. H. Baldwin, Jr., at a Meeting in the Interest of Tuskegee Institute at Madison Square Garden Concert Hall," (address, Tuskegee Institute Donors, New York, New York, December 4, 1889), (BTWPLC), Microfilm: Reel no. 392, 1–2.

136. William Baldwin Jr. to Booker T. Washington, New York, New York, March 7, 1904, (BTWPLC), Microfilm: Reel no. 23, 1.

137. Washington to William Baldwin Jr., New York, New York, March 7, 1904, (BTWPLC), Microfilm: Reel no. 23, 1.

138. William Baldwin Jr., "Extracts from Address of Mr. Wm. H. Baldwin, Jr., at a Meeting in the Interest of Tuskegee Institute at Madison Square Garden Concert Hall," (address, Tuskegee Institute Donors, New York, New York, December 4, 1889), (BTWPLC), Microfilm: Reel no. 392, 1.

139. Ibid.

140. Washington, *My Larger Education: Being Chapters from My Experience*, 15 & 19; Scott and Stowe, *Booker T. Washington: Builder of a Civilization*, 289–90.

141. Baldwin, "Extracts from Address of Mr. Wm. H. Baldwin, Jr., at a Meeting in the Interest of Tuskegee Institute at Madison Square Garden Concert Hall," (address, Tuskegee Institute Donors, New York, New York, December 4, 1889), (BTWPLC), Microfilm: Reel no. 392, 2.

142. William Baldwin Jr. to William P. Bancroft, New York, New York, April 6, 1899, (BTWPLC), Microfilm: Reel no. 392, 1–2.

143. Washington, *Up From Slavery*, 119.

144. Ibid., 149.

145. Spencer, *Booker T. Washington and the Negro's Place in American Life*, 115.

146. Scott and Stowe, *Booker T. Washington: Builder of a Civilization*, 289.

147. Holsey, "Public Relations Intuitions of Booker T. Washington," 8. As an aside, the author has observed the bronze memorial tablet at Tuskegee University.

148. Even though *Up From Slavery* helped to generate funds, it is still representative of Washington's life. Most of the information in it is probably true, except of course for the part at the end of chapter 4 in which Washington writes that the Ku Klux Klan no longer exists in the South. *Up From Slavery* is similar to Washington's first autobiography, *The Story of My Life and Work*, although that is not as well written. As a result of this, its market was mainly African Americans. In certain sections, though, the first autobiography reveals more of Washington. However, there are great similarities between the two personal histories, especially in regard to Washington's earlier life and his efforts to make Tuskegee Institute a success. Moreover, most of Washington's numerous books and articles are in a sense autobiographical and are generally consistent with his autobiographies. For those interested in these issues, besides consulting Washington's first two autobiographies, consider these works: Fitzgerald, "The Story of My Life and Work: Booker T. Washington's Other Autobiography," 35–40, and Gibson, "Strategies and Revisions of Self-Representation in Booker T. Washington's Autobiographies," 370–93.

149. Carnegie, *The Gospel of Wealth*, 3–13; Thimm, *Business Ideologies in the Reform-Progressive Era, 1880–1914*, 58–79; Hofstadter, *Social Darwinism in American Thought*, 31–50.

150. Spencer, *Booker T. Washington and the Negro's Place in American Life*, 113. Over a hundred years ago, Horatio Alger wrote a popular series of rags-to-riches books. These books reflected the national gospel of achievement and success through hard work and honest dealings.

151. Scott and Stowe, *Booker T. Washington: Builder of a Civilization*, 256–60.

152. George Eastman to Booker T. Washington, Rochester, New York, January 2, 1902, in HBTWPV6, 370; David Page Morehouse to Booker T. Washington, Oswego, New York, December 26, 1913, in HBTWPV12, 382–383.

153. Washington, *Up From Slavery*, 114–15.

154. Ibid.

155. Ibid., 120.

156. Washington to Julius Rosenwald, Tuskegee, Alabama, September 12, 1912, in HBTWPV12, 8.

157. Amory Howe Bradford to Booker T. Washington, Montclair, New Jersey, June 7, 1898, in HBTWPV4, 434.

158. Washington, "Chapters From My Experience I," *The World's Work*, October 1910, (BTWPLC), Microfilm: Reel no. 415, 13,521; Washington, *My Larger Education: Being Chapters from My Experience*, 48.

159. John Davison Rockefeller Jr. to Booker T. Washington, New York, New York, June 24, 1903, in HBTWPV7, 183.

160. Washington, "Looking After the Waste," October 29, 1908, in *HBTWPV9*, 670.

161. Washington, *Up From Slavery*, 117; Washington to the editor of the *New York Tribune*, Tuskegee, Alabama, August 26, 1900, in HBTWPV5, 605–606.

162. Collis Potter Huntington to Booker T. Washington, New York, New York, October 28, 1898, in HBTWPV4, 499–500.

163. Collis Potter Huntington to Booker T. Washington, New York, New York, November 14, 1898, (BTWPLC), Microfilm: Reel no. 52, 1.

164. Collis Potter Huntington to Booker T. Washington, New York, New York, December 28, 1898, (BTWPLC), Microfilm: Reel no. 52, 1.

165. Washington, "A Commencement Address in Washington, D.C.," (commencement address, Armstrong Manual Training School, Washington, D.C., June 16, 1905), in HBTWPV8, 314; Washington, *Up From Slavery*, 117.

166. Washington, *Tuskegee and Its People: Their Ideals and Achievements*, 25 & 43; Scott and Stowe, *Booker T. Washington: Builder of a Civilization*, 258–60.

167. James Fowle Baldwin Marshall to Booker T. Washington, Weston, Massachusetts, October, 1890, in HBTWPV3, 85–86; Meyers, *History of the Great American Fortunes*, 537–38.

168. James Fowle Baldwin Marshall to Booker T. Washington, Weston, Massachusetts, October, 1890, in HBTWPV3, 86.

169. Washington to George Foster Peabody, Tuskegee, Alabama, July 3, 1905, (BTWPLC), Microfilm: Reel no. 67, 1.

170. Washington, *The Negro in Business*, 206.

171. George Foster Peabody to Booker T. Washington, Abenia, New York, September 7, 1906, (BTWPLC), Microfilm: Reel no. 67, 1; Washington to George Foster Peabody, New York, New York, October 13, 1906, (BTWPLC), Microfilm: Reel no. 67, 1.

172. Washington to George Foster Peabody, New York, New York, March 9, 1905, in HBTWPV8, 212; George Foster Peabody to Booker T. Washington, New York, New York, January 16, 1905, in HPTWPV8, 177–78.

173. Washington, "Mr. Robert C. Ogden," for the *Metropolitan Magazine*, 1910, (BTWPLC), Microfilm: Reel no. 415, 1–6.

174. Ibid., 3.

175. Washington, *The Negro in Business*, 208.

176. Ibid., 210 & 212.

177. Scott and Stowe, *Booker T. Washington: Builder of a Civilization*, 216.

178. Washington, "An Article in the *New York Evening Post*," New York, New York, May 29, 1909, in HBTWPV10, 122–26; Mathews, *Booker T. Washington: Educator and Interracial Interpreter*, 180–81.

179. Washington to Julius Rosenwald, Tuskegee, Alabama, September 12, 1912, in HBTWPV12, 8; Washington to George Eastman, Tuskegee, Alabama, June 2, 1915, in HBTWPV13, 317.

180. Scott and Stowe, *Booker T. Washington: Builder of a Civilization*, 219.

181. Spencerianism was a philosophy created by Herbert Spencer, an English social philosopher.

182. "How to Get Workmen," "How to Handle Workmen," and "How to Systematize Your Factory," (BTWPLC), Microfilm: Reel no. 15, 1–2.

183. Carnegie, *The Gospel of Wealth*, 1–239; Harlan, *Booker T. Washington: The Wizard of Tuskegee, 1901–1915*, 134.

184. Harlan, *Booker T. Washington: The Wizard of Tuskegee, 1901–1915*, 134.

185. Washington, "A Town Owned by Negroes: Mound Bayou, Miss, An Example of Thrift and Self-Government," (BTWPLC), Microfilm: Reel no. 415, 9,130.

186. Redding, *The Lonesome Road: The Story of the Negro's Part in America*, 93–100 & 105–21.

187. Ibid., 111–13.

188. Washington, "A Town Owned by Negroes: Mound Bayou, Miss., An Example of Thrift and Self-Government," (BTWPLC), Microfilm: Reel no. 415, 9, 125–126.

189. Washington, *The Negro in Business*, 64–72.

190. Meier, "Booker T. Washington and the Town of Mound Bayou," 396–401; Harlan, *Booker T. Washington: The Wizard of Tuskegee, 1901–1915*, 218–25.

191. Flynn, "Booker T. Washington: Uncle Tom or Wooden Horse," 268.

192. Montgomery, "Negroes in Business," 733.

193. "Charles Banks and the Bank of Mound Bayou," 419.

194. Harlan, *Booker T. Washington: The Wizard of Tuskegee, 1901–1915*, 218–25; Redding, *The Lonesome Road: The Story of the Negro's Part in America*, 114–18.

195. Jackson, *A Chief Lieutenant of the Tuskegee Machine: Charles Banks of Mississippi*, 183.

196. Ibid., 166.

197. "Charles Banks No Quitter," 7; Jackson, *A Chief Lieutenant of the Tuskegee Machine: Charles Banks of Mississippi*, 41–58.

198. Scott and Stowe, *Booker T. Washington: Builder of a Civilization*, 216–17.

199. Ibid., 216.

200. Emmett Scott to Charles Banks, Tuskegee, Alabama, June 12, 1914, BTWPLC Special Correspondence, Container no. 8, 1–2; Charles Banks to Emmett Scott, Mound Bayou, Mississippi, August 25, 1914, (BTWPLC), Special Correspondence, Container no. 8, 1.

201. National Negro Business League, *Report of the Seventeenth Annual Session Held at Kansas City, Missouri, August, 16, 17, 18. Record of the National Negro Business League: Part 1, Annual Conference Proceedings and Organizational Records, 1900–1909*. (New York Schomburg Center for Research), Microfilm: Reel no. 3, 62–65.

202. Washington to Charles Banks, June 10, 1907, (BTWPLC), Microfilm: Reel no. 23, 1; Charles Banks to Booker T. Washington, Mound Bayou, Mississippi, September 16, 1907, (BTWPLC), Microfilm: Reel no. 23, 1–2; Charles Banks to Booker T. Washington, Mound Bayou, Mississippi, September 20, 1907, (BTWPLC), Microfilm: Reel no. 23, 1.

203. Moton, "The Significance of Mr. Washington's Lecture Trip in Mississippi," 692.

204. Banks, "Mississippi Negroes and their Progress," Mound Bayou, Mississippi,

1907, BTWPLC Microfilms: Reel no. 23, 1–3; "Mississippi Negro Business League Annual Announcement," Mound Bayou, Mississippi, May 22, 1908, (BTWPLC), Microfilm: Reel no. 24, 1.

205. Washington, *My Larger Education: Being Chapters from My Experience*, 213. In making the above statement, Washington was probably referring to what he called "the better class of whites," who, in his mind, were the progressive Southern whites who wanted to improve the South in general and race relations in particular.

206. Washington, "Extracts from an Address at the Opening of the Mound Bayou Cotton-Oil Mill," (address, Mound Bayou Cotton-Oil Mill, Mound Bayou, Mississippi, November 25, 1912), in HBTWPV12, 56; Washington to Isaiah T. Montgomery, Tuskegee, Alabama, January 25, 1915, in HBTWPV13, 234.

Chapter 3. The Entrepreneurial Ideas of Booker T. Washington

1. Young, "The Educational Philosophy of Booker T. Washington: A Perspective for Liberation," 234.

2. Anderson, *The Education of Blacks in the South, 1860–1935*, 33–109; Calista, "Booker T. Washington: Another Look," 240–55; Cummings, "Historical Setting for Booker T. Washington and the Rhetoric of Compromise, 1895," 75–82; Delaney, *Learning by Doing: A Projected Educational Philosophy in the Thought of Booker T. Washington*, 102–103; Du Bois, *The Souls of Black Folk*, 30–42; Flynn, "Booker T. Washington: Uncle Tom or Wooden Horse," 262–74; Friedman, "Life 'in the Lion's Mouth': Another Look at Booker T. Washington," 337–51.

3. Washington, *Working With The Hands*, 84.

4. Washington, "Chapters From My Experience III," *The World's Work*, December 1910, (BTWPLC), Microfilm: Reel no. 415, 13,785–786; It has been argued that Booker T. Washington learned the correlative or project method of education not at Hampton Institute, but after he had graduated. If this is the case, this means that Washington had advanced beyond the teachings he had received at Hampton Institute under Samuel Chapman Armstrong's guidance. See page 46 of Sherer's work, *Subordination or Liberation?* (1977), listed in my bibliography.

5. Scott and Stowe, *Booker T. Washington: Builder of a Civilization*, 274–78; Sherer, *Subordination or Liberation?*, 46.

6. Matthews, *Black-Belt Diamonds: Gems from the Speeches, Addresses, and Talks to Students of Booker T. Washington*, 52. For example, Washington noted: "When I speak of industrial development I do not mean that no attention should be given to what is called higher education. I favor every kind of education."

7. Washington, *The Future of The American Negro*, 86.

8. Ibid., 87.

9. Washington, "The Relation of Industrial Education to National Progress," 239.

10. Washington, "Unimproved Opportunities," *Character Building*, 129.

11. Washington, *Report of The Fourth Annual Convention of the National Negro Business League, Held at Nashville, Tennessee, August 19, 20, and 21, 1903*, 19.

12. Washington, "Delivered Before the Boston Unitarian Club," (address, Boston Unitarian Club, Boston, Massachusetts, 1888), Box 113, Unnamed Folder, BTWCTU, 7–8.

13. Washington, "Our Opportunity Through The South," in HBTWPV2, 308.

14. Washington, "Atlanta Exposition Address," (address, Atlanta Exposition, Atlanta, Georgia, September 18, 1895), in *African American Political Thought, 1890–1930: Washington, Du Bois, Garvey, and Randolph*, ed. Wintz, 24.

15. Washington, *Report of The Tenth Annual Convention of the National Negro Business League, Held in Louisville, Kentucky, August 18–20, 1909*, 71.

16. Washington, *Report of The Seventh Annual Convention of the National Negro Business League, Held at Atlanta, Georgia, August 29, 30, and 31, 1906*, 64; Flynn, "Booker T. Washington: Uncle Tom or Wooden Horse," 268.

17. Washington, *Up From Slavery*, 143–45.

18. Washington, "Address of Booker T. Washington, Principal, Tuskegee Normal and Industrial Institute, Tuskegee, Alabama, Before the Union League Club, Brooklyn, On Abraham Lincoln, The Emancipator," (address, Union League Club, Brooklyn, New York, February 12, 1896), Box 113, Unnamed Folder, BTWCTU, 4.

19. Washington, *The Negro in Business*, 27.

20. Washington, "Why Should Negro Business Men Go South?," in HBTWPV8, 399.

21. See page xii of Burrows' work, *The Necessity of Myth: A History of the National Negro Business League, 1900–1945*.

22. Washington, "Extracts From Address Delivered by Booker T. Washington at the Annual Fair and Convocation of the Farmers Improvement Society," (address, Farmers Improvement Society, October 1900), Box 114, Unnamed Folder, BTWCTU, 2.

23. Washington, *The National Negro Business League Proceedings, Volume One*, 26.

24. Washington, "The Atlanta Exposition Address," (address, Atlanta Exposition, Atlanta, Georgia, September 18, 1895), Tuskegee University Archives, 9.

25. Ibid., 2.

26. Booker T. Washington, *Report of The Fifth Annual Convention of the National Negro Business League, Held at Indianapolis, Indiana, August 31st, September 1 and 2 A.D., 1904*. 18.

27. Washington, *The Future of The American Negro*, 228–30.

28. Washington, Du Bois, Dunbar, Chesnutt, and Others. *The Negro Problem: 4 Series of Articles By Representative American Negroes of To-Day*, 19.

29. Washington, "An Address before the National Negro Business League in Chicago, August 21, 1912," (address, National Negro Business League, Chicago, Illinois, August 21, 1912), in HBTWPV11, 583.

30. Washington, *Report of The Sixth Annual Convention of the National Negro Business League, Held at New York City, August 16, 17 and 18, 1905*, 66.

31. Washington, "Extracts From Address Delivered by Booker T. Washington at the Annual Fair and Convocation of the Farmers Improvement Society," (address, Farmers Improvement Society, October 1900), Box 114, Unnamed Folder, BTWCTU, 6–7.

32. Washington, "Speech to the National Negro Business League, August 18, 1915," (speech, National Negro Business League, Boston, Massachusetts, August 18, 1915), in *African American Political Thought, 1890-1930: Washington, Du Bois, Garvey, and Randolph*, ed. Wintz, 77.

33. National Negro Business League, "Hints and Help for Local Negro Business Leagues: How to Organize Form of Constitution," Box 42, Folder 280, The National Negro Business League, BTWCTU, 9.

34. Washington, Du Bois, Dunbar, Chesnutt, and Others. *The Negro Problem: A Series of Articles By Representative American Negroes of To-Day*, 28-29.

35. Washington, *The Future of The American Negro*, 232-33.

36. Speech by Booker T. Washington, "Delivered Before the Boston Unitarian Club 1888," (speech, Boston Unitarian Club, Boston, Massachusetts, 1888), Box 113, Unnamed Folder, *BTWCTU*, 2.

37. Washington, "An Address before the National Negro Business League, Boston, Massachusetts, August 18, 1915," (address, National Negro Business League, Boston, Massachusetts, August 18, 1915), in HBTWPV13, 350.

38. A review of many of the Booker T. Washington Papers at Tuskegee University and the Library of Congress confirms that Washington responded to his letters on a timely basis.

39. Washington, *The Future of The American Negro*, 100-104.

40. Washington, "The South as an Opening for a Business Career," (BTWPLC), Microfilm: Reel No. 409, 16.

41. Washington, *Report of The Ninth Annual Convention of the National Negro Business League, Held at Baltimore, Md., August 19, 20, and 21, 1908*, 93.

42. Washington, *Report of The Fourth Annual Convention of the National Negro Business League, Held at Nashville, Tennessee, August 19, 20, and 21, 1903*, 19.

43. Scott and Stowe, *Booker T. Washington: Builder of a Civilization*, 272.

44. Washington, *Up From Slavery*, 37.

45. Washington, *The Negro in Business*, 197.

46. Ibid., 194-98.

47. Washington, "The South as an Opening for a Business Career," 14-15.

48. Washington, *Up From Slavery*, 135.

49. Ibid., 128-40.

50. Washington, *The National Negro Business League Proceedings, Volume 1*, 26.

51. Washington and Du Bois, *The Negro in the South: His Economic Progress in Relation to His Moral and Religious Development*, 73-74.

52. See chapter 1 in Cash's *The Mind of the South*.

53. Washington, *Report of The Fifth Annual Convention of the National Negro Business League, Held at Indianapolis, Indiana, August 31, September 1 and 2 A.D., 1904*, 19.

54. Ibid.

55. Washington, "The Negro and the Labor Problem of the South," in *African*

American Political Thought, 1890–1930: Washington, Du Bois, Garvey, and Randolph, ed. Wintz, 55.

56. Washington, *Report of The Sixth Annual Convention of the National Negro Business League, Held at New York City, August 16, 17, and 18, 1905,* 67.

57. Washington, *The Story of My Life and Work,* 177–84.

58. Ibid., 179–80.

59. Washington, "The South as an Opening for a Business Career," 17.

60. Scott and Stowe, *Booker T. Washington: Builder of a Civilization,* 9.

61. "Annual Report Edition of the Principal and Treasurer, 1914–15," 12–13.

62. Scott and Stowe, *Booker T. Washington: Builder of a Civilization,* 80.

63. Washington, "Industrial Training For The Negro," in HBTWPV4, 373.

64. Washington, see chapter 7 of *The Future of the American Negro,* in HBTWPV5, 369–70.

65. Ibid., 370.

66. Washington, *Up From Slavery,* 66–67.

67. "Annual Catalog Edition, 1914–15," 46–50.

68. Washington, *The Future of The American Negro,* 230–31.

69. Washington and Du Bois, *The Negro in the South: His Economic Progress in Relation to His Moral and Religious Development,* 73–74.

70. Scott and Stowe, *Booker T. Washington: Builder of a Civilization,* 69–71; Washington, *Character Building,* 87–93.

71. Washington, *The Future of The American Negro,* 74.

72. Hamilton, ed., "The Talented Tenth," *The Writings of W.E.B. Du Bois,* 50–55.

73. Du Bois, *Atlanta University Publications, nos. 1–6, 1896–1901,* publication no. 4., 50.

74. Du Bois, in reflecting back on his life in 1940, said that he thought his idea of the Talented Tenth was elitist. See pages 216–17 of Du Bois' autobiography, *Dusk of Dawn: An Essay Toward an Autobiography of a Race Concept,* and another autobiography, *The Autobiography of W.E.B. Du Bois: A Soliloquy on Viewing My Life from the Last Decade of Its First Century,* 370–71.

75. Washington, *The Negro in Business,* 2.

76. Washington, "Extracts From Address Delivered by Booker T. Washington at the Annual Fair and Convocation of the Farmers Improvement Society," (address, Farmers Improvement Society, October 1900), Box 114, Unnamed Folder, BTWCTU, 9.

77. Washington, *The Negro in Business,* 17.

78. Matthews, *Black-Belt Diamonds: Gems from the Speeches, Addresses, and Talks to Students of Booker T. Washington,* 61.

79. Ibid., 4.

80. Washington, *Report of the Seventh Annual Convention of the National Negro Business League Held at Atlanta, Georgia, August 29, 30 and 31, 1906,* 62.

81. Washington, "An Address before the National Negro Business League in Chi-

cago, August 21, 1912," (address, National Negro Business League, Chicago, Illinois, August 21, 1912), in HBTWPV11, 579.

82. Booker T. Washington to Charles William Anderson, Tuskegee, Alabama, November 9, 1910, in HBTWPV10, 452.

83. As will be discussed in chapter 5, when the National Negro Business League was established in 1900, Washington and other members of the executive committee mandated that all discussions at the annual meetings deal exclusively with business issues.

84. Washington, *Report of the Ninth Annual Convention of the National Negro Business League, Held in Baltimore, Maryland, August 19, 20, 21, 1908*, Tuskegee University Archives, 89–90; Washington, *Report of the Tenth Annual Convention of the National Negro Business League, Held in Louisville, Kentucky, August 18–20, 1909*, Tuskegee University Archives, 73.

Chapter 4. The Negro Farmers' Conference: Helping Those Near and Far

1. Meier, "Notes and Documents: Toward A Reinterpretation of Booker T. Washington," *Journal of Southern History* 23: 220–27.

2. Harlan, "Booker T. Washington in Biographical Perspective," Vol. 75, No. 6 (October 1970), 581–599; Harlan, "The Secret Life of Booker T. Washington," 393–416.

3. Harlan, "The Secret Life of Booker T. Washington," 393–416.

4. Poxpey, "The Washington-Du Bois Controversy and Its Effects on the Negro Problem," 128–52; Calista, "Booker T. Washington: Another Look," 240–55; Flynn, "Booker T. Washington: Uncle Tom or Wooden Horse," 262–74; Friedman, "Life 'In the Lion's Mouth': Another Look at Booker T. Washington," 335–51.

5. Washington, Du Bois, Dunbar, Chesnutt, and Others, *The Negro Problem: A Series of Articles by Representative American Negroes of To-Day*, 23–24.

6. Washington, *Up From Slavery*, 72–78.

7. Ibid., 77.

8. Washington, *Tuskegee & Its People: Their Ideals and Achievements*, vi; Williams, "Local Conditions Among Negroes V: Tuskegee Institute Extension Work in Macon County, Alabama," 471–78.

9. Washington, *The Future of the Negro*, 120–21.

10. Sterling, ed., *The Trouble They Seen: The Story of Reconstruction in the Words of African Americans*, 248–74; Smith, *Black Voices from Reconstruction, 1865–1877*, 78–84; Washington, *The Story of the Negro: The Rise of the Race from Slavery: Volume II*, 30–56.

11. Washington, *The Negro in Business*, 18. On page 18, Washington wrote: "As soon as the colored farmer acquires a sufficiently large amount of land he becomes of necessity a businessman. The methods he must employ in conducting his plantation and disposing of his crops make him one." Rome, "American Farmers as Entrepreneurs, 1870–1900," 37–49.

12. Washington, "How I Came To Call The First Negro Conference," [Tuskegee, Alabama, April 1899], an article in the A.M.E. Church Review, in HBTWPV5, 101.

13. Ibid., 96.

14. Ibid.

15. Thrasher, *Tuskegee: Its Story and Its Work*, 164.

16. Washington, "How I Came To Call The First Negro Conference," 98.

17. Washington to William Torrey Harris, Tuskegee, Alabama, May 4, 1892, in HBTWPV3, 226.

18. Banks, "The Tuskegee Conferences," 246.

19. Ibid.

20. Thrasher, *Tuskegee: Its Story and Its Work*, 165; "The Declarations of the First Tuskegee Negro Conference," Tuskegee, Alabama, February 23, 1892, in HBTWPV3, 217–19.

21. Banks, "The Tuskegee Conferences," 246–47; Shower, "The Tuskegee Conferences," 138–40; Jones, "The Tuskegee Negro Conferences," 204–207; Scoville, "The Tuskegee Negro Conferences," 201–203; "The Tuskegee Conferences," 196–99; Williams, "Local Conditions Among Negroes: V Tuskegee Institute Extension Work in Macon County, Alabama," 471–78; "The Tuskegee Conferences," 200–201; Thrasher, "The Tuskegee Conference 1909," (BTWPLC), Microfilm: Reel no. 752, 1–7; Avery, "The Twentieth Tuskegee Conference," 73–78; Williams, "The Tuskegee Negro Conference," 74–76; Avery, "The Tuskegee Conference of 1913," 177–79; "The Tuskegee Conference and Negro Farming," 67–68; Davis, "Tuskegee Institute and Its Conferences," 157–67; "The Tuskegee Farmers' Conference," 133–34.

22. Washington, "How I Came To Call The First Negro Conference," 99; Jones, "The Role of Tuskegee Institute in the Education of Black Farmers," 255.

23. Thrasher, *Tuskegee: Its Story and Its Work*, 165.

24. Jones, "The Role of Tuskegee Institute in the Education of Black Farmers," 255.

25. Washington, *The Story of My Life and Work*, 312.

26. McMurry, *George Washington Carver: Scientist & Symbol*, 44.

27. George Washington Carver to Booker T. Washington, Ames, Iowa, April 12, 1896, in HBTWPV4, 159; Miller, *George Washington Carver: God's Ebony Scientist*, 59–79.

28. Ibid.

29. Campbell, *The Movable School Goes To The Negro Farmer*, 82; George Washington Lovejoy to Booker T. Washington, Mobile, Alabama, December 31, 1896, in HBTWPV4, 250–51.

30. Hines, "George W. Carver and the Tuskegee Agricultural Experiment Station," 73–83.

31. Later examples of such bulletins published by George W. Carver and disseminated to farmers are as follows: "How to Grow the Tomato and 115 Ways to Prepare it for the Table," Bulletin no. 36, Tuskegee, Alabama: Tuskegee Institute Press, 1936; "How to Grow the Peanut and 105 Ways of Preparing it for Human Consumption," Bulletin no. 31, Tuskegee, Alabama: Tuskegee Institute Press, 1983; "How the Farmer

Can Save His Sweet Potatoes: And Ways of Preparing Them for the Table," Bulletin no. 38, Tuskegee, Alabama: Tuskegee Institute Press, 1937.

32. Jones, "The Role of Tuskegee Institute in the Education of Black Farmers," 259.

33. Ibid.

34. Work, "Short Course For Farmers," 866; Williams, "Local Conditions Among Negroes: V Tuskegee Institute Extension Work in Macon County, Alabama," 477.

35. Work, "Short Course For Farmers," 866.

36. Ibid.

37. Ibid.

38. Ibid.

39. Davis, "Tuskegee Institute and Its Conferences," 158–61; Washington, "Chapters From My Experience III," in *The World's Work*, December 1910, (BTWPLC), Microfilm: Reel no. 415, 13,789.

40. Washington, "An Article in the Annals of the American Academy of Political and Social Science," in HBTWPV11, 505–506.

41. Williams, "Local Conditions Among Negroes: V Tuskegee Institute Extension Work in Macon County, Alabama," 473.

42. "A Circular Announcing The Negro Farmer," Tuskegee, Alabama, ca. November 1913, in HBTWPV12, 362–63.

43. Campbell, *The Movable School Goes To The Negro Farmer*, 88 (b); Graham and Lipscomb, *Dr. George Washington Carver, Scientist*, 138–39.

44. Mayberry, "The Tuskegee Moveable School: A Unique Contribution to National and International Agriculture and Rural Development," 87.

45. Campbell, *The Movable School Goes To The Negro Farmer*, 93.

46. "An Item in the *Tuskegee Student*," Tuskegee Institute, Tuskegee, Alabama, November 17, 1906, in HBTWPV9, 130–34.

47. Jones, "The South's Negro Farm Agent," 39.

48. McMurry, *George Washington Carver: Scientist & Symbol*, 58–63.

49. Dr. Seaman Knapp originally had doubts concerning hiring African Americans as farm agents, especially in the South, because he thought that it might arouse racial prejudice and be a waste of government funds.

50. Washington, "A Memorandum of Agreement between Tuskegee Institute and the General Education Board," Tuskegee, Alabama, November 9, 1906, in HBTWPV9, 121–22; Jones, "The South's First Black Farm Agents," 638.

51. Washington, "A Farmers' College on Wheels," 8,352–354.

52. Campbell, *The Movable School Goes To The Negro Farmer*, 92–132; James, "The Tuskegee Institute Movable School, 1906–1923," 201–209; Jones, "Thomas M. Campbell: Black Agricultural Leader of the New South," 42–59.

53. Washington, "A Farmers' College on Wheels," 8,354.

54. Ibid.

55. James, "The Tuskegee Institute Movable School, 1906–1923," 206.

56. "The Principal's Report to the Board of Trustees of Tuskegee Institute," Tuskegee Institute, Tuskegee, Alabama, May 31, 1915, in HBTWPV13, 298.

57. Work, "The Negro's Industrial Problem: II Farming, Trades, and Business," 43 & 503; Lemon, "The Farmers' Conference at Calhoun," 247–49; "Farmers' Conference at Lane College," 5.

58. Work, "The Negro's Industrial Problem: II Farming, Trades, and Business," 503–504.

59. Jones, "Improving Rural Life for Blacks: The Tuskegee Negro Farmers' Conference, 1892–1915," 114.

60. Ibid.

61. Harlan, *Booker T. Washington: The Making of a Black Leader, 1856–1901*, 200.

62. Ferguson, "Caught in 'No Man's Land': The Negro Cooperative Demonstration Service and the Ideology of Booker T. Washington, 1900–1918," 33–54.

63. "Southern Agriculture and the Negro," 515; Scott, "The Tuskegee Negro Conference," 180–81; Bowen, "Doing Things at the Tuskegee Institute," 252; Washington, "Twenty-Five Years of Tuskegee," 7,435–7,437; Washington, *The Story of the Negro: The Rise of the Race from Slavery: Volume II*, 45–46; "An Account of a Tour of Macon County, Alabama," Tuskegee, Alabama, June 3, 1911, in HBTWPV11, 177–79; Washington, "The Negro as a Farmer," (BTWPLC), Microfilm: Reel no. 416, 175–81; Washington, "Industrial Education and Public Schools," 231; "Some Tangible Results of the Tuskegee Negro Conference," 4–5; "Tuskegee Annual Conference Holds Monster Meeting," 1; Aery, "Tuskegee Conference Now Helps The Nation," 8; Aptheker, ed., *Against Racism: Unpublished Essays, Papers, Addresses, 1887–1961 of W.E.B. Du Bois*, 116; Rogers, *World's Great Men of Color: Volume II*, 397; Harris, *The Harder We Run: Black Workers since the Civil War*, 32–33.

64. Strauss, *Qualitative Analysis for Social Scientists*, 20–21, 27–33, & 55–81. Applying Anselm Strauss's coding techniques to many of Washington's speeches and writings on the farmers' conference proves this point. Strauss's techniques, which were used in chapter 3 to uncover Booker T. Washington's business ideas, are a form of content analysis that offers researchers procedures by which to rigorously analyze documents to disclose underlying themes.

65. All the materials presented in the footnotes on the Negro Farmers' Conference and activities related to it were rigorously scrutinized for recurring themes.

66. Thrasher, "The Tuskegee Conference," 5.

67. Washington, "Addresses to the Colored Farmers of Alabama," 364.

68. Washington, *Working With The Hands*, 139.

69. Washington, "Important to Colored Farmers in Macon and Adjacent Counties in Alabama," 7.

70. Washington, *Up From Slavery*, 76.

71. Washington, "Chickens, Pigs and People," 293–94.

72. Washington, "Grow One Pig at Least, Says Dr. Washington," 10.

73. Scott and Stowe, *Booker T. Washington: Builder of a Civilization*, 174.

74. Carver, "Helps for the Hard Times," 1.

75. Thrasher, *Tuskegee: Its Story and Its Work*, 182–85; Washington, *A New Negro for a New Century*, 418; Washington, "The Advancement of Colored Women," 183–89.

76. "The Rural Negro in the South," (BTWPLC), Microfilm: Reel no. 410, 5–11; Isaiah T. Montgomery to Booker T. Washington, Mound Bayou, Mississippi, September 6, 1904, in HBTWPV8, 61–63; Holmes, "Whitecapping: Agrarian Violence in Mississippi, 1902–1906," 165–85.

77. Washington, "The Rural Negro in the South," 1–11.

78. "The Declarations of the First Tuskegee Negro Conference," Tuskegee, Alabama, February 23, 1892, in HBTWPV3, 18; "Tuskegee Negro Farmers' Conference Breaks Record Attendance," 5.

79. "Galley Proof: Tuskegee Negro Conference," (BTWPLC), Microfilm: Reel no. 755, 1.

80. Washington, *The Negro in Business*, 18.

81. "Winners From the Soil: Colored Heroes of the Farm," from the *Negro Farmer* 1: 4; "Winners From the Soil: Colored Heroes of the Farm," from the *Negro Farmer* 2: 4–5; "Winners From the Soil: Colored Heroes of the Farm," from the *Negro Farmer* 2: 9–10; "Winners From the Soil: Colored Heroes of the Farm," from the *Negro Farmer* 2: 9–10; "Winners From the Soil: Colored Heroes of the Farm," from the *Negro Farmer* 2: 9.

82. "Winners From the Soil: Colored Heroes of the Farm," from the *Negro Farmer* 1: 2.

83. Ibid.

84. "Winners From the Soil: Colored Heroes of the Farm," from the *Negro Farmer* 2: 5; "Winners From the Soil: Colored Heroes of the Farm," from the *Negro Farmer* 2: 8–9.

85. Washington, "Negro Enterprise I: A Negro Potato King," 115–18.

86. Washington, *The Negro in Business*, 23–29.

87. Ibid.

88. Ibid., 27.

89. Ibid.

90. Ibid.

91. Ibid.

92. Ibid.

93. Junius G. Groves to Emmett J. Scott, Edwardville, Kansas, September 15, 1914, (BTWPLC), Microfilm: Reel no. 755, 1.

94. Haynes, "The Movement of Negroes from the Country to the City," 230–36.

95. Scott and Stowe, *Booker T. Washington: Builder of a Civilization*, 183–84.

Chapter 5. The National Negro Business League: A History and Analysis

1. Butler, *Entrepreneurship and Self-Help Among Black Americans: A Reconsideration of Race and Economics*, 64–68; Pryor, *Wealth Building Lessons of Booker T. Washington for a New Black America*.

2. "Resolution and Recommendations Adopted by the National Negro Business

League at its First Meeting held in Boston, August 23 and 24, 1900," (BTWPLC), Microfilm: Reel no. 752, 1–2.

3. Washington, *The Negro in Business*, 199.

4. Thornbrough, "More Light on Booker T. Washington and the New York Age," 34–49.

5. Scott and Stowe, *Booker T. Washington: Builder of a Civilization*, 185.

6. Washington, "Important to Colored Men and Women Engaged in Business Throughout the Country," June 15, 1900, Tuskegee, Alabama, (BTWPLC), Microfilm: Reel no. 416, 1–2.

7. Drinker, *Booker T. Washington: The Master Mind of a Child of Slavery*, 119.

8. Washington, "Important to Colored Men and Women Engaged in Business Throughout the Country," June 15, 1900, Tuskegee, Alabama, (BTWPLC), Microfilm: Reel no. 416, 2.

9. Harlan, *Booker T. Washington: The Making of a Black Leader, 1856–1901*, 266–71; Harlan, "Booker T. Washington and the National Negro Business League," in *Seven in Black: Reflections on the Negro Experience in America*, eds. Slade and Herrenkohl, 76–79; Burrows, *The Necessity of Myth: A History of the National Negro Business League, 1900–1945*, 23 & 35–39; Marable, *How Capitalism Underdeveloped Black America*, 145.

10. Du Bois, "The Growth of the Niagara Movement," *Voice of the Negro* 3: 43–45; Du Bois, *The Autobiography of W.E.B. Du Bois: A Soliloquy on Viewing My Life from the Last Decade of Its First Century*, 214.

11. Du Bois, *Atlanta University Publications, Numbers 1–6, 1896–1901*, publication No. 4, 50.

12. William Edward Burghardt Du Bois to Booker T. Washington, Atlanta, Georgia, May 16, 1900, in HBTWPV5, 526 & footnote no. 1; Burrows, *The Necessity of Myth: A History of the National Negro Business League, 1900–1945*, 33–37.

13. Harlan's Tuskegee Machine Thesis, stated simply, argues that Booker T. Washington, in attempting to retain his hegemonic leadership over African Americans, which was often viewed as controversial, had numerous willing accomplices throughout the nation that helped him to retain his stronghold. They were often in important key positions. They not only alerted Washington to his unknown enemies, but helped to sabotage some of their efforts to bring Washington down.

14. Holt, "The Lonely Warrior: Ida B. Wells-Barnett and the Struggle for Black Leadership," in *Black Leaders of the Twentieth Century*, eds. Franklin and Meier, 50–51.

15. William Edward Burghardt Du Bois to Booker T. Washington, Atlanta, Georgia, July 12, 1899, in HBTWPV5, 152–53; Booker T. Washington to William Edward Burghardt Du Bois," Tuskegee, Alabama, October 26, 1899, in HBTWPV5, 245.

16. William Edward Burghardt Du Bois to Booker T. Washington, Atlanta, Georgia, April 10, 1900, in HBTWPV5, 480.

17. William Edward Burghardt Du Bois to Booker T. Washington, Atlanta, Georgia, July 3, 1901, in HBTWPV6, 165.

18. Du Bois' list of businessmen consisted of the businessmen that he and his as-

sociates at Atlanta University included in their study of African-American entrepreneurs.

19. William Edward Burghardt Du Bois to Booker T. Washington, Atlanta, Georgia, May 16, 1900, in HBTWPV5, 526.

20. Washington, "The American Negro and His Economic Value," December 1900, in HBTWPV5, 704–709; Washington, "The Negro in Business," *Gunton's Magazine*, March 1901, (BTWPLC), Microfilm: Reel no. 414, 215–16; Washington, "National Negro Business League," Box 33, Folder 230, The National Negro Business League, BTW-CTU, 3.

21. Du Bois attributed the conferences at Tuskegee and Hampton Institute as factors that influenced the work of the Atlanta University conferences. See Du Bois, *The Autobiography of W. E. B. Du Bois: A Soliloquy on Viewing My Life from the Last Decade of Its First Century*, 213–14.

22. William Edward Burghardt Du Bois to Booker T. Washington, Atlanta, Georgia, February 11, 1901, in HBTWPV6, 33; Scott, "The Tuskegee Negro Conference," 180–81.

23. William Edward Burghardt Du Bois to Booker T. Washington, Atlanta, Georgia, March 4, 1902, in HBTWPV6, 412–13.

24. The event called the Boston Riot occurred on July 30, 1903. Washington was scheduled to speak at an NNBL rally that was held at the African Methodist Episcopal Church in Boston. Monroe Trotter, one of the publishers of the anti-Washington paper *The Guardian*, and several of his supporters (excluding Du Bois) attended the rally with the sole intent of confronting Washington on his educational and leadership stances. As Washington began to speak, Trotter and his supporters heckled him almost nonstop. Then Trotter arose, asked Washington several loaded questions, and inquired, "Is the rope and the torch all the race is to get under your leadership?" Disruption continued until the rally was out of control. Police were called in to remove Trotter and his supporters. All the while, Washington waited patiently until the disruption was over and then continued the rally as though nothing had ever occurred. The next day, these events were reported in newspapers across the country as the Boston Riot, and Trotter was jailed for thirty days. Trotter's treatment greatly disturbed Du Bois and further alienated him from Washington. For more information, see Rudwick's work, "Race Leadership Struggle: Background of the Boston Riot of 1903," 16–24.

25. Du Bois, *The Souls of Black Folks*, 30–42.

26. Broderick, "The Fight Against Booker T. Washington," in *Booker T. Washington and His Critics: The Problem in American Civilization*, ed. Hawkins, 40–49; Walden, "The Contemporary Opposition to the Political Ideas of Booker T. Washington," 103–15.

27. William Edward Burghardt Du Bois to Booker T. Washington, Atlanta, Georgia, February 17, 1900, in HBTWPV5, 443–44.

28. Du Bois, "The Growth of the Niagara Movement," 43–45.

29. Meier, *Negro Thought in America 1880–1915*, 42–58; Meier, "Negro Class Structure and Ideology in the Age of Booker T. Washington," 258.

30. Washington, *The Negro in Business*, 199.

31. Ibid., 199–200.

32. Washington, *The National Negro Business League Proceedings Volume 1, 1900*, 25.

33. *Programme of Second Annual Session of the National Negro Business League to be Held at Chicago, Illinois, Handel Hall, 46–48 Randolph St., August 21, 22, 23, 1901*, 3.

34. Gaines, *Uplifting the Race: Black Leadership, Politics, and Culture in the Twentieth Century*, 95.

35. Edwin B. Jourdain to Emmett Jay Scott, New Bedford, Massachusetts, August 19, 1902, in HBTWPV6, 502–505.

36. "Resolutions and Recommendations Adopted by the National Negro Business League at its First Meeting held in Boston, August 23 and 24, 1900," (BTWPLC), Microfilm: Reel no. 752, 2.

37. The members of the NNBL Committee on Regulations and Rules were Giles B. Jackson, W. R. Pettiford, M. M. Lewey, Daniel Lucas, and William L. Reed.

38. "Resolutions and Recommendations Adopted by the National Negro Business League at its First Meeting held in Boston, August 23 and 24, 1900," (BTWPLC), Microfilm: Reel no. 752, 2.

39. Washington, *The National Negro Business League Proceedings Volume 1, 1900*, 213–14.

40. Washington to Emmett Jay Scott, Boston, Massachusetts, August 24, 1900, in HBTWPV5, 605.

41. Scarborough, "The Negro as a Factor in Business," 455–59.

42. *Programme of Second Annual Session of the National Negro Business League to be Held at Chicago, Illinois, Handel Hall, 46–48 Randolph St., August 21, 22, 23, 1901*, 2.

43. "The National Negro Business League," 513–15.

44. "The National Negro Business League," Nashville, Tennessee, August 19, 1903, (BTWPLC), Microfilm: Reel no. 752, 1.

45. Washington, *Report of the Fifth Annual Convention of the National Negro Business League, Held at Indianapolis, Indiana, August 31st, September 1st and 2nd A. D. 1904*, 21.

46. "New York Meeting of the National Negro Business League," 5.

47. Washington, *The Negro in Business*, view the fourth page prior to page 1.

48. Washington, "Speech to the National Negro Business League, August 18, 1915," (speech, National Negro Business League, Boston, Massachusetts, August 18, 1915), Wintz, ed., *African American Political Thought, 1890–1930: Washington, Du Bois, Garvey, and Randolph*, 73–74.

49. Burrows, *The Necessity of Myth: A History of the National Negro Business League, 1900–1945*, 47.

50. Ibid.

51. Washington, *The Negro in Business*, 198.

52. Barbour, "An Account of the National Negro Business Convention," September 14, 1901, Chicago, Illinois, in HBTWPV6, 206–209.

53. Nannie Helen Burroughs to Booker T. Washington, July 8, 1914, Washington, D.C., in HBTWPV13, 82–83.

54. Washington to Nannie Helen Burroughs, July 13, 1914, Tuskegee, Alabama, in HBTWPV13, 87.

55. Scott and Stowe, *Booker T. Washington: Builder of a Civilization*, 199.

56. "The National Negro Business League," (BTWPLC), Microfilm: Reel no. 752, 1.

57. E. Brown to Booker T. Washington, August 22, 1906, Birmingham, Alabama, Box 28, Folder 217, National Negro Business League, BTWCTU, 1.

58. Ibid.

59. Fred R. Moore to Booker T. Washington, October 4, 1906, Tuskegee, Alabama, Box 33, Folder 230, National Negro Business League, BTWCTU, 4.

60. Washington to G. M. Howell, July 5, 1906, Box 26, Folder 211, National Negro Business League, BTWCTU, 1.

61. Circular Letter by Fred R. Moore, March 16, 1904, Brooklyn, New York, (BTWPLC), Microfilm: Reel no. 752, 1; Fred R. Moore, "Organizing Local Business Leagues," 626–27.

62. Washington to Fred R. Moore, November 2, 1903, Brooklyn, New York, 1903, Box 1, ALHCTU, 1–2.

63. Circular Letter by Fred R. Moore, New York, New York, Box 26, Folder 212, National Negro Business League, BTWCTU, 1.

64. Ibid., 2.

65. Washington to Robert A. Frank, Hotel Manhattan, New York, New York, December 16, 1908, in HBTWPV9, 701; Margaret James Murray Washington to Julius Rosenwald, Tuskegee Institute, Tuskegee, Alabama, December 10, 1915, in HBTWPV13, 479.

66. Washington to Andrew Carnegie, Boston, Massachusetts, December 16, 1910, in HBTWPV10, 507–508; James Bertram to Booker T. Washington, New York, New York, December 20, 1910, Box 1, ALHCTU, 1; Washington to Emmett Jay Scott, Tuskegee, Alabama, January 8, 1911, in HBTWPV10, 538–39.

67. Washington to Fred R. Moore, July 3, 1906, New York, New York, Box 26, Folder 212, National Negro Business League, BTWCTU, 1.

68. Ingham and Feldman, *African-American Business Leaders: A Biographical Dictionary*, 467.

69. Fred R. Moore to Booker T. Washington, February 20, 1906, New York, New York, Box 19, Folder 188, National Negro Business League, BTWCTU, 2; Fred R. Moore to Booker T. Washington, March 2, 1906, New York, New York, Box 20, Folder 192, National Negro Business League, BTWCTU, 1–2; Fred R. Moore to Booker T. Washington, July 23, 1906, Valdosta, Georgia, Box 26, Folder 212, National Negro Business League, BTWCTU, 1.

70. Ibid.

71. Fred R. Moore to Booker T. Washington, April 2, 1906, New York, New York, Box 21, Folder 197, National Negro Business League, BTWCTU, 1; Fred R. Moore to

Booker T. Washington, June 26, 1906, New York, New York, Box 24, Folder 206, National Negro Business League, BTWCTU, 1–8.

72. Washington to Ford Havis, November 28, 1910, Tuskegee, Alabama, Box 1, ALHCTU, 1.

73. National Negro Business League, "Hints and Helps for Local Negro Business Leagues: How to Organize-Form of Constitution," Box 42, Folder 280, National Negro Business League, BTWCTU, 7–15; Booker T. Washington, Emmett J. Scott, and Fred R. Moore, "Making Your Local League More Effective," (BTWPLC), Microfilm: Reel no. 752, 1.

74. The correspondence between Washington and his NNBL national organizers are replete with letters discussing the inactivity of many local leagues. Evidence concerning this issue is offered within the next few pages of this book.

75. Moore, "Progressive Business Men of Brooklyn," 304–308; Bruce, "The Necessity for Business Leagues," 338–39; Burrell, "History of the Business of Colored Richmond," 316–22; Crawford, "Business Negroes of Chattanooga," 534–37; Lewis, "Colored Business Men of Jacksonville," 474–76.

76. "National Negro Business League at Louisville," 1.

77. Work, *Negro Yearbook, 1914–15*, 304–308.

78. In giving his annual address for the NNBL meeting in 1909, Washington stated that there were at least five hundred leagues, not exactly five hundred. *Report of the Tenth Annual Convention of the National Negro Business League, Held in Louisville, KY., August 18–20, 1909*, 71.

79. Theodore W. Jones to Booker T. Washington, June 12, 1906, Chicago, Illinois, Box 1, ALHCTU, 1.

80. "National Negro Business League at Louisville," 1; "Program: Tenth Annual Session: National Negro Business League, Louisville, Kentucky, Wednesday, Thursday, Friday: August 18, 19, 20, 1909" (BTWPLC), Microfilm: Reel no. 752, 6–7.

81. Washington to Fred R. Moore, June 26, 1906, Box 24, Folder 206, National Negro Business League, BTWCTU, 1.

82. Washington to Fred R. Moore, July 3, 1906, Box 26, Folder 212, National Negro Business League, BTWCTU, 1.

83. Ibid.

84. Washington to Fred R. Moore, July 12, 1906, Box 26, Folder 212, National Negro Business League, BTWCTU, 1; Fred R. Moore to Booker T. Washington, July 14, 1906, Box 26, Folder 212, National Negro Business League, BTWCTU, 1.

85. Ingham and Feldman, *African-American Business Leaders: A Biographical Dictionary*, 469.

86. Burrows, *The Necessity of Myth: A History of the National Negro Business League, 1900–1945*, 83.

87. Ibid.; Tyler, "Thrifty Center of Business: Encouraging Report of Race Progress in South," 7.

88. Ralph Waldo Tyler to Booker T. Washington, Washington, D.C., July 19, 1913, in HBTWPV12, 237–40.

89. Washington, "Speech to the National Negro Business League, August 18, 1915," (speech, National Negro Business League, Boston, Massachusetts, August 18, 1915), *African American Political Thought, 1890-1930: Washington, Du Bois, Garvey, and Randolph*, ed. Wintz, 74.

90. Ibid.

91. Harris, *The Negro as Capitalist: A Study of Banking and Business among American Negroes*, 177-84; Frazier, *Black Bourgeoisie*, 134 & 139; Harlan, "Booker T. Washington and the National Negro Business League," in *Seven in Black: Reflections on the Negro Experience in America*, eds. Slade and Herrenkohl, 86-87; Burrows, *The Necessity of Myth: A History of the National Negro Business League 1900-1945*, xii, 26, & 175-76.

92. Harlan, "Booker T. Washington and the National Negro Business League," in *Seven in Black: Reflections on the Negro Experience in America*, eds. Slade and Herrenkohl, 86; Burrows, *The Necessity of Myth: A History of the National Negro Business League, 1900-1945*, 34.

93. Washington, "Why Should Negro Business Men Go South?" 19.

94. "An Account of a Speech in Washington, D.C.," Washington, D.C., April 7, 1894, in HBTWPV3, 400-401.

95. Washington, "A Speech before the National Educational Association," (speech, National Educational Association, Madison, Wisconsin, July 16, 1884), in HBTWPV2, 257; Washington, "The South as an Opening for a Business Career," (speech, Washington, D.C., November 20, 1891), (BTWPLC), Microfilm: Reel no. 409, 4-5; Washington, "The Negro in Business," 95 & 214; Washington, *The Negro in Business*, 40-41, 43-47, 51, 107-108, 269-270, 279-280, and so on. Besides these cited examples, *The Negro in Business* is full of examples of African Americans conducting business in the open market; Washington, "Durham, North Carolina, a City of Negro Enterprises," *The Independent*, March 30, 1911, (BTWPLC), Microfilm: Reel no. 415, 644 & 649.

96. Washington, "An Address Before the National Negro Business League in Chicago," (address, National Negro Business League, Chicago, Illinois, August 21, 1912), in HBTWPV11, 582.

97. Washington, *The Negro in Business*, 13.

98. Washington, "An Address Before the National Negro Business League," (address, National Negro Business League, Philadelphia, Pennsylvania, August 20, 1913), in HBTWPV12, 237-40.

99. Anderson, *The Education of Blacks in the South, 1860-1935*, 102; Washington, "The Case of the Negro," 583.

100. Washington, "The Relation of the Races in the South," 272-79.

101. Washington, *The Future of the American Negro*, 86-87.

102. Washington to the editor of the *Tuskegee News*, Tuskegee, Alabama, October 21, 1914, in HBTWPV12, 147.

103. "The Negro Business League," 518; Harlan, "Booker T. Washington and the National Negro Business League," in *Seven in Black: Reflections on the Negro Experience in America*, eds. Slade and Herrenkohl, 79-80.

104. James Bertram to Booker T. Washington, New York, New York, December 20, 1910, 1.

105. "Resolutions," 1909, (BTWPLC), Microfilm: Reel no. 752, 1.

106. Circular from Booker T. Washington and Emmett J. Scott, Tuskegee, Alabama, October 12, 1903, Box 1, ALHCTU, 1; Circular from Booker T. Washington and Emmett Scott, Tuskegee Institute, Tuskegee, Alabama, October, 16, 1908, Box 44, Folder 286, National Negro Business League, BTWCTU, 1.

107. Carter, "The Accountant as a Factor in Business," (speech, NNBL, Topeka, Kansas, August 16, 1907), 619–24.

108. Nannie Helen Burroughs to Emmett Jay Scott, Washington, D.C., June 29, 1915, in HBTWPV13, 333.

109. Charles Banks to Booker T. Washington, Mound Bayou, Mississippi, May 23, 1906, Box 1, ALHCTU, 1.

110. I. B. Beale to Booker T. Washington, Box 28, Folder 217, National Negro Business League, BTWCTU, 1–2.

111. Albon L. Holsey was an author, a Tuskegee Institute employee, the secretary of Tuskegee Instutute after Emmett J. Scott left in 1917, and a national organizer for the NNBL. He orchestrated in 1929 a collected business effort for the NNBL. He decided that the NNBL should sponsor a national cooperative grocery store. The goal was to organize African-American grocers into cooperative buying units, create a standardized store service, promote cooperative advertising, and use the local league chapters as coordinating agencies. This national organization was called the Colored Merchants Association (CMA). For more information on the CMA, see Oak's work, *The Negro's Adventure in General Business* , 62–65.

112. Frazier, *Black Bourgeoisie*, 139; Harlan, "Booker T. Washington and the National Negro Business League," in *Seven in Black: Reflections on the Negro Experience in America*, eds. Slade and Herrenkohl, 82.

113. Washington, *Report of the Seventh Annual Convention of the National Negro Business League Held at Atlanta Georgia, August 29, 30 and 31, 1906*, 62; "Mission of the Business League: Bishop Cottrell Calls Attention to Its Usefulness," 1915, (BTWPLC), Microfilm: Reel no. 757, 1.

114. Frazier, *Black Bourgeoisie*, 134; Harlan, "Booker T. Washington and the National Negro Business League," in *Seven in Black: Reflections on the Negro Experience in America*, eds. Slade and Herrenkohl, 87; Burrows, *The Necessity of Myth: A History of the National Negro Business League, 1900–1945,* 58.

115. Scott and Stowe, *Booker T. Washington: Builder of a Civilization*, 221.

116. Weare, *Black Business in the New South: A Social History of the North Carolina Mutual Life Insurance Company* , 146–47

117. Newstelle, "A Negro Business League at Work," 43–47; Uspean, "Report of D. Uspean [a] Delegate from [the] Business League [of] Montgomery, Alabama," (BTWPLC), Microfilm: Reel no. 755, 1–3.

118. Giles Beecher Jackson to Booker T. Washington, Richmond, Virginia, January 24, 1901, HBTWPV6, 14–16.

119. National Negro Business League, "Hints and Helps for Local Negro Business Leagues: How to Organize-Form of Constitution," 11.

120. Washington to Mrs. W. A. Parker, March 2, 1904, Box 1, ALHCTU, 1.

121. Washington, "Important to Colored Men and Women Engaged in Business Throughout the Country," June 15, 1900, Tuskegee, Alabama, BTWCTU, 1–2.

122. Washington, *The Negro in Business*, 199.

123. Washington, "The Negro in Business," 212–14; Washington, *The National Negro Business League Proceedings Volume 1, 1900*, 212.

124. *Programme of Second Annual Session of the National Negro Business League to be Held at Chicago, Illinois, Handel Hall, 46–48 Randolph St., August 21, 22, 23, 1901*, 3–4.

125. Bessie Nance to Booker T. Washington, Chicago, Illinois, April 7, 1904, Box 1, ALHCTU, 2; Washington, *The Negro in Business*, 30.

126. Maggie L. Walker to Booker T. Washington, Richmond, Virginia, November 17, 1905, Box 1, ALHCTU, 1; "Program [of the] Ninth Annual Session [of the] National Negro Business League, Baltimore, Maryland, Wednesday, Thursday and Friday, August 19th, 20th, and 21st, 1908," Box 42, Folder 280, National Negro Business League, BTWCTU, 6.

127. Washington, "Women as Economic Factors," 187.

128. Work, "The Negro's Industrial Problem: II Farming, Trades, and Business," 505–506.

129. Schuyler, "Madam C. J. Walker: Pioneer Big Business Woman of America," 250–58 & 264.

130. "Noted Business Woman Crosses The Great Divide," 1; Hine and Thompson, *A Shining Thread of Hope*, 203–205.

131. Ingham and Feldman, *African-American Business Leaders: A Biographical Dictionary*, 686.

132. Ibid.

133. Hine and Thompson, *A Shining Thread of Hope*, 203; Ingham and Feldman, *African-American Business Leaders: A Biographical Dictionary*, 686.

134. Madame C. J. Walker to Booker T. Washington, Indianapolis, Indiana, May 5, 1914, in HBTWPV13, 14–15; Washington to Madame C. J. Walker, Tuskegee, Alabama, May 22, 1914, in HBTWPV13, 30.

135. Margaret James Murray Washington to Julius Rosenwald, Tuskegee Institute, Tuskegee, Alabama, December 10, 1915, in HBTWPV13, 479.

136. Washington, "The Negro in Business," 94; Washington, *The Negro in Business*, 51, 108, & 152.

137. "Annual Report of the Fifteenth Annual Convention: National Negro Business League, Held at Muskogee, Oklahoma, August 19–21, 1914," (BTWPLC), Microfilm: Reel no. 754, 43; Keyes, "Big Business for Negroes," 240.

138. Washington, *The Negro in Business*, 152.

139. Murray, "The Upward Struggle," 510.

140. "The Negro Business League," from the *Southern Workman*, Vol. 31: 513–15;

"The Negro Business League," from the *Southern Workman,* Vol. 34: 467–68; "The Negro Business League," from the *Southern Workman,* Vol. 35: 519–20; "The Negro Business League," from the *Southern Workman,* Vol. 36: 515–16; "The Baltimore Session of the National Negro Business League," Box 42, Folder 280, National Negro Business League, BTWCTU, 1–6; "Louisville Meeting of the National Negro Business League," 467–69; "New York Meeting of the National Negro Business League," 469–70; "The Negro Business League," from the *Southern Workman,* Vol. 41: 497–500; "The Negro Business League," from the *Southern Workman,* Vol. 42: 517–19; Washington, "The Negro in Business," from the *Southern Workman,* Vol. 41: 523–24; Potter, "Booker T. Washington, a Visit to Florida," 744–45.

141. Oak, author of *The Negro's Adventure in General Business*, stated that: "Partly as a result of the activities of the League, especially in the first two decades of its formation, and partly as a result of general improvement in the economic, social, and educational life of the Negro, colored business made rapid progress during the first three decades of the twentieth century." See page 47 therein.

142. "Growth of Negro Business," 62. These numbers appear to be a good estimate because for 1930 Abram Harris came up with a figure of seventy thousand African-American-owned-and-operated businesses. See *The Negro as Capitalist*, page 53.

143. For more evidence, also see Work's essay, "The Negro In Business Enterprise," 306–307. Using the census for the year 1910, he estimated that there were forty-three thousand African-American businesses operating.

144. Frazier, *Black Bourgeoisie*, 132; Higgs, *Competition and Coercion: Blacks in the American Economy, 1865–1914*, 90–91.

145. Washington was an evolutionist not in the biological sense, but in terms of African-American economic, social, and political development; he believed in a step-by-step process that would ultimately lead to progression.

146. Washington, "What I Am Trying To Do," 106; Burrows, *The Necessity of Myth: A History of the National Negro Business League, 1900–1945*, 69–70.

147. Butler, "Why Booker T. Washington Was Right," in *A Different Vision: African American Economic Thought*, ed. Boston, 174–93.

148. Delaney, *Learning by Doing: A Projected Educational Philosophy in the Thought of Booker T. Washington*, 112.

Chapter 6. Fundraising, Management, and Industrial Education: Booker T. Washington as a Business Executive and Promoter of the Tuskegee Spirit

1. Besides the faculty, staff, and students, in the early days, Olivia A. Davidson was the other driving force that helped maintain and develop Tuskegee Institute. According to historian Carolyn A. Dorsey, Davidson was the cofounder of Tuskegee Institute. This author, who agrees with Professor Dorsey, heard her express her remarks at the Booker T. Washington Family Reunion held at Tuskegee Institute on June 27, 1998.

2. McPherson, *The Abolitionist Legacy: From Reconstruction to the NAACP*, 158.

3. Washington, *Up From Slavery*, 80.

4. Dorsey, "Despite Poor Health: Olivia Davidson Washington's Story," 69–72.
5. Hine and Thompson, *A Shining Thread of Hope*, 196.
6. Washington, *Up From Slavery*, 83.
7. Washington, *The Story of My Life and Work*, 85–86.
8. Ibid., 116.
9. Washington, *The Story of My Life and Work*, 85; Washington, *Up From Slavery*, 82–83.
10. Washington, *Up From Slavery*, 82–83.
11. Washington, "Chapter 7: The Struggles and Success of the Workers at Tuskegee from 1882 to 1884," in HBTWPV1, 43.
12. Franklin and Moss Jr., *From Slavery to Freedom: A History of African Americans*, 7th ed., 268.
13. Washington, *Up From Slavery*, 112.
14. Ibid., 111–21.
15. Willcox, "Tuskegee's Contribution To National Efficiency," 447; Ford, "Two Theological Students Hear Booker T. Washington," 135.
16. Edwards, *Twenty-Five Years in the Black Belt*, 18–25; Du Bois, *Black Reconstruction in America 1860–1880*, 637–69; Rose, *Rehearsal for Reconstruction: The Port Royal Experiment*, 229–35.
17. "The Principal's Report to the Board of Trustees of Tuskegee Institute," Tuskegee Institute, Tuskegee, Alabama, May 31, 1915, in HBTWPV13, 312–13.
18. Washington, *Up From Slavery*, 114–15.
19. Brown, "Booker T. Washington As A Philosopher," 35.
20. Matthew Anderson to Booker T. Washington, Philadelphia, Pennsylvania, September 17, 1902, in HBTWPV6, 516–22; George Richards Lyman to Booker T. Washington, Pasadena, California, December 27, 1911, in HBTWPV11, 429.
21. Whitfield, "Three Masters of Impression Management: Benjamin Franklin, Booker T. Washington, and Malcolm X as Autobiographers," 416.
22. Holsey, "Public Relations Intuitions of Booker T. Washington," 12; Enck, "Tuskegee Institute and Northern White Philanthropy: A Case Study in Fund Raising, 1900–1915," 338; "Annual Report Edition of the Principal and Treasurer, 1914–15," 13–15; "Annual Report Edition of the Principal and Treasurer, 1915," 15–16; Washington to George Eastman, Tuskegee, Alabama, December 4, 1903, *George Eastman House: International Museum of Photography and film*, Archival Division, Rochester, New York; Washington to George Eastman, Boston, Massachusetts, December 15, 1903, *George Eastman House: International Museum of Photography and film*, Archival Division, Rochester, New York.
23. Washington to Charles Winter Wood, Tuskegee, Alabama, March 13, 1915, in HBTWPV13, 254–55; Greer, "Large Audience Hears Booker T. Washington," 3; Enck, "Tuskegee Institute and Northern White Philanthropy: A Case Study in Fund Raising, 1900–1915," 337–38.
24. Andrew Carnegie to Booker T. Washington, Fernandina, Florida, February 7,

1907, in HBTWPV9, 213–14; Spencer Jr., *Booker T. Washington and the Negro's Place in American Life*, 115–16.

25. Enck, "Tuskegee Institute and Northern White Philanthropy: A Case Study in Fund Raising, 1900–1915," 336.

26. Ibid.

27. "The Principal's Report to the Board of Trustees of Tuskegee Institute," Tuskegee Institute, Tuskegee, Alabama, May 31, 1915, in HBTWPV13, 310–11.

28. Scott and Stowe, *Booker T. Washington: Builder of a Civilization*, 271.

29. Ibid., 250–52.

30. "The Principal's Report to the Board of Trustees of Tuskegee Institute," Tuskegee Institute, Tuskegee, Alabama, May 31, 1915, 307.

31. Stokes, "Tuskegee Institute, the First Fifty Years," 1–99, Tuskegee University Archives; *Seventh Annual Report of the Year Ending May Thirty-First, 1888*, 27; *Eighth Annual Financial Report of the Tuskegee Normal and Industrial Institute for the Year Ending May Thirty-First, 1889*, 19–30; *Fourteenth Annual Financial Report of the Tuskegee Normal and Industrial Institute, Tuskegee, Alabama, for the year Ending May 31, 1895*, 73–90; Washington, "The Relation of the Races in the South," 278; Warren Logan to John H. Washington, Box 2, Folder April-May 1903, WLPTU, 1; "Normal—School Printing Office Orders for All Kinds of Job Printing," *The Southern Letter*, (BTWPLC), Microfilm: Reel no. 425, 4. The following is a list of transactions recorded between Tuskegee Institute representatives (for example, O. Davidson, B. T. Washington, and W. Logan) and Tuskegee Institute patrons in the Tuskegee Probate Court: Book 39, December 23, 1893, 153; Book 41, August 8, 1894, 438; Book 44, August 9, 1895, 443; Book 46, May 24, 1895, 87; Book 44, July 1896, 549; Book 47, February 22, 1896; and Book 62, December 1901, 52.

32. Washington, *Up From Slavery*, 90.

33. Washington, *Working With the Hands*, 200–18.

34. Harlan, *Booker T. Washington: The Making of a Black Leader, 1856-1901*, 272–87.

35. Davis, "Hampton at Tuskegee," 527–28; Hill, *Booker T's Child: The Life and Times of Portia Marshall Washington Pittman*, 14.

36. "A Reminiscence by Frank P. Chisholm," New York City, ca. December 1915, in HBTWPV13, 489.

37. Gardner, "The Educational Contributions of Booker T. Washington," 508–10.

38. Scott and Stowe, *Booker T. Washington: Builder of a Civilization*, 274–79.

39. Washington to Ruth Anna Fisher, Tuskegee, Alabama, November 14, 1906, in HBTWPV9, 125–26.

40. Scott and Stowe, *Booker T. Washington: Builder of a Civilization*, 273–74.

41. Washington, *Up From Slavery*, 157.

42. Porter, *The Rise of Big Business*, 17–20.

43. Washington to Warren Logan, Crawford House, Boston, Massachusetts, December 14, 1901, Box 1, WLPTU; Washington to T. W. Talley, Crawford House, Boston,

Massachusetts, December 14, 1901, Box 1, WLPTU; Washington to Miss Melissa Jones, Crawford House, Boston, Massachusetts, December 16, 1901, Box 1, WLPTU.

44. Scott and Stowe, *Booker T. Washington: Builder of a Civilization*, 276–78.

45. Davis, "Hampton at Tuskegee," 528.

46. W. Logan was employed at Tuskegee Institute in 1882 and E. J. Scott in 1897. Logan was employed at Tuskegee Institute for forty-two years and Scott for twenty-two.

47. Both W. Logan and E. J. Scott were seriously considered as successors to Washington following his death. The job, however, went to an outsider—Robert Russa Moton of Hampton Institute.

48. Washington, *The Story of My Life and Work*, 104.

49. "A Codicil to Washington's Will," Tuskegee, Alabama, June 13, 1911, in HBTWPV11, 212–13.

50. Booker T. Washington to George Washington Carver, Tuskegee, Alabama, June 22, 1898, in HBTWPV4, 435; Washington to Warren Logan, Muskegon, Michigan, December 30, 1901, Box 1, WLPTU, 1.

51. Consult pages 5, 6, & 14 of the *Letter Book: Correspondence of Letters Sent and Received*, Tuskegee University Archives.

52. Washington, "How Students May Contribute Toward the Support of Their School," 48–51.

53. Washington to Warren Logan, Crawford House, Boston, Massachusetts, December 12, 1901, Box 1, WLPTU, 1; Washington to Warren Logan, Hotel Manhattan, New York, New York, April 6, 1903, Box 2, Folder April-May 1903, WLPTU, 1; Washington to Warren Logan, June 1, 1910, Box 66, Folder 385, WLPTU, 1; Washington to Warren Logan, June 13, 1910, Box 66, Folder 385, WLPTU, 1; Washington to Warren Logan, July 7, 1910, WLPTU, 1.

54. "Digest of Mr. D. C. Smith's Report, of November 16th [1908]," (BTWPLC), Microfilm: Reel no. 78, 1–2.

55. Washington to Warren Logan," aboard Congressional Limited, Pennsylvania Railroad, April 1, 1898, in HBTWPV4, 399.

56. Washington to Warren Logan, Hotel Manhattan, New York, New York, April 3, 1904, WLPTU, Box 2, Folder 188, 1; Washington to Warren Logan, Tuskegee, Alabama, June 15, 1910, Box 66, Folder 385, WLPTU, 1.

57. Washington to Warren Logan, Tuskegee Institute, Tuskegee, Alabama, February 13, 1915, in HBTWPV13, 238–39.

58. Washington, "Educational Engineers," 505.

59. Charles W. Hare to Booker T. Washington, March 17, 1902, (BTWPLC), Microfilm: Reel no. 51, 1.

60. "Annual Report Edition of the Principal and Treasurer, 1914–15," 19.

61. "Annual Report Edition of the Principal and Treasurer, 1915," 16.

62. Washington, *Working With the Hands*, 186.

63. Scott and Stowe, *Booker T. Washington: Builder of a Civilization*, 161.

64. "By-Laws, Tuskegee Co-operative Building and Loan Association," Box 1, Folder 1901–1902, JHPCTU, 1–9.

65. "Ten shares of Stock Issued to John H. Palmer," March 1904, Box 1, Folder 1901–1902, JHPCTU.

66. Palmer, "A Building and Loan Association at Tuskegee," 410.

67. Ibid.

68. Ibid.

69. "The Tuskegee Co-operative Building and Loan Association Stockholder's Booklet belong to John H. Palmer," March 1895, Box 1, Folder 1901–1902, JHPCTU.

70. Washington to Warren Logan, Crawford House, Boston, Massachusetts, July 5, 1895, in HBTWPV3, 564.

71. *The Thirteenth Annual Report of the Principal of the Tuskegee Normal and Industrial Institute*, 3–5. Silas C. Dizer and his wife gave the funds for the Dizer Fund.

72. Ibid.

73. Washington to Warren Logan," Tuskegee, Alabama, October 24, 1899, in HBTWPV5, 243–44.

74. Bruce, "Does Tuskegee Educate?" 19.

75. Sisk, "Negro Education in the Alabama Black Belt, 1875–1900," 126–35; Washington, "The Awakening of the Negro," 322–28.

76. Washington, *The Future of the American Negro*, 107; Spencer Jr., *Booker T. Washington and the Negro's Place in American Life*, 79.

77. Quote from Smock's book, *Booker T. Washington in Perspective*, 15.

78. Gill, "Booker T. Washington's Philosophy of Black Education: A Reassessment," 216–17.

79. Bruce, "III, Tuskegee Institute," in *American Education: Its Men Ideas and Institutions: From Servitude to Service*, ed. Cremin, 93–94.

80. Washington, *Up From Slavery*, 71.

81. Bruce, "III, Tuskegee Institute," 90.

82. Stokes, "Tuskegee Institute, the First Fifty Years," 1–99.

83. "The Catalog of Tuskegee Normal School" Tuskegee, Alabama, ca. January 1882, in HBTWPV2, 169–72; Washington, *Working With the Hands*, 84–97.

84. Washington, "A Sunday Evening Talk," (lecture, Tuskegee Institute, Tuskegee, Alabama, April 28, 1895), in HBTWPV3, 548–53; Washington, "A Sunday Evening Talk," (lecture, Tuskegee Institute, Tuskegee, Alabama, December 2, 1905), in HBTWPV8, 456–60.

85. Washington, *Character Building*, table of contents.

86. Ibid., 265.

87. Ibid., 170.

88. Edwards, *Twenty-Five Years in the Black Belt*, 23–24; Campbell, *The Movable School Goes To The Negro Farmer*, 67–68; Reid, "The Story of a Farmer," in *Tuskegee & Its People: Their Ideals and Achievements*, ed. Washington, 165; Scott and Stowe, *Booker T. Washington: Builder of a Civilization*, 224.

89. "Brick-Making As An Industry," (BTWPLC), Microfilm: Reel no. 416, 1.

90. Washington, "An Address Before the National Colored Teachers Associa-

tion," (address, National Colored Teachers Association, St. Louis, Missouri, July 30, 1911), in HBTWPV11, 279–82; "An excerpt from an Article in *The Nautilus:* Why I Made Tuskegee An Industrial School," February 1912, in HBTWPV11, 470–75; Work, "Tuskegee Institute More Than an Educational Institution," 197–205.

91. Anderson, *The Education of Blacks in the South, 1860–1935*, 102–103; Whitfield, "Three Masters of Impression Management: Benjamin Franklin, Booker T. Washington, and Malcolm X as Autobiographers," 416; Spivey, *Schooling for the New Slavery: Black Industrial Education, 1868–1915*, 45–70.

92. Du Bois, "Industrial Education—Will It Solve the Negro Problem," 333–39; Horton, "Industrial Education—Will It Solve the Negro Problem?" 436–39; Anderson, *The Education of Blacks in the South, 1860–1935*, 33–109.

93. Heningburg, "The Relation of Tuskegee Institute to Education in the Lower South," 161.

94. Park, "Tuskegee and Its Mission," 347–54.

95. Palmer, "Former Students of Tuskegee in Business," 124.

96. Washington, *Tuskegee & Its People: Their Ideals and Achievements*, 164–72.

97. Moton, "The Scope and Aim of Tuskegee Institute," 152–54.

98. Washington, *Tuskegee & Its People: Their Ideals and Achievements*, 167–68.

99. Ibid., 285–98.

100. Ibid., 298.

101. "Booker Washington—The Neighbors' View," 781.

Chapter 7. Washington's Broad Economic Influence on African-American Life and History

1. Meier, *Negro Thought in America, 1880–1915*, 42–58.

2. For the context of this chapter, 1900 to 1972 defines the period in which we will consider Washington's influence on the extensive promotion of twentieth-century African-American business development.

3. Cruse, *The Crisis of the Negro Intellectual*, 19–21, 330, 426, & 558; Cruse, *Rebellion or Revolution?*, 164–66; Cruse, *Plural But Equal: A Critical Study of Blacks and Minorities and America's Plural Society*, 305 & 309.

4. Cruse, *Rebellion or Revolution?*, 165.

5. Ibid.

6. Ibid.

7. Any quality study involving African-American urban history from 1900 to about 1972 that covers the business community will substantiate this point.

8. Payton Jr., "Afro-American Realty Company," 682–91; Dailey, "Booker T. Washington and the Afro-American Realty Company," 184–201.

9. Osofsky, *Harlem: The Making of a Ghetto: Negro New York, 1890–1930*, 94.

10. Washington, *The Negro in Business*, 153.

11. "Growth of the Afro-American Realty Company," 102–18.

12. Ibid., 116.

13. Fordham, "The Buffalo Cooperative Economic Society, Inc., 1928-1961: A Black Self-help Organization," 42.

14. Ibid.

15. Ibid., 41-49.

16. Lamon, *Black Tennesseans 1900-1930*, 4-5, 168-69, & 176-78.

17. Napier, "Mr. Napier's Address," (speech, Kansas City, Missouri, August 16, 1916) National Negro Business League, *Report of the Seventeenth Annual Session Held at Kansas City, Missouri, August 16-18, 1916*; *Record of the National Negro Business League: Part I, Annual Conference Proceedings and Organizational Records, 1900-1919* (New York: Schomburg Center for Research), Microfilm: Reel no. 3, 73-75.

18. J. C. Napier was also a lawyer, and he served as the register of the U.S. Treasury.

19. Lamon, *Black Tennesseans 1900-1930*, 176.

20. James Carrol Napier to Booker T. Washington, Washington, D.C., April 1, 1913, in HBTWPV12, 153-54.

21. Lamon, *Black Tennesseans 1900-1930*, 176.

22. Clark, "James Carroll Napier: National Negro Leader," 246.

23. Washington to James Carroll Napier, Tuskegee, Alabama, July 7, 1903, in HBTWPV7, 199-200.

24. James Carroll Napier to Booker T. Washington, Nashville, Tennessee, July 21, 1903, in HBTWPV7, 216-17.

25. Washington, *The Negro in Business*, page following the forward page, which is titled "Past Presidents."

26. John and James Knox—brothers that graduated from Tuskegee Institute and implemented Washington's business philosophy—established an undertaking business in Mobile, Alabama, and published a local newspaper, *The Mobile Weekly Advocate*. See *The Afro-American* 22: 7; Other evidence can be found in: Spear, *Black Chicago: The Making of a Negro Ghetto 1890-1920*, 71-84; Barr, *Black Texans: A History of Negroes in Texas 1528-1971*, 153; Gerber, *Black Ohio and the Color Line 1860-1915*, 379-80; Kusmer, *A Ghetto Takes Shape: Black Cleveland, 1870-1930*, 140-43; Watkins, "Voices Beyond the Dark Tower: Expanding the Boundaries of the Inquiry into the Harlem Renaissance," (unpublished paper presented at the Monroe Fordham Conference at Buffalo State College, October 23, 1999), 10-11 (these pages cover Washington's economic influence on the African-American community of Oakland, California); Moore, *Leading the Race: The Transformation of the Black Elite in the Nation's Capital, 1880-1920*, 135-36.

27. Bussel, "'The Most Indispensable Man in His Community': African-American Entrepreneurs in West Chester, Pennsylvania, 1865-1925," 344-45.

28. Drake and Cayton, *Black Metropolis: A Study of Negro Life in a Northern City*, 430-69; "A Man and His Products," 48.

29. Marable, *How Capitalism Underdeveloped Black America*, 146-47; Myrdal, *An American Dilemma: The Negro Problem and Modern Democracy*, 304-305.

30. "A. G. Gaston," 32.

31. Jenkins and Hines, *Black Titan: A. G. Gaston and the Making of a Black Millionaire*, 35–37.

32. Ibid., 35.

33. Ibid., 41.

34. Ibid., 70–72.

35. Dr. Martin Luther King Jr. and other members of the Southern Christian Leadership Conference stayed at the Gaston Motel during the 1963 Birmingham civil rights campaign. The hotel was bombed at the end of the campaign.

36. Gaston, "Investment in Life," in *Many Shades of Black*, eds. Wormley and Fenderson, 185–91.

37. Ingham and Feldman, *African-American Business Leaders: A Biographical Dictionary*, 259.

38. Gaston died in 1996.

39. Ingham and Feldman, *African-American Business Leaders: A Biographical Dictionary*, 268.

40. "How Herman Russell Built His Business . . . Brick By Brick," 178.

41. Ibid., 182.

42. Johnson, *Succeeding Against the Odds*, 243.

43. *Jet* magazine, Supreme Beauty Products, Johnson Publishing Company, the Ebony Fashion Show, etc.

44. Ingham and Feldman, *African-American Business Leaders: A Biographical Dictionary*, 376.

45. Johnson, *Succeeding Against the Odds*, 91.

46. Ibid., 68–69.

47. Ibid., 299–300.

48. "The National Business League After 70 Years of More Downs Than Ups, NBL Looks for a Turning Point," 37–38 & 41; Dreyfus, "Rowboating in the Economic Mainstream: The NBL Keeps Moving Despite Rough Waters," 43–45.

49. "Business Campaign Launched By League," 1; "Leader Among Business Men," 7; "Race Merchants Form Business Association," 1; "New Women's Store Opens in Fifth Ward is Beautiful Place," 4; "Negro Capitalists Gather in Atlanta," *Amsterdam News*, 6; Berry Gordy's mother named their family store after Booker T. Washington. Berry Gordy is known for founding Motown Records. Consult his autobiography, *To Be Loved: The Music, The Magic, The Memories of Motown: An Autobiography*, 23.

50. Daniel, *Women Builders*, 28–52.

51. "Maggie L. Walker (1867–1934), Entrepreneur, Feminist, Civil Rights Activist, Newspaper Fonder, Lecturer," 1,190.

52. Brown, "Womanist Consciousness: Maggie Lena Walker and the Independent Order of Saint Luke," in *Black Women in America: Social Science Perspective*, eds. Malson, Mudimbe-Boyi, O'Barr, and Wyer, 173–96.

53. "Profiles," 214.

54. Darney, "Maggie L. Walker: A Tribute To A Friend," 216.

55. Ingham and Feldman, *African-American Business Leaders: A Biographical Dictionary*, 673.

56. White, "I Remember Maggie Walker," 56.

57. "A Distinguished Business Woman," 304–305; Simmons, "Maggie Lena Walker and The Consolidated Bank and Trust Company," 345–49. Mrs. Walker was the first African-American woman in the United States to form and head a bank.

58. Washington, "The Negro in Business," 345; Washington, "Negro Disfranchisement and the Negro in Business," 314; "Notes on Racial Progress," Box 60, Folder 356 (January of 1910), BTWCTU.

59. Park, "Advance Report for the National Negro Business League," Box 33, Folder 230 (August 29, 1906), BTWCTU; Bruce, "The New York Meeting of the National Negro Business League," 31–32; Work, "The Negro in Business Enterprise," 306.

60. Washington, *The Negro in Business*, 95; Washington, *The Story of the Negro: The Rise of the Race from Slavery*, 219.

61. Maggie L. Walker to Booker T. Washington, Richmond, Virginia, November 17, 1908, Box 1, ALHCTU.

62. Ingham and Feldman, *African-American Business Leaders: A Biographical Dictionary*, 679; Interview with Ms. Celia Suggs, of the Maggie Lena Walker National Historic Site, 4–22–00.

63. Marlowe, *A Right Worthy Grand Mission: Maggie Lena Walker and the Quest for Black Economic Empowerment*, 111, 124–125, 138, 157.

64. Ms. Celia Suggs (historian, Maggie Lena Walker National Historic Site), in discussion with the author, April 22, 2000.

65. Marlowe, *A Right Worthy Grand Mission: Maggie Lena Walker and the Quest for Black Economic Empowerment*, 124–25.

66. "Business Men Reorganize," 7.

67. Schweninger, *Black Property Owners in the South 1790–1915*, 173.

68. Jacques-Garvey, ed., *Philosophy and Opinions of Marcus Garvey*, 126.

69. Marcus Garvey to Booker T. Washington, Kingston, Jamaica, W.I., September 8, 1914, Hill and Rudisell, eds., *The Marcus Garvey and Universal Negro Improvement Association Papers: Volume I, 1826-August 1919*, 66–67; "Enclosure," Kingston, Jamaica, W.I., September 8, 1914, Hill and Rudisell, eds., *The Marcus Garvey and Universal Negro Improvement Association Papers: Volume I, 1826-August 1919*, 68–69; "To Marcus Mosiah Garvey," Tuskegee, Alabama, September 17, 1914, in HBTWPV13, 133–34; "To Marcus Mosiah Garvey," Tuskegee, Alabama, April 27, 1915, in HBTWPV13, 284.

70. "Newspaper Report: Improvement Association Proposal to Establish Industrial Farm in Jamaica," *Daily Chronicle*, August 3, 1915, in *The Marcus Garvey and Universal Negro Improvement Association Papers: Volume I, 1826-August 1919*, eds. Hill and Rudisell, 128; Jacques-Garvey, *Garvey & Garveyism*, 13.

71. "Improvement Association Proposal To Establish Industrial Farm In Jamaica," Daily Chronicle, August 3, 1915, in *The Marcus Garvey and Universal Negro Improvement Association Papers: Volume I, 1826-August 1919*, eds. Hill and Rudisell, 128

72. Washington to Marcus Mosiah Garvey, Tuskegee, Alabama, September 17, 1914, in HBTWPV13, 133–34; Washington to Marcus Mosiah Garvey, Tuskegee, Alabama, October 2, 1915, in HBTWPV13, 376.

73. Jacques-Garvey, *Garvey & Garveyism*, 130–31.

74. Essien-Udom and Jacques-Garvey, eds., *More Philosophy and Opinions of Marcus Garvey: Volume 3*, 20–27; Hill and Bair, eds., *Marcus Garvey: Life and Lessons*, 252–59.

75. Jacques-Garvey, ed., *Philosophy and Opinions of Marcus Garvey*, 48.

76. Essien-Udom and Garvey, eds., *More Philosophy and Opinions of Marcus Garvey: Volume 3*, 101–13; Hill and Bair, eds., *Marcus Garvey: Life and Lessons*, 233–39.

77. Martin, *Race First: The Ideological and Organizational Struggles of Marcus Garvey and the Universal Negro Improvement Association*, 33.

78. According to Garvey, "Outside of Booker Washington and Frederick Douglass, there [was] not another aristocratic Negro in America. Douglass and Washington [were] the only two Negroes in this country who went out and did service so as to make themselves singular among the Negroes of America. It was not a matter of money that made these two men big Negroes. It was nobility of soul, of spirit, to do service to suffering humanity, and that made them different from the rest of the people. That made them aristocrats among their own." See Marcus Garvey, "Address to UNIA Supporters in Philadelphia, October 21, 1919," (address, UNIA, Philadelphia, Pennsylvania, October 21, 1919), in *African American Political Thought 1890–1930: Washington, Du Bois, Garvey, and Randolph*, 207, edited by Wintz. Moreover, besides naming one of the Black Star Steamship Line's ships after Booker T. Washington, another was named after Frederick Douglass.

79. Marcus Garvey to Booker T. Washington, Kingston, Jamaica, W.I., September 8, 1914, in *The Marcus Garvey and Universal Negro Improvement Association Papers: Volume I, 1826-August 1919*, eds. Hill and Rudisell, 67.

80. "Garveyism" refers to the school of thought that encompasses the economic, political, and social thoughts of Marcus Garvey.

81. Gardell, *In The Name of Elijah Muhammad: Louis Farrakhan and the Nation of Islam*, 49–50.

82. Lincoln, *The Black Muslims in America*, 94; Clegg III, *An Original Man: The Life and Times of Elijah Muhammad*, 41 & 70.

83. Essien-Udom, *Black Nationalism: A Search for an Identity in America*, 60 & 63.

84. Muhammad, *The Supreme Wisdom*, 49.

85. Cruse, *Rebellion or Revolution?*, 211.

86. Muhammad, *Message To The Blackman in America*, 192–205.

87. Tyler, "The Protestant Ethic Among The Black Muslims," *Phylon* 27: 5–14.

88. Malcolm X, *The Autobiography of Malcolm X*, 275.

89. Farrakhan, *A Torchlight for America*, 83–87.

90. Work, "Inter-Racial Cooperation," 310–15; Fisher, "National Negro Business League," 342–46; Johnson, "The Social Philosophy of Booker T. Washington," 115; Jones, "Booker T. Washington: Apostle of Self-Determination and Cooperation," 136;

Rhetta, "Correspondence," 344; Simmons, "Washington Remains Without a Peer," 2, Magazine Section, 18–20; Upson, "A Great Negro Conservative: What Would Booker T. Washington Say Now?" 2; Wilson, *Blueprint for Black Power: A Moral, Political and Economic Imperative for the Twenty-First Century*, 510; Yette, "Booker T. Washington: His Wise Words Still Apply," 114, 2-A; "Master Mind: Builder of Civilization," 10; Larsha, "Silence Covers the Plan of the Man," 5-A; "Washington and Du Bois Reconsidered," A-2; Wright, "The Importance of Booker T. Washington to Black Conservatism," 4; Conley, "Opinions: Pleasing 'The Wizard,'" A-3; Kendrick, "To Tell The Truth: Were These Two Men So Different?" A-7; "The Great Divide," 70–72; Mtima, "African-American Economic Empowerment Strategies for the New Millennium-Revisiting the Washington-Du Bois Dialectic," 403.

    91. Williams, "Booker T. Washington: An Appreciation," 34–42.

    92. Ibid., 34.

    93. Ibid.

    94. Ibid., 36.

    95. Jerkins, "Apostle of Industrial Education," 143.

    96. Stone, "Drop Your Bucket Where You Are," 6.

    97. Ibid.

    98. Ibid.

    99. Brock, "Cast Down Your Buckets Where You Are," 23.

    100. Butler, "Why Booker T. Washington Was Right," in *A Different Vision: African American Economic Thought*, ed. Boston, 190.

    101. Carroll, ed., *Uncle Tom or New Negro? African Americans Reflect on Booker T. Washington and Up From Slavery One Hundred Years Later*, 113–14. I would argue that the themes Hutchinson discussed did not begin with Washington, but they were institutionalized and popularized best by him, particularly those concerning African-American business development. However, Hutchinson makes crucial points.

Conclusion

    1. For example, bricklaying, carpentry, and tailoring.

Bibliography

Primary Sources (Collections)

Albon L. Holsey Collection, Tuskegee University Archives.
Booker T. Washington Collection, Tuskegee University Archives.
Booker T. Washington Collection, Schomburg Research Center, New York Public Library.
Booker T. Washington Papers, Manuscript Division, Library of Congress, Washington, D.C.
Booker T. Washington Collection, George Eastman House: International Museum of Photography and Film, Rochester, New York.
John H. Palmer Collection, Tuskegee University Archives.
National Negro Business League Collection, Tuskegee University Archives.
Robert Russa Moton Papers, Tuskegee University Archives.
Warren N. Logan Papers, Tuskegee University Archives.

Primary Sources (Interviews)

Nash, Jessie Jr. Interview by author. March 28, 1995. Canisus College.
Suggs, Celia. Phone interview by author. April 22, 2000. Maggie Lena Walker National Historic Site.
Wilson, Cynthia. Interview by author. December 3, 1997. Tuskegee University, Tuskegee, Alabama.

Primary Sources (Letters)

Baldwin, William, Jr., to Booker T. Washington, January 21, 1898, New York. *The Booker T. Washington Papers*, Washington, D.C.: The Library of Congress Microfilms: Reel no. 392.
Baldwin, William, Jr., to Daniel C. Smith, April 7, 1898, New York. *The Booker T. Washington Papers*, Washington, D.C.: The Library of Congress Microfilms: Reel no. 392.

Baldwin, William, Jr., to Booker T. Washington, September 27, 1898, New York. *The Booker T. Washington Papers*, Washington, D.C.: The Library of Congress Microfilms: Reel no. 392.

Baldwin, William, Jr., to Booker T. Washington, October 11, 1898, New York. *The Booker T. Washington Papers*, Washington, D.C.: The Library of Congress Microfilms: Reel no. 392.

Baldwin, William, Jr., to Booker T. Washington, January 21, 1899, New York. *The Booker T. Washington Papers*, Washington, D.C.: The Library of Congress Microfilms: Reel no. 392.

Baldwin, William, Jr., to William P. Bancroft, March 6, 1899, New York. *The Booker T. Washington Papers*, Washington, D.C.: The Library of Congress Microfilms: Reel no. 23.

Baldwin, William, Jr., to Booker T. Washington, January 26, 1900, New York. *The Booker T. Washington Papers*, Washington, D.C.: The Library of Congress Microfilms: Reel no. 392.

Baldwin, William, Jr., to Booker T. Washington, March 7, 1904, New York. *The Booker T. Washington Papers*, Washington, D.C.: The Library of Congress Microfilms: Reel no. 23.

Baldwin, William, Jr., to Booker T. Washington, May 16, 1904, New York. *The Booker T. Washington Papers*, Washington, D.C.: The Library of Congress Microfilms: Reel no. 23.

Groves, Junis G., to Emmett J. Scott, September 15, 1914, Edwardsville, Kansas. *The Booker T. Washington Papers*, Washington, D.C.: The Library of Congress Microfilms: Reel no. 755.

Hare, Charles W., to Booker T. Washington, March 17, 1902, *The Booker T. Washington Papers*, Washington, D.C.: The Library of Congress Microfilms: Reel no. 51.

Huntington, Collis Potter, to Booker T. Washington, November 14, 1898, New York. *The Booker T. Washington Papers*, Washington, D.C.: The Library of Congress Microfilms: Reel no. 52.

Huntington, Collis Potter, to Booker T. Washington, December 28, 1898, New York. *The Booker T. Washington Papers*, Washington, D.C.: The Library of Congress Microfilms: Reel no. 52.

Peabody, George Foster to Booker T. Washington, September 7, 1906, Abenia, New York. *The Booker T. Washington Papers*, Washington, D.C.: The Library of Congress Microfilms: Reel no. 67.

Rhetta, Barnett M. "Correspondence." *Opportunity* 14, no. 11 (November 1936): 344.

Smith, Daniel C., to Booker T. Washington, July 10, 1898, Brooklyn, New York. *The Booker T. Washington Papers*, Washington, D.C.: The Library of Congress Microfilms: Reel no. 392.

Washington, Booker T., to Henry Davis, March 13, 1901, Tuskegee, Alabama. *The Booker T. Washington Papers*, Washington, D.C.: The Library of Congress Microfilms: Reel no. 752.

Washington, Booker T., to William Baldwin Jr., March 7, 1904, New York. *The Booker*

T. Washington Papers, Washington, D.C.: The Library of Congress Microfilms: Reel no. 23.

Washington, Booker T., to George Foster Peabody, July 3, 1905, Tuskegee, Alabama. *The Booker T. Washington Papers*, Washington, D.C.: The Library of Congress Microfilms: Reel no. 67.

Washington, Booker T., to George Foster Peabody, October 13, 1906, New York. *The Booker T. Washington Papers*, Washington, D.C.: The Library of Congress Microfilms: Reel no. 67.

Primary Sources (Probate Court Records)

The following is a list of transactions recorded between Tuskegee Institute representatives (for example, O. Davidson, B. T. Washington, and W. Logan) and Tuskegee Institute patrons in the Tuskegee Probate Court:

(1) Book 39, December 23, 1893, p. 153.
(2) Book 41, August 8, 1894, p. 438.
(3) Book 44, August 9, 1895, p. 443.
(4) Book 46, May 24, 1895, p. 87.
(5) Book 44, July 1896, p. 549.
(6) Book 47, February 22, 1896, p. 479.
(7) Book 62, December 1901, p. 52.

Primary Sources (Annual Reports, Books, Journal Articles, Newspapers, Notes, Reports, Speeches, etc.)

"A Distinguished Business Woman." *Voice of the Negro* 2 (1905): 304–305.

"A Few Successful Business Colored Men." *New York Freeman* (March 28, 1885). University of Buffalo Microfilms: Reel 1: 2.

"A Letter Written by a Negro Causes a Commotion." *Montgomery Adviser* 4 (August 1888), 24, no. 13: 1.

"A Lynching Carnival Expected and the Victim to be a Negro." *Montgomery Adviser* 13 (July 1888), 23, no. 321: 1.

"A Negro Moved to Montgomery for Safe Keeping." *Montgomery Adviser* 12 (July 1888), 23, no. 320: 2.

"A Northern Lynching." *Outlook* 95 (July 1910): 597–98.

"A Successful Business Man." *New York Freedman* (February 20, 1886). University of Buffalo Microfilms: Reel 1: 1.

Abbott, Lyman. *Silhouettes of My Contemporaries*. New York: Doubleday, Page & Company, 1921.

Aery, William Anthony. "The Negro in Business: Stories of Success." *Southern Workman* 43 (October 1913): 522–27.

———. "Successful Business Men of the Negro Race." *Southern Workman* 41 (November 1912): 604–606.

———. "Tuskegee Conference Now Helps The Nation." *Norfolk Journal and Guide* 18 (February 1922), 22, no. 7: 8.

———. "The Tuskegee Conference of 1913." *Southern Workman* 42 (March 1913): 177–79.

———. "The Twentieth Tuskegee Conference." *Southern Workman* 40 (February 1911): 73–78.

Alexander, Charles. "National Negro Business League." *Alexander's Magazine* 1 (September 1905): 24–29.

"Annual Catalog Edition, 1914–15." The *Tuskegee Institute Bulletin* (1915).

"Annual Report Edition of the Principal and Treasurer, 1915." The *Tuskegee Institute Bulletin* 9, no. 1 (January–March 1915).

"Annual Report Edition of the Principal and Treasurer, 1914–15." The *Tuskegee Institute Bulletin* 9, no. 3 (October-December 1914–1915).

Annual Report of the Fifteenth Annual Convention [of the] National Negro Business League, Held at Muskogee, Oklahoma, August 19–21, 1914. The Booker T. Washington Papers, Washington, D.C.: The Library of Congress Microfilms: Reel no. 754.

Aptheker, Herbert, ed. *A Documentary History of The Negro People in the United States, 1910–1932.* Secaucus, New Jersey: The Citadel Press, 1973.

———, ed. *Against Racism: Unpublished Essays, Papers, Addresses, 1887–1961 of W.E.B. Du Bois.* Amherst: Massachusetts Press, 1985.

Armstrong, Samuel C. *Education for Life.* Hampton, Virginia: Hampton Normal & Agricultural Institute Press, 1914.

"At Home and Afield: Death of Booker T. Washington." *Southern Workman* 44 (December 1915): 691–92.

Baker, Ray Stannard. *Following the Color Line.* New York: Harper Torchbooks, 1964.

Baldwin, William H. Jr. "Extracts from Address of Mr. Wm. H. Baldwin, Jr., at a Meeting in the Interest of Tuskegee Institute at Madison Square Garden Concert Hall." Speech to Tuskegee Institute Donors, New York, New York, 4 December 1889. *The Booker T. Washington Papers*, Washington, D.C.: The Library of Congress Microfilms: Reel no. 392.

Banks, Charles. "Mississippi Negro Business League Annual Announcement." Speech to the National Negro Business League, Mound Bayou, Mississippi, 22 May 1908. *The Booker T. Washington Papers*, Washington, D.C.: The Library of Congress Microfilms: Reel no. 24: 1.

———. "Mississippi Negroes and their Progress." 1907, Mound Bayou, Mississippi. *The Booker T. Washington Papers*, Washington, D.C.: The Library of Congress Microfilms: Reel no. 23: 1–3.

Banks, Frank D. "The Tuskegee Conferences." *Southern Workman* 32 (April 1903): 246–47.

Blassingame, John W., and John R. McKivigan, eds. *The Frederick Douglass Papers: Series One, Speeches, Debates, and Interviews, Volume 5, 1881–95.* New Haven, Connecticut: Yale University Press, 1992.

Blayton, J. B. "Are Negroes Now in Business, Business Men?" *Journal of Negro History* 18 (1933): 56–65.

———. "The Negro in Banking." *Bankers Magazine* 133 (December 1936): 511–14.

"Booker T. Washington." *World's Work* 31 (January 1916): 250–51.

"Booker T. Washington On Negro Education." *NEA Bulletin* 13 (November 1924): 310.

"Booker T. Washington—The Neighbors' View." *Outlook* 111 (December 1, 1915): 781–83.

"Booking." *Southern Workman* 3 (March 1874). Cornell University Microfilms 3,631: 18.

"Boston's Business Basis: What the Colored Competitor Must Offer." The *New York Age* (November 19, 1887). University of Buffalo Microfilms: Reel no. 1: 4.

Bowen, J.W.E. "Doing Things at the Tuskegee Institute." *Voice of the Negro* 2 (1905): 249–53.

"Brick-Making as an Industry." *The Booker T. Washington Papers*, Washington, D.C.: The Library of Congress Microfilms: Reel no. 416: 1.

Brown, E. C. "I Am Making Money For Others." *Alexander's Magazine* 1 (December 1905): 57.

Bruce, John E. "The Necessity for Business Leagues." *Voice of the Negro* 1 (1904): 338–39.

Bruce, Roscoe Conklin. "Does Tuskegee Educate? The *Colored American Magazine* 8 (January 1905): 17–21.

———. "The New York Meeting of the National Negro Business League." *Alexander's Magazine* 1 (September 1905): 30–32.

———. "Tuskegee and Its Mission: A Review of the Events of the Twenty-Fifth Anniversary Celebration of Mr. Washington's School." The *Colored American Magazine* 10 (May 1906): 347–54.

Burrell, W. P. "History of the Business of Colored Richmond." *Voice of the Negro* 1 (1904): 316–22.

"Business Campaign Launched By League." The *Chicago Defender* 6 (February 1915), 10, no. 6: 1.

"Business Men Reorganize: Local League In Richmond, Va., Takes on New Life." The *Afro-American* (March 28, 1914), 22, no. 30: 7.

"Buying Land." *Southern Workman* 3 (August 1874). Cornell University Microfilms 3,631: 58.

Caffey, Francis G. "Suffrage Limitations at the South." *Political Science Quarterly* 20 (1905): 53–67.

Campbell, Thomas Monroe. *The Movable School Goes to the Negro Farmer*. Tuskegee, Alabama: Tuskegee Institute Press, 1992.

Carnegie, Andrew. *The Gospel of Wealth*. Cambridge: Harvard University Press, 1962.

Carter, William H. "The Accountant as a Factor in Business." *Southern Workman* 36 (November 1907): 619–24.

Carver, George Washington. "Helps for the Hard Times." The *Negro Farmer* 2 (February 27, 1915): 1.
———. "How the Farmer Can Save His Sweet Potatoes: And Ways of Preparing Them for the Table." Bulletin no. 38 (November 1936). Tuskegee, Alabama: Tuskegee Institute Press, 1937.
———. "How to Grow the Peanut and 105 Ways of Preparing it for Human Consumption." Bulletin no. 31 (June 1925). Tuskegee, Alabama: Tuskegee Institute Press, 1983.
———. "How to Grow the Tomato and 115 Ways to Prepare it for the Table." Bulletin no. 36 (April 1918). Tuskegee, Alabama: Tuskegee Institute Press, 1936.
"Charles Banks and the Bank of Mound Bayou." The *Colored American Magazine* 10 (June 1906): 419–22.
"Charles Banks No Quitter." The *Negro Farmer* 2 (January 30, 1915): 7.
Clement, Richardson. "What are Negroes Doing in Durham?" *Southern Workman* 42 (July 1913): 385.
Crawford, R. J. "Business Negroes of Chattanooga." *Voices of the Negro* 1 (1904): 534–37.
Cremin, Lawrence A., ed. *American Education: Its Men Ideas and Institutions: From Servitude to Service*. New York: Arno Press & the *New York Times*, 1969.
Darney, Wendell P. "Maggie L. Walker: A Tribute To A Friend." *Opportunity* 13 (July 1935): 216 & 221.
Davis, J. E. "Hampton at Tuskegee." *Southern Workman* 44 (October 1915): 529–37.
———. "Tuskegee Institute and Its Conferences." *Southern Workman* 43 (March 1914): 157–67.
Decosta-Willis, Miriam, ed. *The Memphis Diary of Ida B. Wells: An Intimate Portrait of the Activist as a Young Woman*. Boston: Beacon Press, 1995.
Denison, John H. "Samuel Chapman Armstrong." The *Atlantic Monthly* 73 (January 1894): 90–98.
"Digest of Mr. D. C. Smith's Report, of November 16 [1908]." *The Booker T. Washington Papers*, Washington, D.C.: The Library of Congress Microfilms: Reel no. 78: 1–2.
"Disfranchising the Negro." The *Nation* 69 (July-December 1889): 384–85.
Dodd, Donald B., and Wynelle S. Dodd. *Historical Statistics of the South 1790–1970*. Tuscaloosa, Alabama: University of Alabama Press, 1973.
Dodson, N. Barnett. "Fine Prospects For Business: Tour of Ralph W. Tyler Starts Big Revival." The *Afro-American* 29 (November 1913), 22, no. 14: 2.
"Does the Negro Prefer to Patronize the White?" *Colored American Magazine* 13 (November 1907): 328.
"Don't Put Off Work Today for Tomorrow." *Southern Workman* 2 (March 1873). Cornell University Microfilms 3,631: 2.
Du Bois, W.E.B. *Atlanta University Publications, nos. 1–6, 1896–1901*. New York: Octagon Books, Inc., 1968.
———. *The Atlanta University Publications: nos. 1, 2, 4, 8, 9, 11, 13, 14, 15, 16, 17, 18*. New York: Arno Press and the *New York Times*, 1968.

———. *The Autobiography of W.E.B. Du Bois: A Soliloquy on Viewing My Life from the Last Decade of Its First Century*. New York: International Publishers Company, Inc., 1968.

———. "The Burden." *Crisis* 1 (March 1911): 28-29.

———. "The Business League." *Crisis* 4 (October 1912): 285.

———. *Dusk of Dawn: An Essay Toward an Autobiography of a Race Concept*. New Brunswick, New Jersey: Transaction Publishers, 1992.

———. *The Education of Black People: Ten Critiques, 1906-1960*. Edited by Herbert Aptheker. New York: Monthly Review Press, 1973.

———. "The Growth of the Niagara Movement." *Voice of the Negro* 3 (1906): 42-45.

———. "Industrial Education—Will It Solve the Negro Problem?" *The Colored American Magazine* 7 (May 1904): 333-39.

———. *The Philadelphia Negro: A Social Study*. New York: Schocken Books, Inc., 1970.

———. *The Souls of Black Folk*. New York: Bantam Books, 1989.

Durham, John Stephens. "The Labor Unions and the Negro." *The Atlantic Monthly* 81 (January 1889): 222-31.

Dyke, Charles Bartlett. "The Tuskegee Negro Conference." *Southern Workman* 29 (April 1900): 232-34.

Edwards, Harry Stillwell. "The Negro and the South." *The Colored American Magazine* 11 (July 1906): 51-55.

Edwards, Thomas J. "Classes of Negro Farmers in Macon County, Alabama: Fifth Paper, Landowners." *Southern Workman* 40 (December 1911): 672-75.

———. "Classes of Negro Farmers in Macon County, Alabama: First Paper, Wage-Earners." *Southern Workman* 40 (August 1911): 459-62.

———. "Classes of Negro Farmers in Macon County, Alabama: Second Paper, Share-Croppers." *Southern Workman* 40 (September 1911): 533-36.

———. "Classes of Negro Farmers in Macon County, Alabama: Third Paper, Landowners." *Southern Workman* 40 (November 1911): 635-38.

———. "Classes of Negro Farmers in Macon County, Alabama: Third Paper, Renters." *Southern Workman* 40 (October 1911): 559-61.

Edwards, William J. *Twenty-Five Years in the Black Belt*. Tuscaloosa, Alabama: University of Alabama Press, 1993.

Eighth Annual Financial Report of the Tuskegee Normal and Industrial Institute for the Year Ending May Thirty-First, 1889. Tuskegee, Alabama: Normal School Press, 1889.

Ellavich, Marie, and Kenneth Estell, *African American History in the Press: Volume II: 1870-1899*. Detroit, Michigan: Gale Research Inc., 1996.

Emerson, J. S. "A Reminiscence of General Armstrong." *Outlook* 48 (1893). University of Buffalo Microfilms: Reel no. 386: 710-11.

Essien-Udom, E. U., and Amy Jacques-Garvey, eds. *More Philosophy and Opinions of Marcus Garvey: Volume 3*. Totowa, New Jersey: Frank Cass and Company, 1977.

"Farmers' Conference at Lane College." *The Negro Farmer* 1 (March 28, 1914): 5.

Farrakhan, Louis. *A Torchlight for America*. Chicago: FCN Publishing Company, 1993.

Fisher, Isaac. "National Negro Business League." *Southern Workman* LXVII (November 1938): 342-46.

Foote, William H. "Character Sketch of Booker T. Washington." The *Colored American Magazine* 8 (December 1904): 706-13.

"Forced Labor in America." *Outlook* 90 (December 19, 1908): 846-48.

Ford, E. C. "Two Theological Students Hear Booker T. Washington." *Negro History Bulletin* 17 (March 1954): 135.

Fortune, T. Thomas. "What Does the White South Expect of the Black South?" The *Colored American Magazine* 11 (December 1906): 393-397.

Fourteenth Annual Financial Report of the Tuskegee Normal and Industrial Institute, Tuskegee, Alabama, for the year Ending May 31, 1895. Tuskegee, Alabama: Press of the Normal Industrial School, 1895.

Franklin, John Hope. "Booker T. Washington, Revisited." The *New York Times* (August 1, 1991), 140: A21 (L).

Frissell, H. B. "Rural Segregation." *Southern Workman* 44 (March 1915): 137-38.

"Gallery of Proof: Tuskegee Negro Conference." *The Booker T. Washington Papers*, Washington, D.C.: The Library of Congress Microfilms: Reel no. 755: 1.

Ginzburg, Ralph. *100 Years of Lynchings*. Baltimore, Maryland: Black Classic Press, 1988.

Gordy, Berry Jr. *To Be Loved: The Music, The Magic, The Memories of Motown: An Autobiography*. New York: Warner Books, Inc., 1994.

"Gospel of Co-Operation." *New York Freedman* (February 13, 1886). University of Buffalo Microfilms: Reel 1: 1.

"Growth of Negro Business." *Literary Digest* 83 (October 25, 1924): 62.

"Growth of the Afro-American Realty Company." *The Colored American Magazine* 10 (February 1906): 102-18.

Hamilton, Kenneth. "Introduction and Overview to the National Negro Business League Papers in the Library of Congress." Library of Congress, Washington, D.C.

Hamilton, Virginia, ed. *"The Talented Tenth," The Writings of W.E.B. Du Bois*. New York: Thomas Y. Crowell Company, 1975.

Harlan, Louis. "Twenty Years with Booker T." November 29, 1984. Tuskegee University Archives.

Harlan, Louis and John W. Blassingame, eds. *The Booker T. Washington Papers: Volume 1: The Autobiographical Writings*. Urbana: University of Illinois Press, 1972.

Harlan, Louis, Pete Daniel, Stuart B. Kaufman, Raymond W. Smock, and William M. Welty, eds. *The Booker T. Washington Papers: Volume 2, 1860-89*. Urbana: University of Illinois Press, 1972.

Harlan, Louis, Stuart B. Kaufman, Barbara S. Kraft, and Raymond W. Smock, eds. *The*

Booker T. Washington Papers: Volume 4, 1895-98. Urbana: University of Illinois Press, 1975.

Harlan, Louis, Stuart B. Kaufman, and Raymond W. Smock, eds. *The Booker T. Washington Papers: Volume 3, 1889-95.* Urbana: University of Illinois Press, 1974.

Harlan, Louis, and Raymond W. Smock. *The Booker T. Washington Papers: Volume 7, 1903-4.* Urbana: University of Illinois Press, 1977.

Harlan, Louis, and Raymond W. Smock, eds. *The Booker T. Washington Papers: Volume 12, 1912-14.* Urbana: University of Illinois Press, 1982.

Harlan, Louis, Raymond W. Smock, Sadie M. Harlan, and Susan Valenza. *The Booker T. Washington Papers: Volume 14: Cumulative Index.* Urbana: University of Illinois Press, 1989.

Harlan, Louis, Raymond W. Smock, and Barbara S. Kraft, eds. *The Booker T. Washington Papers: Volume 5, 1899-1900.* Urbana: University of Illinois Press, 1976.

Harlan, Louis, Raymond W. Smock, and Barbara S. Kraft, eds. *The Booker T. Washington Papers: Volume 6, 1901-2.* Urbana: University of Illinois Press, 1977.

Harlan, Louis, Raymond W. Smock, and Geraldine McTigue, eds. *The Booker T. Washington Papers: Volume 8, 1904-6.* Urbana: University of Illinois Press, 1979.

Harlan, Louis, Raymond W. Smock, and Geraldine McTigue, eds. *The Booker T. Washington Papers: Volume 11, 1911-12.* Urbana: University of Illinois Press, 1981.

Harlan, Louis, Raymond W. Smock, Geraldine McTigue, and Nan E. Woodruff, eds. *The Booker T. Washington Papers: Volume 10, 1909-11.* Urbana: University of Illinois Press, 1981.

Harlan, Louis, Raymond W. Smock, and Nan E. Woodruff, eds. *The Booker T. Washington Papers: Volume 9, 1906-8.* Urbana: University of Illinois Press, 1980.

Haynes, George E. "The Movement of Negroes From the Country to the City." *Southern Workman* 42 (April 1913): 230-36.

Hibbard, Benjamin H. "Tenancy in the Southern States." *Quarterly Journal of Economics* 27 (November-August 1912-13): 482-96.

Hill, Robert A., and Barbara Bair, eds. *Marcus Garvey: Life and Lessons.* Berkeley, California: University of California Press, 1987.

Hill, Robert A., and Carol A. Rudisell, eds. *The Marcus Garvey and Universal Negro Improvement Association Papers: Volume I, 1826-August 1919.* Berkeley, California: University of California Press, 1983.

Hill, Roy L. *Booker T's Child: The Life and Times of Portia Marshall Washington Pittman.* Washington, D.C.: Three Continents Press, 1993.

———. *Booker T's Child: The Life and Times of Portia Marshall Washington Pittman.* Newark, New Jersey: McDaniel Press, 1974.

Holsey, Albon L. "Negro Business." *Messenger* 9 (November 1927): 321.

———. "Negro in Business Aided by Racial Appeal." *Forbes* 21 (January 15, 1928): 42-48.

———. "Public Relations Intuitions of Booker T. Washington." *Public Opinion Quarterly* XII (Summer 1948): 227-35.

"Homes for All." *Southern Workman* 2 (August 1873). Cornell University Microfilms 3,631: 2.

Horton, Dr. Edward A. "Industrial Education—Will It Solve the Negro Problem? The *Colored American Magazine* 7 (June 1904): 436–39.

"How to Get Workmen," "How to Handle Workmen," and "How to Systematize Your Factory." *The Booker T. Washington Papers*, Washington, D.C.: The Library of Congress Microfilms: Reel no. 15.

"Important to Colored Men and Women Engaged in Business Throughout the Country." *The Booker T. Washington Papers*, Washington, D.C.: The Library of Congress Microfilms: Reel no. 416: 1.

"Industry." *Southern Workman* 1 (July 1872). Cornell University Microfilm 3,631: 4.

Jacques-Garvey, Amy. *Garvey and Garveyism*. New York: Collier Books, 1970.

———, ed. *Philosophy and Opinions of Marcus Garvey*. New York: Maxwell Macmillan International, 1992.

James, Felix. "The Tuskegee Institute Moveable School, 1906–1923." *Agricultural History* 45 (July 1971): 201–209.

Johnson, Clifton. "Tuskegee, A Typical Alabama Town." *Outlook* 72 (November 1, 1902): 519–26.

Johnson, John H. *Succeeding Against the Odds*. New York: Warner Books, Inc., 1989.

Jones, Thomas Jesse. "The Negroes of the Southern States and the U.S. Census of 1910." *Southern Workman* 41 (August 1912): 459–72.

———. "Social Studies in the Hampton Curriculum: IV United States Census and Actual Conditions." *Southern Workman* 35 (April 1906): 233–39.

———. "Social Studies in the Hampton Curriculum: IV United States Census and Actual Conditions (Concluded)." *Southern Workman* 35 (May 1906): 311–18.

———. "The Tuskegee Negro Conference." *Southern Workman* 34 (April 1905): 204–207.

Keyes, John B. "'Big Business' For Negroes." *Southern Workman* 44 (April 1915): 239–41.

Knox, John B. "Reduction of Representation in the South." *Outlook* 79 (January-April 1905): 169–71.

"Labor." *Southern Workman* 3 (March 1874). Cornell University Microfilms 3,631: 18.

Lane, Linda Rochell. *A Documentary of Mrs. Booker T. Washington*. Lewiston, New York: Edwin Mellen Press, 2001.

"Large Audience Hears Booker T. Washington." *Chicago Defender* (July 17, 1915), 10, no. 29: 3.

"Leader Among Business Men: Success of Cornellus C. Cook of Shreveport, La." The *Afro-American* (January 15, 1916), 24, no. 21: 7.

Lemon, John W. "The Farmers' Conference at Calhoun." *Southern Workman* 32 (April 1903): 247–49.

Letter Book: Correspondence of Letters Sent and Received. Tuskegee University Archives.

Lewis, W. L. "Colored Business Men of Jacksonville." *Voice of the Negro* 2 (1905): 474–76.

Lodge, Henry Cabot, and Terence V. Powderly. "The Federal Election Bill." *North American Review* 151 (September 1890): 257–73.

Lord, Nathalie. "Booker Washington's School Days at Hampton." *Southern Workman* 31 (May 1902): 255–59.

"Louisville Meeting of the National Negro Business League." *Southern Workman* 38 (September 1909): 467–69.

Ludlow, Helen W. "The Negro in Business in Hampton and Vicinity." *Southern Workman* 33 (September 1904): 491–01.

Matthews, Victoria Earle. *Black-Belt Diamonds: Gems from the Speeches, Addresses, and Talks to Students of Booker T. Washington.* New York: Negro University Press, 1969.

McAdam, Cyril H. "Booker T. Washington's Recent Trip Through the Southwest." The *Colored American Magazine* 10 (January 1906): 765–83.

McLaughlin, Andrew C. "Mississippi and the Negro Question." The *Atlantic Monthly* 70 (July-December 1892): 828–37.

Miller, Kelly. "Booker T. Washington Five Years After." Pages 3–16, Archival Department, Schomburg Research Center, New York Public Library.

"Mission of the Business League: Bishop Cottrell Calls Attention to Its Usefulness." *The Booker T. Washington Papers*, Washington, D.C.: The Library of Congress Microfilms: Reel no. 757.

Montgomery, Isaiah T. "Negroes in Business." *Outlook* 69 (1901): 733–34.

Moore, Fred R. "Circular Letter." Brooklyn, New York. *The Booker T. Washington Papers*, Washington, D.C.: The Library of Congress Microfilms: Reel no. 752.

———. "Circular Letter." March 16, 1904, Brooklyn, New York. *The Booker T. Washington Papers*, Washington, D.C.: The Library of Congress Microfilms: Reel no. 752.

———. "Organizing Local Business Leagues." The *Colored American Magazine* (October 1904): 624–28.

Moore, William P. "Progressive Business Men of Brooklyn." *Voices of the Negro* 1 (1904): 304–308.

"More Farmers, Journalists, Lawyers, etc., Wanted." *New York Globe* (August 25, 1883). University of Buffalo Microfilms: Reel 1: 2.

Moton, Robert R. "The Negro and the South's Industrial Life." *Southern Workman* 43 (July 1914): 411–18.

———. "The Scope and Aim of Tuskegee Institute." *Journal of Educational Sociology* 7 (November 1933): 151–56.

———. "The Significance of Mr. Washington's Lecture Trip in Mississippi." *Southern Workman* 37 (December 1908): 691–95.

———. "Signs of Growing Co-Operation." *Southern Workman* 43 (October 1914): 552–59.

———. "The Washington Party in North Carolina." *Southern Workman* 39 (December 1910): 646–49.

Muhammad, Elijah. *Message To The Blackman in America*. Chicago, Illinois: Muhammad Mosque of Islam No. 2., 1965.

———. *The Supreme Wisdom*. New York: Shabazz Publication, 1957.

Murray, William. "The Upward Struggle." The *Colored American Magazine* 9 (September 1905): 503–20.

"National Negro Business League at Louisville." The *Tuskegee Student* 21 (September 11, 1909): 1.

"National Negro Business League [Nashville, Tenn. August 19, 1903]." *The Booker T. Washington Papers*, Washington, D.C.: The Library of Congress Microfilms: Reel no. 752: 1.

National Negro Business League. *Report of the Seventeenth Annual Session Held at Kansas City, Missouri, August, 16, 17, 18. Record of the National Negro Business League: Part 1, Annual Conference Proceedings and Organizational Records, 1900–1909*. Schomburg Research Center, New York Public Library Microfilms: Reel no. 3: 62–87.

"National Negro Business League." *Southern Workman* 37 (September 1908): 467–68.

"Needs of the Race." *New York Globe* (October 20, 1883). University of Buffalo Microfilms: Reel 1: 1.

"Negro Business League." *Southern Workman* 36 (October 1907): 515–16.

"Negro Business League." *Southern Workman* 35 (October 1906): 519–20.

"Negro Business League." *Southern Workman* 34 (September 1905): 467–68.

"Negro Labor." *Southern Workman* 9 (1880). Cornell University Microfilms 3,631: 45.

"Negro Suffrage in the South." *Outlook* 74 (June 13, 1903): 399–403.

"New York Meeting of the National Negro Business League." *Southern Workman* 39 (September 1910): 469–70.

"New York Meeting of the National Negro Business League." The *Colored American Magazine* 8 (January 1905): 51.

"New Women's Store Opens in Fifth Ward is Beautiful Place." The *Houston Informer* (September 25, 1920), 2, no. 19: 4.

Newstelle, G. M. "A Negro Business League at Work." *Southern Workman* 44 (January 1915): 43–47.

"Normal-School Printing Office Orders for All Kinds of Job Printing." *Southern Letter*. *The Booker T. Washington Papers*, Washington, D.C.: The Library of Congress Microfilms: Reel no. 425: 4.

"Noted Business Woman Crosses The Great Divide." *Cleveland Advocate* (May 31, 1919), 6, no. 4.

"Notes on Racial Progress." Box 60, Folder 356 (January 1910), *The Booker T. Washington Collection*, Tuskegee University Archives.

"Nothing to Do!" *Southern Workman* 3 (April 1874). Cornell University Microfilms 3,631: 26.

Oates, W. C. "Industrial Development of the South." *North American Review* 161 (1895): 566–74.
"Organize for Big Campaign." *The New York Age* (March 30, 1916), 29, no. 27: 1 & 5.
"What Negroes are Spending in New York and Number of Businesses They Ought to Support." *The Booker T. Washington Papers*, Washington, D.C.: The Library of Congress Microfilms: Reel no. 416.
Palmer, John H. "A Building and Loan Association at Tuskegee." *Southern Workman* 31 (July 1902): 410–11.
———. "Former Students of Tuskegee in Business." *Southern Workman* 31 (February 1902): 124.
Park, Robert E. "Tuskegee and Its Mission." *The Colored American Magazine* 10 (May 1906): 347–54.
Parks, P. C. "Conditions Among Negro Farmers." *Southern Workman* 40 (February 1911): 100–104.
Payton, Philip A. Jr. "Afro-American Realty Company." *The Colored American Magazine* 8 (November 1904): 682–91.
Pierce, Joseph. *Negro Business and Business Education*. New York: Harper and Brothers Publishing, 1947.
"Practice and Theory." *Southern Workman* 3 (October 1874). Cornell University Microfilms 3,631: 75.
"Praying and Working." *Southern Workman* 2 (March 1873). Cornell University Microfilms 3,631: 4.
"President Wilson and the Color Line." *Literary Digest* 47 (August 23, 1913): 270–71.
"Program: Tenth Annual Session National Negro Business League, Louisville, Kentucky, Wednesday, Thursday, Friday, August 18, 19, 20, 1909." *The Booker T. Washington Papers*, Washington, D.C.: The Library of Congress Microfilms: Reel no. 752: 1–8.
"Programme of the Second Annual Session of the National Negro Business League to be Held at Chicago, Illinois, Handel Hall, 46–48 Randolph St., August 21, 22, 23, 1901." *The Booker T. Washington Papers*, Washington, D.C.: The Library of Congress Microfilms: Reel no. 752: 1–8.
"Race Merchants Form Business Association." *The Cleveland Advocate* (August 17, 1918), 5, no. 15: 1.
Randolph, A. Philip. "The Co-operative Movement Among Negroes." *The Messenger* 1 (1918): 23.
———. "Unionism Among Negroes." *The Messenger* 1 (1918): 24.
———. "What are Negroes Doing in Durham?" *Southern Workman* 42 (July 1913): 385–93.
"'Rapid Fire' Discussion and 'Quizzes.' Example of How the National Negro Business League Annual Meetings are Run." *The Booker T. Washington Papers*, Washington, D.C.: The Library of Congress Microfilms: Reel no. 754: 1.
Reed, Thomas B. "The Federal Control of Elections." *North American Review* 150 (June 1890): 671–80.

"Resolutions and Recommendations Adopted by the National Negro Business League at Its First Meeting Held in Boston, August 23 and 24, 1900." *The Booker T. Washington Papers*, Washington, D.C.: The Library of Congress Microfilms: Reel no. 752.

"Resolutions [of National Negro Business League, 1909]." *The Booker T. Washington Papers*, Washington, D.C.: The Library of Congress Microfilms: Reel no. 752.

Richards, Theora. *Economic Power: The Original Plan of Booker T. Washington*. Brooklyn, New York: Richards Research Enterprise, 1987.

Richardson, Clement. "Early Days at Tuskegee." *Southern Workman* 42 (June 1913): 333–35.

Rosengarten, Theodore. *All God's Dangers: The Life of Nate Shaw*. New York: Alfred A. Knopf, 1974.

Scarborough, W. S. "The Negro as a Factor in Business." *Southern Workman* 30 (August 1901): 455–59.

Scott, Emmett J. "The Tuskegee Negro Conference." *Voice of the Negro* 1 (1904): 177–83.

———. "Twenty Years After: An Appraisal of Booker T. Washington." *Journal of Negro Education* 5 (October 1936): 543–54.

Scott, Emmett J. and Lyman B. Stowe. *Booker T. Washington: Builder of a Civilization*. New York: Doubleday, Page & Company, 1917.

Scoville, William H. "The Tuskegee Negro Conferences." *Southern Workman* 35 (April 1906): 201–203.

Seventh Annual Report of the Year Ending May Thirty-First, 1888. Tuskegee, Alabama: School Press, 1888.

Sharpton, Al and Anthony Walton. *Go and Tell Pharaoh: The Autobiography of The Reverend Al Sharpton*. New York: Doubleday, 1996.

Shower, Susan H. "The Tuskegee Conferences." *Southern Workman* 33 (March 1904): 138–40.

Simmons, Roscoe Conkling. "Washington Remains Without a Peer." *Chicago Defender* 2 (June 18, 1949), magazine section: 18–20.

Simmons, Thomas Murray. *Booker Taliaferro Washington Family Journal*, Issue Number 1 (Winter 1996).

Smith, C. C. "Helping the Negro to Help Himself." *Outlook* 78 (November 19, 1904): 727–30.

Smith, Jessie Carney Smith and Carrell Peterson Horton, eds. *Historical Statistics of Black America: Agriculture to Labor & Employment*. New York: Gale Research Inc., 1995.

Smith, Wilford H. "Is the Negro Disfranchised?" *Outlook* 79 (April 1905): 1,047–1,049.

"Some Tangible Results of the Tuskegee Negro Conference." *The Negro Farmer* 2 (January 30, 1915): 4–5.

"Southern Agriculture and the Negro." *Southern Workman* 31 (October 1902): 515.

"Southern Peonage and Immigration." *Nation* 85 (December 19, 1908): 557.

Spaulding, C. C. "Business in Negro Durham." *Southern Workman* LXVI (December 1937): 364–68.

———. "Is The Negro Meeting the Test in Business?" *Journal of Negro History* 18 (1933): 66–70.

Stewart, Ruth Ann. *Portia: The Life of Portia Washington Pittman, the Daughter of Booker T. Washington*. New York: Doubleday & Company, Inc., 1977.

Stokes, Anson Phelp. "Tuskegee Institute, the First Fifty Years." Tuskegee University Archives.

"Success in Business." *Southern Workman* 3 (August 1874). Cornell University Microfilms 3,631: 58.

Sutton W. S. "The Contribution of Booker T. Washington to the Education of the Negro." *School and Society* 4 (September 23, 1916): 457–63.

Talbot, Edith Armstrong. *Samuel Chapman Armstrong: A Biographical Study*. New York: Negro University Press, 1969.

"The Alabama Case." *Outlook* 74 (May 9, 1903): 95.

"The Alabama Decision." *Nation* 76 (April 1903): 346.

"The Best Defense." *Outlook* 74 (August 15, 1903): 927–29.

"The Burden." *Crisis* 1 (December 1910): 26–27.

"The Burden." *Crisis* 3 (April 1912): 253.

"The Epidemic of Savagery." *Outlook* 69 (September 7, 1901): 9–11.

"The Labor Problem in the South." *New York Globe* (April 22, 1883). University of Buffalo Microfilms: Reel no. 1: 2.

"The Late Colored Convention." *Harper's Weekly* (October 27, 1883): 674.

"The National Negro Business League." *The Booker T. Washington Papers*, Washington, D.C.: The Library of Congress Microfilms: Reel no. 752.

"The National Negro Business League." *Southern Workman* 31 (October 1902): 513–15.

"The Negro Business League." *Southern Workman* 32 (September 1903): 404–405.

"The Negro Business League." *Southern Workman* 41 (September 1912): 497–500.

"The Negro Business League." *Southern Workman* 42 (October 1913): 517–19.

"The Negro in Business." *Southern Workman* 43 (October 1914): 523–24.

"The Negro in the South." *New York Globe* (April 21, 1883). University of Buffalo Microfilms: Reel no. 1: 2.

"The President Mr. Cleveland and the Coal Strike." *Outlook* 89 (August 22, 1908): 869–70.

"The Rural Negro in the South." 1907. *The Booker T. Washington Papers*, Washington, D.C.: The Library of Congress Microfilms: Reel no. 410: 1–11.

"The Tenth Annual Meeting of the National Negro Business League will be held in the City of Louisville, Kentucky, 1900–1909, Wednesday, Thursday and Friday, Aug. 18th, 19th and 20th, 1909." *The Booker T. Washington Papers*, Washington, D.C.: The Library of Congress Microfilms: Reel no. 752: 1–2.

"The Tuskegee Conference and Negro Farming." *Southern Workman* 43 (February 1914): 67–68.

"The Tuskegee Farmers' Conference." *Southern Workman* 44 (March 1915): 133–34.
"The Tuskegee Meeting in New York." *Southern Workman* 37 (February 1908): 67–68.
"The Tuskegee Negro Conference." *Southern Workman* 21 (March 1892): 40–48.
"The Tuskegee Negro Conferences." *Southern Workman* 36 (April 1907): 196–99.
"The Tuskegee Negro Conferences." *Southern Workman* 37 (April 1908): 200–201.
Thirteenth Annual Report of the Principal of the Tuskegee Normal and Industrial Institute. Tuskegee, Alabama: Tuskegee Institute Press, 1894.
Thrasher, Max Bennett. "The Alabama Constitutional Convention." *Outlook* 68 (June 1901): 437–39.
———. *Tuskegee: Its Story and Its Work*. New York: Negro University Press, 1969.
———. "The Tuskegee Conference." *The Booker T. Washington Papers*, Washington, D.C.: The Library of Congress Microfilms: Reel no. 752: 1–7.
"Throng of 1,200 Attend Rites for S. L. Walker." The *Buffalo Criterion*. (January 3–9, 1970): 1.
"To the Members of the National Negro Business League." *The Booker T. Washington Papers*, Washington, D.C.: The Library of Congress Microfilms: Reel no. 754: 1.
Tourge, Albion W. *The Invisible Empire*. Barton Rouge, Louisiana: Louisiana State University Press, 1880.
"Tuskegee Annual Conference Holds Monster Meeting." *Chicago Defender* (January 30, 1915), 10, no. 5: 1.
"Tuskegee Negro Farmers' Conference Breaks Record Attendance." *The Negro Farmer* 1 (February 14, 1914): 5.
Tyler, Ralph W. "Persistence In Business Wins: Review of Race Thrift In Kansas City, Mo." The *Afro-American* (February 14, 1914), 22, no. 25: 2.
———. "Pushing Ahead in Business: Chances For Success Along Many Lines Are Good in Evansville, Ind." The *Afro-American* (January 24, 1914), 22, no. 22: 2.
———. "Thrifty Center of Business: Encouraging Report of Race Progress in South." The *Afro-American* (October 4, 1913), 22, no. 6: p. 7.
"Up From Dependency." *The Wall Street Journal* (March 25, 1992): A12 (W) & (E).
U.S. Bureau of the Census, *Negro Population, 1790–1915*. Washington, D.C.: Government Printing Office, 1918.
Uspean, D. "Report of . . . [a] Delegate from Business League, Montgomery, Ala." *The Booker T. Washington Papers*, Washington, D.C.: The Library of Congress Microfilms: Reel no. 755: 3.
Waldron, Rev. J. Milton. "Inside View of the Condition and Needs of the Colored People of the South." The *Colored American Magazine* 6 (October 1903): 714–19.
Ware, Edward T. "The Atlanta Riots." *Outlook* 84 (November 3, 1906): 557–66.
Washington, Booker T. "A Farmers' College on Wheels." The *World's Work* 13 (December 1906): 8,352–354.
———. "A Home Talk at Hampton." *Southern Workman* 37 (August 1908): 456–57.
———. *A New Negro for a New Century*. Miami, Florida: Mnemosyne Publishing, Inc., 1969.

———. "A Notable Instance of the Negro in Politics." The *Colored American Magazine* 10 (June 1906): 387-89.

———. "A Town Owned by Negroes: Mound Bayou, Miss, An Example of Thrift and Self-Government." The *World's Work* 14 (July 1907): 9,125-134.

———. "Address Delivered Before the New England Club." Address, New England Club, Boston, Massachusetts, January 2, 1899. *The Booker T. Washington Papers*, Washington, D.C.: The Library of Congress Microfilms: Reel no. 409: 12-14.

———. "Address Delivered By Booker T. Washington—Education." Address, Augusta, Georgia, April 27, 1899. *The Booker T. Washington Papers*, Washington, D.C.: The Library of Congress Microfilms: Reel no. 409: 1-6.

———. "An Address Delivered in the Interest of Hampton Institute." Address, Hampton Institute, Springfield, Massachusetts, April 26, 1892. *The Booker T. Washington Papers*, Washington, D.C.: The Library of Congress Microfilms: Reel no. 409: 9-10.

———. "An Address Delivered on Old South." Address, Tuskegee Institute Donors, Boston, Massachusetts, December 15, 1891. *The Booker T. Washington Papers*, Washington, D.C.: Library of Congress Microfilms: Reel no. 409: 1-6.

———. "Addresses to the Colored Farmers of Alabama." Address, Colored Farmers of Alabama. *Annals of the American Academy* 7 (March 1896): 363-64.

———. "The Atlanta Exposition Address (1895)." Address, Atlanta Exposition, Atlanta, Georgia, 1895. Tuskegee University Archives, Tuskegee University.

———. "The Awakening of the Negro." The *Atlantic Monthly* 78 (1896): 322-28

———. "Boley, A Negro Town in the West." *Outlook* 88 (January 4, 1908): 28-31.

———. "The Case of the Negro." The *Atlantic Monthly* 84 (November 1899): 577-87.

———. *Character Building*. New York: Doubleday, Page & Company, 1902.

———. "Chapters From My Experience I." The *World's Work* (October 1910). *The Booker T. Washington Papers*, Washington, D.C.: Library of Congress Microfilms: Reel no. 415: 13,505-522.

———. "Chapters From My Experience II." The *World's Work* (November 1910). *The Booker T. Washington Papers*, Washington, D.C.: Library of Congress Microfilms: Reel no. 415: 13,627-640.

———. "Chapters From My Experience III." The *World's Work* (December 1910). *The Booker T. Washington Papers*, Washington, D.C.: Library of Congress Microfilms: Reel no. 415: 13,783-794.

———. "Chapters From My Experience V." The *World's Work* (February 1911). *The Booker T. Washington Papers*, Washington, D.C.: Library of Congress Microfilms: Reel no. 415: 14,032-14,039.

———. "Chapters From My Experience VI." The *World's Work* (April 1911). *The Booker T. Washington Papers*, Washington, D.C.: Library of Congress Microfilms: Reel no. 415: 14,230-238.

———. "Chickens, Pigs and People." *Outlook* 68 (June 1, 1901): 291-300.

———. "Durham, North Carolina, a City of Negro Enterprises." The *Independent*

(March 30, 1911). *The Booker T. Washington Papers*, Washington, D.C.: Library of Congress Microfilms: Reel no. 415: 642–50.

———. "Education and Getting Down to Business." *Southern Workman* 38 (September 1909): 479–80.

———. "Educational Engineers." *Southern Workman* 39 (July 1910): 504–506.

———. "Extracts from Address Delivered in Birmingham, Alabama." Address, Birmingham, Alabama, January 1, 1900. *The Booker T. Washington Papers*, Washington, D.C.: The Library of Congress Microfilms: Reel no. 409: 1–3.

———. "Extracts from Address Delivered in Pensacola, Florida." Address, Pensacola, Florida, May 10, 1900. *The Booker T. Washington Papers*, Washington, D.C.: The Library of Congress Microfilms: Reel no. 409: 1–5.

———. *Frederick Douglass*. Philadelphia, Pennsylvania: George W. Jacobs & Company, 1907.

———. "Fruits of Industrial Training." *Southern Workman* 32 (December 1903): 620–26.

———. *The Future of the American Negro*. Boston: Small, Maynard & Company, 1900.

———. "The Golden Rule in Atlanta." *Outlook* 84 (December 15, 1906): 913–16.

———. "Grow One Pig at Least, Says Dr. Washington." The *Negro Farmer* 1 (October 24, 1914): 10.

———. "Hampton Institute Anniversary." Address, Hampton Institute, Hampton, Virginia, April 12, 1898. *The Booker T. Washington Papers*, Washington, D.C.: The Library of Congress Microfilms: Reel no. 409: 1–3.

———. "How Students May Contribute Toward the Support of Their School." *Southern Workman* 38 (January 1909): 48–51.

———. "Important to Colored Farmers in Macon and Adjacent Counties in Alabama." The *Negro Farmer* 1 (October 24, 1914): 7.

———. "Industrial Education and Public Schools." *Annals of the American Academy of Political and Social Science* 49 (1913): 219–32.

———. *The Man Farthest Down*. New York: Doubleday, Page & Company, 1912.

———. *My Larger Education: Being Chapters From My Experience*. Miami, Florida: Mnemosyne Publishing, Inc., 1969.

———. "The National Negro Business League." *The Booker T. Washington Papers*, Washington, D.C.: The Library of Congress Microfilms: Reel no. 752.

———. *The National Negro Business League Proceedings, Volume One*. Boston, Massachusetts: J. R. Hamm, Publisher, 1901.

———. "The Negro and His Relation to the Economic Progress of the South." Address, Southern Industrial Convention, Huntsville, Alabama, October 12, 1899. *The Booker T. Washington Papers*, Washington, D.C.: The Library of Congress Microfilms: Reel no. 409: 1–8.

———. "The Negro as a Farmer." *North American Review* 195 (1912): 175–81.

———. "Negro Disfranchisement and the Negro in Business." *Outlook* 93 (October 9, 1909): 310–16.

---. "Negro Enterprise I: A Negro Potato King." *Outlook* 77 (May 14, 1904): 115-18.

---. *The Negro in Business*. Wichita, Kansas: DeVore and Sons, Inc., 1992.

---. "The Negro in Business." *American Illustrated Magazine* LXI (January 1906): 340-45.

---. "The Negro in Business." The *Colored American Magazine* 10 (February 1906): 91-99.

---. "The Negro in Business." *Gunton's Magazine* (March 1901): 208-19.

---. "The Negro in Business." *The Raven: The California Monthly* 6 (1905): 178-79.

---. "The Negro's Part in the South's Upbuilding." *Voice of the Negro* 1 (January 1904): 28-30.

---. "The Privilege of Service." *Southern Workman* 36 (December 1907): 684-88.

---. *Putting the Most into Life*. New York: Crowell, 1906.

---. "The Relation of Industrial Education to National Progress." *Southern Workman* 37 (April 1908): 237-41.

---. "The Relation of the Races in the South." The *Union Seminary Magazine* 11 (April-May 1900): 272-79.

---. *Report of The Fifth Annual Convention of the National Negro Business League, Held at Indianapolis, Indiana, August 31st, September 1st and 2d A.D.* Pensacola, Florida: M. M. Lewey, *Florida Sentinel*, 1904.

---. *Report of The Fourth Annual Convention of the National Negro Business League, Held at Nashville, Tennessee, August 19, 20, and 21, 1903*. Wilberforce, Ohio: Charles Alexander Publisher, 1903.

---. *Report of The Ninth Annual Convention of the National Negro Business League, Held at Baltimore, Md., August 19, 20, and 21, 1908.* Tuskegee University Archives.

---. *Report of The Seventh Annual Convention of the National Negro Business League, Held at Atlanta, Georgia, August 29, 30, and 31, 1906*. Boston, Massachusetts: Charles Alexander, Printer, 1906.

---. *Report of The Sixth Annual Convention of the National Negro Business League, Held at New York City, August 16, 17 and 18, 1905*. Boston, Massachusetts: Charles Alexander, Printer, 1905.

---. *Report of The Tenth Annual Convention of the National Negro Business League, Held in Louisville, Kentucky, August 18-20, 1909.* Nashville, Tennessee: A.M.E. Sunday School Union Print, 1909.

---. "Mr. Robert C. Ogden." The *Metropolitan Magazine* (1910). *The Booker T. Washington Papers*, Washington, D.C.: The Library of Congress Microfilms: Reel no. 415: 1-6.

---. "Signs of Progress Among the Negroes." *Century Magazine* 59 (1900): 472-78.

---. "Some Results of the Armstrong Idea." *Southern Workman* 38 (March 1909): 170-81.

---. "The South and the Negro." *Southern Workman* 34 (July 1905): 400-405.

---. *Sowing and Reaping*. New York: H. M. Caldwell, 1900.

---. *The Story of My Life and Work*. New York: Negro University Press, 1969.

———. *The Story of the Negro: The Rise of the Race from Slavery: Volumes I & II*. New York: Peter Smith, 1940.

———. "The Successful Training of the Negro." *The World's Work* 6 (August 1903): 3,731–751.

———. "Teamwork." *Southern Workman* 44 (December 1915): 651–53.

———. *Tuskegee and Its People: Their Ideals and Achievements*. New York: D. Appleton and Company, 1905.

———. "Twenty-Five Years of Tuskegee." *The World's Work* 11 (April 1906): 7,433–450.

———. *Up From Slavery*. New York: Dell Publishing Company, 1968.

———. *Up From Slavery*. New York: Airmont Publishing Company, 1967.

———. *Up From Slavery*. New York: Doubleday & Company, 1901.

———. "The Value of Educating the Negro." *Southern Workman* 33 (October 1904): 558–64.

———. "What Co-operation Can Accomplish." *Southern Workman* 43 (December 1914): 660–64.

———. "What I Am Trying To Do." *The World's Work* 27 (November 1913): 101–107.

———. "Why Should Negro Business Men Go South." *Charities* 15 (October 7, 1905): 17–19.

———. "Women as Economic Factors." The *FRA* 5 (September 1910): 187–88.

———. *Working with the Hands*. New York: Doubleday, Page & Company, 1904.

Washington, Booker T., and W.E.B. Du Bois. *The Negro in the South: His Economic Progress in Relation to His Moral and Religious Development*. New York: Carol Publishing Group, 1970.

Washington, Booker T., and W.E.B. Du Bois, Paul Laurence Dunbar, Charles W. Chesnutt, and Others. *The Negro Problem: 4 Series of Articles by Representative American Negroes of To-Day*. New York: James Pott & Company, 1969.

Washington, E. David, ed. *Selected Speeches of Booker T. Washington*. Garden City, New Jersey: Doubleday, Doran & Company, Inc., 1932.

Wells-Barnett, Ida B. *On Lynchings, Southern Horrors, A Red Record, Mob Rule in New Orleans*. New York: Arno Press and the *New York Times*, 1969.

"What Negroes are Spending in New York and Number of Businesses They Ought to Support." *The Booker T. Washington Papers*, Washington, D.C.: The Library of Congress Microfilms: Reel no. 416: 1–2.

White, Alvin E. "I Remember Maggie Walker." *Sepia* 2 (1905): 56–59.

Wilkeson, Frank. "The Labor Problem." *New York Globe* (February 17, 1883): 2.

Willcox, William G. "Tuskegee's Contribution to National Efficiency." *Southern Workman* XLV (August 1916): 446–48.

Williams, W.T.B. "Booker T. Washington: An Appreciation." *Southern Workman*, XLV (January 1916): 34–42.

———. "Local Conditions Among Negroes V: Tuskegee Institute Extension Work in Macon County, Alabama." *Southern Workman* 36 (September 1907): 471–78.

———. "The Tuskegee Negro Conference." *Southern Workman* 41 (February 1912): 74–76.

"Winners From the Soil: Colored Heroes of the Farm." The *Negro Farmer* 1 (January 31, 1914): 2.

"Winners From the Soil: Colored Heroes of the Farm." The *Negro Farmer* 1 (June 6, 1914): 4.

"Winners From the Soil: Colored Heroes of the Farm." The *Negro Farmer* 1 (March 14, 1914): 2.

"Winners From the Soil: Colored Heroes of the Farm." The *Negro Farmer* 1 (March 28, 1914): 5.

"Winners From the Soil: Colored Heroes of the Farm." The *Negro Farmer* 2 (August 14, 1915): 9–10.

"Winners From the Soil: Colored Heroes of the Farm." The *Negro Farmer* 2 (August 28, 1915): 9–10.

"Winners From the Soil: Colored Heroes of the Farm." The *Negro Farmer* 2 (July 3, 1915): 4–5.

"Winners From the Soil: Colored Heroes of the Farm." The *Negro Farmer* 2 (March 13, 1915): 8–9.

"Winners From the Soil: Colored Heroes of the Farm." The *Negro Farmer* 2 (October 9, 1915): 9.

Wintz, Cary D., ed. *African American Political Thought, 1890–1930: Washington, Du Bois, Garvey, and Randolph*. Armonk, New York: M. E. Sharpe, 1996.

Woodson, Carter G. "Insurance Business Among Negroes." *Journal of Negro History* 14 (1929): 202–26.

———. *The Mis-Education of the Negro*. Trenton, New Jersey: African World Press, Inc., 1993.

Work, Monroe N. "Inter-Racial Cooperation." *Social Forces* 3 (1924/25): 310–15.

———. "The Negro in Business Enterprise." *Southern Workman* XLVI (May 1917): 304–309.

———. *Negro Year Book, 1914–15*. Tuskegee, Alabama: Negro Yearbook Publishing Company, 1915.

———. *Negro Year Book and Annual Encyclopedia of the Negro 1912*. Tuskegee, Alabama: Tuskegee Institute Press, 1912.

———. *Negro Year Book and Annual Encyclopedia of the Negro 1913*. Tuskegee, Alabama: Tuskegee Institute Press, 1913.

———. "The Negro's Industrial Problem: Learning How To Work." *Southern Workman* 43 (August 1914): 436–39.

———. "The Negro's Industrial Problem: II Farming, Trades, and Business." *Southern Workman* 43 (September 1914): 503–509.

———. "Short Course for Farmers." *Outlook* 91 (April 17, 1909): 866–68.

———. "Tuskegee Institute More Than an Educational Institution." *Journal of Educational Sociology* 7 (November 1933): 197–205.

Wormley, Stanton. L. and Lewis H. Fenderson. *Many Shades of Black*. New York: William Morrow and Company, 1969.

Wright, R. R. Jr. "The Economic Condition of Negroes in the North: VI Negroes in Business in the North." *Southern Workman* 38 (January 1909): 36–44.

———. "The Economic Condition of Negroes in the North, Tendencies Downward: Third Paper: Poverty Among Northern Negroes." *Southern Workman* 40 (December 1911): 700–709.

X, Malcolm. *The Autobiography of Malcolm X*. New York: Ballantine Books, 1965.

"Young Men of Business." The *Afro-American* (October 4, 1913), 22, n0.6: 7.

Secondary Sources (Books, Dissertations, Masters' Theses, Journal Articles, Newspapers, Conference Papers, etc.)

"A. G. Gaston." *Black Enterprise* 6 (July): 31–33.

"A Man and His Products." *Black Enterprise* 6 (August 1975): 47–50.

Alexander, Adele L. "Grandmother, Grandfather, W.E.B. Du Bois and Booker T. Washington." *Crisis* 90 (1983): 8–11.

Alilunas, Leo J. "What Our Schools Teach About Booker T. Washington and W.E.B. Du Bois." *Journal of Negro Education* 42 (1973): 176–86.

Allen, Robert L. *Black Awakening in Capitalist America: An Analytic History*. New York: Doubleday and Company, Inc., 1970.

Anderson, Claud. *Black Labor, White Wealth: The Search for Power and Economic Justice*. Edgewood, Maryland: Duncan & Duncan, Inc. 1994.

Anderson, James D. *The Education of Blacks in the South, 1860–1935*. Chapel Hill, North Carolina: University of North Carolina Press, 1988.

Ayers, Edward L. *The Promise of the New South: Life After Reconstruction*. New York: Oxford University Press, 1992.

Baida, Peter. *Poor Richard's Legacy: American Business Values from Benjamin Franklin to Michael Milken*. New York: William Morrow & Company, Inc., 1990.

Bailey, Ronald W. *Black Business Enterprise: Historical and Contemporary Perspective*. New York: Basic Books, Inc., 1971.

Barr, Alwyn. *Black Texans: A History of Negroes in Texas 1528–1971*. Austin, Texas: Jenkins Publishing Company, 1973.

Bates, Timothy. *Banking on Black Enterprise: The Potential of Emerging Firms for Revitalizing Urban Economics*. Washington, D.C.: Joint Center for Political and Economic Studies, Inc., 1993.

Becker, Gary S. *The Economics of Discrimination*. Chicago: University of Chicago Press, 1971.

Bell, William K. *A Business Primer for Negroes*. New York: William K. Bell, 1948.

Bennett, Lerone Jr. *Before the Mayflower: A History of Black America*. New York: Penguin Books, 1993.

———. *The Shaping of Black America: The Struggles and Triumphs of African Americans, 1619 to the 1990s*. New York: Penguin Books, 1993.

Bernstein, Barton J. "Case Law in *Plessy v. Ferguson.*" *Journal of Negro History* 47 (July 1962): 192–98.

———. "*Plessy v. Ferguson*: Conservative Sociological Jurisprudence." *Journal of Negro History* 48 (July 1963): 196–205.

"Black Economic Well-Being Since the 1950s." The *Review of Black Political Economy* 12 (Spring 1984): 3–39.

Blake, Susan L. "A Better Mouse Trap: Washington's Program and the Colonel's Dream." *CLA Journal* 23 (1980): 49–59.

Bond, Horace Mann. "The Influence of Personalities on the Public Education of Negroes in Alabama, II." *Journal of Negro Education* 6 (April 1937): 172–87.

———. "Negro Education: A Debate in the Alabama Constitutional Convention of 1901." *Journal of Negro Education* 1 (April 1932): 49–59.

———. *Negro Education in Alabama: A Study in Cotton and Steel*. New York: Octagon Books, 1969.

Bontemps, Arna. *100 Years of Negro Freedom*. New York: Dodd, Mead & Company, 1961.

"Booker T. Washington." *Aryan Path* 20 (October 1949): 455.

Boston, Thomas D. *A Different Vision: African American Economic Thought: Volumes I & II*. New York: Routledge Press, 1997.

Boyd, Herb. "Du Bois and Black Economic Development." *Crisis* 99 (1992): 19–20.

Boyd, William K. *The Story of Durham*. Durham, North Carolina: Duke University Press, 1927.

Bracey, John H. Jr., August Meier, and Elliott Rudwick, eds. *Black Nationalism*. Indianapolis, Indiana: Boobs-Merrill Company, Inc., 1970.

Breitman, George. *The Last Year of Malcolm X: The Evolution of a Revolutionary*. New York: Pathfinder Press, 1967.

Breuilly, John. *Nationalism and the State*. Chicago: University of Chicago Press, 1994.

Brewer, William M. "Poor Whites and Negroes in the South Since the Civil War." *Journal of Negro History* 15 (1930): 26–37.

Brock, Randall E. "Cast Down Your Buckets Where You Are." *Crisis* 99 (February 1992): 22–23.

Brooks, R. P. "A Local Study of the Race Problem: Race Relations in the Eastern Piedmont Region of Georgia." *Political Science Quarterly* 26 (June 1911): 193–221.

Brown, W. L. "Booker T. Washington as a Philosopher." *Negro History Bulletin* 20 (1956): 34–37.

Browning, James B. "The Beginnings of Insurance Enterprise Among Negroes." *Journal of Negro History* 22 (1937): 417–32.

Brundage, W. Fitzhugh. *Booker T. Washington and Black Progress: Up From Slavery 100 Years Later*. Gainesville, Florida: University Press of Florida, 2003.

———. *Lynching in the New South: Georgia and Virginia, 1880-1930*. Urbana: University of Illinois Press, 1993.

Bundles, A'Lelia P. "Madame C. J. Walker to Her Daughter A'Lelia Walker—The Last Letter." *Sage: A Scholarly Journal on Black Women* 12 (1984): 34–35.

Butler, Broadus N. "The Great Debate." *Crisis* 85 (1978): 222–30.
Butler, John S. *Entrepreneurship and Self-Help Among Black Americans: A Reconsideration of Race and Economics*. Albany, New York: State University of New York Press, 1991.
Burrows, John H. *The Necessity of Myth: A History of the National Negro Business League, 1900–1945*. Auburn, Alabama: Hickory Hill Press, 1988.
Bussel, Robert. "'The Most Indispensable Man in His Community': African-American Entrepreneurs in West Chester, Pennsylvania, 1865–1925." *Pennsylvania History* 65 (Summer 1998): 324–49.
Calista, Donald J. "Booker T. Washington: Another Look." *Journal of Negro History* 49 (October 1964): 240–55.
Carroll, Rebecca, ed. *Uncle Tom or New Negro? African Americans Reflect on Booker T. Washington and Up From Slavery One Hundred Years Later*. New York: Harlem Moon, 2006.
Cash, Wilbur J. *The Mind of the South*. New York: Alfred A. Knopf, Inc., 1941.
Cason, Clarence E. "Alabama Goes Industrial." The *Virginia Quarterly Review* 6 (April 1930): 161–70.
Chandler, Alfred D. *The Visible Hand: The Managerial Revolution in American Business*. Cambridge: Harvard University Press, 1977.
Clark, Herbert L. "James Carroll Napier: National Negro Leader." *Tennessee Historical Quarterly* 49 (Winter 1990): 243–52.
Clarke, John Henrik, Esther Jackson, Ernest Kaiser, and J. H. O'Dell. *Black Titan W.E.B. Du Bois: An Anthology by the Editors of Freedomways*. Boston: Beacon Press, 1970.
Clegg III, Claude Andrew. *An Original Man: The Life and Times of Elijah Muhammad*. New York: St. Martin's Press, 1997.
Cochran, Thomas C., and William Miller. *The Age of Enterprise: A Social History of Industrial America*. New York: Harper & Row, Publisher, 1961.
———. *The American Business System: A Historical Perspective, 1900–1955*. New York: Harper Torchbooks, 1957.
Conley, Anthony L. "Opinions: Pleasing 'The Wizard.'" The *Indianapolis Recorder* (August 28, 1998), 104, no. 35: A-3.
Cook, Mercer. "Booker T. Washington and the French." *Journal of Negro History* 40 (October 1955): 318–40.
Cox, Oliver C. "The Leadership of Booker T. Washington." *Social Forces* 30 (October 1951): 91–97.
Cronon, E. David. *Black Moses: The Story of Marcus Garvey and the Universal Negro Improvement Association*. Madison, Wisconsin: University of Wisconsin Press, 1969.
Crosby, Earl W. "Limited Success Against Long Odds: The Black County Agent." *Agricultural History* 57 (July 1983): 277–88.
Cross, T. L. *Black Capitalism*. New York: Atheneum, 1969.
Crouthamel, James L. "Springfield Race Riot of 1908." *Journal of Negro History* 45 (1960): 164–81.

Crowe, Charles. "Racial Violence and Social Reform—Origins of the Atlanta Riot of 1906." *Journal of Negro History* 53 (1968): 234–56.
Cruden, Robert. *The Negro in Reconstruction*. Englewood Cliffs, New Jersey: Prentice-Hall, Inc., 1969.
Cruse, Harold. *The Crisis of the Negro Intellectual*. New York: William Morrow and Company, Inc., 1967.
———. *Plural But Equal: a Critical Study of Blacks and Minorities and America's Plural Society*. New York: William Morrow and Company, Inc., 1987.
———. *Rebellion or Revolution?* New York: William Morrow and Company, Inc., 1968.
Cummings, Melbourne. "Historical Setting for Booker T. Washington and the Rhetoric of Compromise, 1895." *Journal of Black Studies* 8 (September 1977): 75–82.
Cunnigen, Donald, Rutledge M. Dennis, and Myrtle Gonza Glascoe. *The Racial Politics of Booker T. Washington*. Oxford, United Kingdom: JAI Press, 2006.
Dagbovie, Pero Gaglo. "'Clean the Ceiling Before Cleaning the Floor': Exploring Eighty Years of Scholarship and Historiography on Booker T. Washington." Masters Thesis, Michigan State University, 1995.
Dailey, Maceo C. "Booker T. Washington and the Afro-American Reality Company." The *Review of Black Political Economy* 8 (Winter 1978): 184–201.
Daniel, Sadie Iola. *Women Builders*. Washington, D.C.: The Associated Publishers, 1970.
Delaney, William H. *Learning By Doing: A Projected Educational Philosophy in the Thought of Booker T. Washington*. New York: Vantage Press, 1974.
Denton, Virginia L. *Booker T. Washington and the Adult Education Movement*. Gainesville, Florida: University Press of Florida, 1993.
———. "Booker T. Washington and the Adult Education Movement, 1865–1915." PhD. dissertation, University of Southern Mississippi, 1988.
Dorsey, Carolyn A. "Despite Poor Health: Olivia Davidson Washington's Story." *SAGE: A Scholarly Journal on Black Woman* 2 (Fall 1985): 69–72.
D'orso, Michael. *Rosewood: Like Judgement Day*. New York: The Berkley Publishing Group, 1996.
Drago, Edmund L. *Black Politicians & Reconstruction in Georgia: A Splendid Failure*. Athens, Georgia: University of Georgia Press, 1992.
Drake, St. Clair and Horace A. Cayton. *Black Metropolis: A Study of Negro Life in a Northern City*. Chicago: University of Chicago Press, 1993.
Dreyfus, Joel. "Rowboating in the Economic Mainstream: The NBL Keeps Moving Despite Rough Waters." *Black Enterprise* 5 (January 1975): 43–45.
Drimmer, Melvin. *Issues in Black History*. Dubuque, Iowa: Kendall-Hunt Publishing Company, 1987.
Drinker, Frederick. *Booker T. Washington*. New York: Negro University Press, 1970.
Du Bois, W.E.B. *Black Reconstruction in America, 1860–1880*. New York: Atheneum, 1935.
Dunn, Frederick. "The Educational Philosophies of Washington, Du Bois, and Hous-

ton: Laying the Foundation for Afrocentrism and Multiculturalism." *Journal of Negro Education* 62 (Winter 1993): 24–34.

Dye, R. Thomas. "Rosewood, Florida: The Destruction of an African American Community." *Historian: A Journal of History* 58 (Spring 1996): 605–22.

Elder, Arlene A. "Chesnutt on Washington: An Essential Ambivalence." *Phylon* 38 (1977): 1–8.

Enck, Henry S. "Tuskegee Institute and Northern White Philanthropy: A Case Study in Fund Raising, 1900-1915." *Journal of Negro History* 65 (Autumn 1980): 336–48.

Essien-Udom, E. U. *Black Nationalism: A Search for an Identity in America*. Chicago: University of Chicago Press, 1962.

Ezeania, Eboh C. "Economic Conditions of Freed Blacks in the United States, 1870-1920." The *Review of Black Political Economy* 8 (Fall 1977): 104–18.

Factor, Robert L. *The Black Response to America: Men, Ideas, and Organization from Frederick Douglass to the NAACP*. Reading, Massachusetts: Addison-Wesley Publishing Company, 1970.

Farley, Reynolds. "The Urbanization of Negroes in the United States." *Journal of Social History* 1 (Spring 1968): 241–58.

Farrison, Edward W. "Booker T. Washington: A Study in Educational Leadership." The *South Atlantic Quarterly* XLI (1942): 313–19.

Ferguson, Karen J. "Caught in 'No Man's Land': The Negro Cooperative Demonstration Service and the Ideology of Booker T. Washington, 1900-1918." *Agricultural History* 72 (Winter 1998): 33–54.

Fishburn, Eleanor and Mildred Sandison Fenner. "Booker T. Washington." *National Education Association Bulletin* 33 (April 1944): 95–96.

Fisher, Dorothy Canfield. "The Washed Window." *American Heritage* 7 (1955): 28–31 & 115.

Fitzgerald, Charlotte D. "The Story of My Life and Work: Booker T. Washington's Other Autobiography." The *Black Scholar* 21 (1991): 35–40.

Fleming, Walter L. "Reorganization of the Industrial System in Alabama After the Civil War." *American Journal of Sociology* 10 (1904–1905): 473–500.

Flynn, John P. "Booker T. Washington: Uncle Tom or Wooden Horse." *Journal of Negro History* 54 (1969): 262–74.

Foner, Eric. *Reconstruction: America's Unfinished Revolution, 1863-1877*. New York: Harper & Row, Publishers, 1988.

Foner, Philip S. "Is Booker T. Washington Correct?" *Journal of Negro History* 55 (October 1970): 343–44.

Fordham, Monroe. "The Buffalo Cooperative Economic Society, Inc., 1928-1961: A Black Self-Help Organization." *Niagara Frontier* (Summer 1976): 41–49.

Forth, Christopher E. "Booker T. Washington and the 1905 Niagara Movement Conference." *Journal of Negro History* 72 (Summer-Autumn 1987): 45–56.

Franklin, John H. *Reconstruction After the Civil War*. Urbana: University of Illinois Press, 1982.

Franklin, John H. and Alfred A. Moss Jr. *From Slavery to Freedom: A History of African Americans*, 7th ed. New York: McGraw-Hill, Inc., 1994.

Franklin, John H. and Alfred A. Moss Jr. *From Slavery to Freedom: A History of African Americans*, 8th ed. New York: McGraw-Hill, Inc., 2000.

Franklin, John H. and August Meier, eds. *Black Leaders of the Twentieth Century*. Chicago: University of Chicago Press, 1994.

Frazier, E. Franklin. *Black Bourgeoisie*. London: Collier-Macmillan Company, 1969.

Fredrickson, George M. *The Black Image in the White Mind: The Debate on Afro-American Character and Destiny, 1817–1914*. New York: Harper Torchbooks, 1971.

———. *White Supremacy: A Comparative Study in American & South African History*. New York: Oxford University Press, 1981.

Friedman, Lawrence J. "Life 'In the Lion's Mouth': Another Look at Booker T. Washington." *Journal of Negro History* 59 (October 1974): 337–51.

Fullinwider, S. P. *The Mind and Mood of Black America*. Homewood, Illinois: The Dorsey Press, 1969.

Gaines, Kevin K. *Uplifting the Race: Black Leadership, Politics, and Culture in the Twentieth Century*. Chapel Hill, North Carolina: University of North Carolina Press, 1996.

Gardell, Mattias. *In The Name of Elijah Muhammad: Louis Farrakhan and the Nation of Islam*. Durham, North Carolina: Duke University Press, 1996.

Gardner, Booker T. "The Educational Contributions of Booker T. Washington." *Journal of Negro Education* 44 (1975): 502–18.

Gatewood, Willard B. "Booker T. Washington and the Ulrich Affair." *Journal of Negro History* 55 (1970): 25–28.

Gavin, Roy. "Benjamin, or 'Pap,' Singleton and His Followers." *Journal of Negro History* 33 (1948): 7–23.

Gelber, Steven M. *Black Men and Businessmen: The Growing Awareness of a Social Responsibility*. Port Washington, New York: Kennikat Press, 1974.

Gerber, David A. *Black Ohio and the Color Line 1860–1915*. Urbana: University of Illinois Press, 1976.

Gibson, Donald B. "Strategies and Revisions of Self-Representation in Booker T. Washington's Autobiographies." *American Quarterly* 45 (September 1993): 370–93.

Giddings, Paula. *When and Where I Enter: The Impact of Black Women on Race and Sex in America*. New York: Bantam Books, 1985.

Gill, Walter Arthur Harris. "Booker T. Washington's Philosophy of Black Education: A Reassessment." The *Western Journal of Black Studies* 16 (Winter 1992): 214–20.

Goldstein, Michael L. "Preface to the Rise of Booker T. Washington: A View from New York City of the Demise of Independent Black Politics, 1889–1902." *Journal of Negro History* LXII (January 1977): 81–99.

Green, Shelley and Paul Pryde. *Black Entrepreneurship in America*. New Brunswick, New Jersey: Transaction Publishers, 1990.

Grimshaw, Allen D. "Lawlessness and Violence in America and Their Special Manifestations in Changing Negro-White Relationships." *Journal of Negro History* 44 (1959): 52–72.

Guess, Jerry M. "Booker T. Washington: The Message, The Legacy, The Challenge." *Crisis* 99 (1992): 25–28.

Guzman, Jessie P. "Monroe Nathan Work and his Contribution: Background and Preparation for Life's Career." *Journal of Negro History* 34 (October 1949): 428–61.

Gyant, LaVerne. "Contributors to Adult Education: Booker T. Washington, George Washington Carver, Alain L. Locke, and Ambrose Caliver." *Journal of Black Studies* 19 (September 1988): 97–110.

Hamilton, Kenneth Marvin. *Black Towns and Profit: Promotion and Development in the Trans-Appalachian West, 1877–1915*. Urbana: University of Illinois Press, 1991.

Harlan, Louis R. "Booker T. Washington in Biographical Perspective." *American Historical Review* 75 (October 1970): 1,581–599.

———. *Booker T. Washington: The Making of a Black Leader 1856–1901*. New York: Oxford University Press, 1972.

———. "Booker T. Washington and the Voice of the Negro, 1904–1907." *Journal of Southern History* 45 (February 1979): 45–62.

———. "Booker T. Washington and the White Man's Burden." *American Historical Review* 71 (January 1966): 441–67.

———. *Booker T. Washington: The Wizard of Tuskegee, 1901–1915*. New York: Oxford University Press, 1983.

———. "The Secret Life of Booker T. Washington." *Journal of Southern History* 37 (1982): 393–416.

Harmon, J. H. "The Negro as a Local Business Man." *Journal of Negro History* 14 (1929): 116–55.

Harmon, J. H., Arnett Lindsay, and Carter G. Woodson. *The Negro as a Businessman*. Washington, D.C.: Association for the Study of Negro Life and History, 1929.

Harris, Abram. *The Negro as Capitalist*. College Park, Maryland: McGrath Publishing Company, 1936.

Harris, H. William. *The Harder We Run: Black Workers since the Civil War*. New York: Oxford University Press, 1982.

Hawkins, Hugh. *Booker T. Washington and His Critics*. Lexington, Massachusetts: D. C. Heath and Company, 1962.

Hedin, Raymond. "Paternal at Last: Booker T. Washington and the Slave Narrative Tradition." *Callaloo* 7 (October 1979): 95–102.

Henderson, Alexa Benson. "Herman E. Perry and Black Enterprise in Atlanta, 1908–1925." *Business History Review* 61 (Summer 1987): 216–42.

Heningburg, Alphonse. "The Relation of Tuskegee Institute to Education in the Lower South." *Journal of Educational Sociology* 7 (November 1933): 157–62.

Henry, Charles P. "Who Won The Great Debate—Booker T. Washington or W.E.B. Du Bois?" *Crisis* 99 (1992): 12–17.

Higgs, Robert. *Competition and Coercion: Blacks in the American Economy, 1865–1914*. Chicago: University of Chicago Press, 1980.

Hine, Darlene Clark and Kathleen Thompson. *A Shining Thread of Hope*. New York: Broadway Books, 1998.

Hines, Linda O. "George W. Carver and the Tuskegee Agricultural Experimental Station." *Agricultural History* 53 (January 1979): 71–83.

Hofstadter, Richard. *Social Darwinism in American Thought*. Boston, Massachusetts: Beacon Press, 1992.

Holmes, William F. "Whitecapping: Agrarian Violence in Mississippi, 1902–1906." *Journal of Southern History* 35 (May 1969): 165–85.

Howard-Pitney, David. "The Jeremiads of Frederick Douglass, Booker T. Washington, and W.E.B. Du Bois and Changing Patterns of Black Messianic Rhetoric, 1841–1920." *Journal of American Ethnic History* 6 (Fall 1986): 47–61.

Huggins, Nathan I., Martin Kilson, and Daniel M. Fox. *Key Issues in Afro-American Experience: Volume II: Since 1865*. New York: Harcourt Brace Jovanovich, Inc., 1971.

Ijere, Martin O. *Survey of Afro-American Experience in the U.S. Economy*. Hicksville, New York: Exposition Press, 1978.

Ingham, John N., and Lynne B. Feldman. *African-American Business Leaders: A Biographical Dictionary*. Westport, Connecticut: Greenwood Press, 1994.

Jackson, David H. "Booker T. Washington's Tour of the Sunshine State, March 1912," *Florida Historical Quarterly* 8 (Winter 2003): 254–78.

———. *A Chief Lieutenant of the Tuskegee Machine: Charles Banks of Mississippi*. Gainesville, Florida: University Press of Florida, 2002.

Jenkins, Carol, and Elizabeth G. Hines. *Black Titan: A. G. Gaston and the Making of a Black American Millionaire*. New York: One World Book, 2004.

Jensen, Beverly. "100 Oldest: The Oldest Black Business in Our Top 100 Is Still Going Strong." *Black Enterprise* 6 (June 1976): 66–74 & 223.

Jerkins, Henry R. "Apostle of Industrial Education." *Opportunity* 18 (May 1940): 142–43.

Johnson, Abby A., and Ronald M. Johnson. "Away From Accommodation: Radical editors and Protest Journalism, 1900–1910." *Journal of Negro History* 62 (1977): 325–38.

Johnson, Charles. "The Rise of the Negro Magazine." *Journal of Negro History* 13 (1928): 7–21.

———. "The Social Philosophy of Booker T. Washington." *Opportunity* 6 (April 1928): 102–105 & 115.

Johnson, Guy. "Negro Racial Movements and Leadership in the United States." *American Journal of Sociology* 43 (January 1937): 57–71.

Jones, Allen. "Improving Rural Life for Blacks: The Tuskegee Negro Farmers' Conference, 1892–1915." *Agricultural History* 65 (Spring 1991): 105–14.

———. "The Role of Tuskegee Institute in the Education of Black Farmers." *Journal of Negro History* 60 (1970): 252–67.

———. "The South's First Black Farm Agents." *Agricultural History* 50 (October 1976): 636–44.

———. "Thomas M. Campbell: Black Agricultural Leader of the New South." *Agricultural History* 53 (January 1979): 42–59.
Jones, Charles A. "Liberalism and American Black Business." Presented at the annual meeting of the National Conference of Black Political Scientists, Hampton, Virginia, March 1994, 1–98.
Jones, Edward H. *Blacks in Business*. New York: Grosset and Dunlap, Publishers, 1971.
Jones, Jacqueline. *Labor of Love, Labor of Sorrow: Black Women, Work and the Family, From Slavery to the Present*. New York: Vintage Books, 1995.
Jones, Lewis W. "The South's Negro Farm Agent." *Journal of Negro Education* 22 (Winter 1953): 38–45.
Jones, Thomas Jesse. "Booker T. Washington: Apostle of Self-Determination and Cooperation." *Opportunity* 12 (May 1934): 136–39.
Katz, William L. *A New Negro for a New Century: Booker T. Washington, N. F. Wood, and Fannie Barrier Williams*. New York: Arno Press & the *New York Times*, 1969.
Kendrick, Louis. "To Tell The Truth: Were These Two Men So Different?" *Pittsburgh New Courier* (September 1998), 89, no. 73: A-7.
Kelly, Don Quinn. "The Political Economy of Booker T. Washington: A Bibliographic Essay." *Journal of Negro Education* 46 (1977): 403–18.
Kilpatrick, James Jackson. "What Was So Wrong With Booker T. Washington?" *Human Events* 25 (March 13, 1965): 13.
Kinzer, Robert H., and Edward Sagarin. *The Negro in American Business: The Conflict Between Separatism and Integration*. New York: Greenberg Publishing, 1950.
Kusmer, Kenneth L. *A Ghetto Takes Shapes: Black Cleveland 1870–1930*. Urbana: University of Illinois Press, 1978.
Lamon, Lester C. *Black Tennesseans 1900–1930*. Knoxville: University of Tennessee Press, 1977.
Larsha, William. "Silence Covers the Plan of the Man." *Tri-State Defender* (March 4, 1998), 47, no. 9: 5-A.
Larson, Charles R. "The Deification of Booker T. Washington." *Negro American Literature Forum* 4 (Winter 1970): 125–26.
Lawrence, David. "Let Booker T. Washington Speak Again." *US News and World Report* 55 (September 2, 1963): 88.
Lee, Roy F. *The Setting for Black Business Development: A Study in Sociology and Political Economy*. Ithaca, New York: Cornell University Press, 1972.
Light, Ivan H. *Ethnic Enterprise in America: Business and Welfare Among Chinese, Japanese, and Blacks*. Berkeley, California: University of California Press, 1972.
Lincoln, C. Eric. *The Black Muslims in America*. Boston: Beacon Press, 1961.
Lipscomb, George D. *Dr. George Washington Carver, Scientist*. Toronto, Canada: Smithers & Bonellie, 1944.
Litwack, Leon F. *Been in the Storm so Long: The Aftermath of Slavery*. New York: Vintage Books, 1980.
Locke, Alain. *The New Negro*. New York: Atheneum, 1968.

Logan, Rayford W. *The Betrayal of the Negro, from Rutherford B. Hayes to Woodrow Wilson*. New York: Collier, 1965.
Logan, Rayford W., and Irving S. Cohen. *The American Negro: Old World Background and New World Experience*. New York: Houghton Mifflin Company, 1967.
MacDonald, Stephen. *Business and Blacks*. Princeton, New Jersey: Dow Jones Books, 1970.
Malson, Micheline R., Elisabeth Mudimbe-Boyi, Jean O'Barr, and Mary Wyer. *Black Women in America: Social Science Perspective*. Chicago: University of Chicago Press, 1990.
Mandle, Jay R. *Not Slave, Not Free: The African American Economic Experience Since the Civil War*. Durham, North Carolina: Duke University Press, 1992.
———. *The Roots of Black Poverty*. Philadelphia, Pennsylvania: Temple University Press, 1978.
Marable, Manning. "Black Conservatives and Accommodation: Thomas Sowell and Others." *Negro History Bulletin* 43 (1982): 32–35.
———. *Black Liberation in Conservative America*. Boston, Massachusetts: South End Press, 1997.
———. "Booker T. Washington and African Nationalism." *Phylon* 35 (1974): 398–406.
———. *How Capitalism Underdeveloped Black America*. Boston, Massachusetts: South End Press, 1983.
———. "The Pan-Africanism of Booker T. Washington: A Reappraisal." The *Claflin College Review* 2 (May 1978): 1–13.
Marlowe, Gertrude W. *A Right Worthy Grand Mission: Maggie Lena Walker and the Quest for Black Economic Empowerment*. Washington, D.C.: Howard University Press, 2003.
Martin, Tony. *Race First: The Ideological and Organizational Struggles of Marcus Garvey and the Universal Negro Improvement Association*. Westport, Connecticut: Greenwood Press, 1976.
"Master Mind: Builder of Civilization." The *New York Beacon* (March 4, 1998), 5, no. 8: 10.
Mathews, Basil. *Booker T. Washington: Educator and Interracial Interpreter*. Cambridge, Massachusetts: Harvard University Press, 1948.
Matthews, Mark D. "Booker T. Washington and His Relationship to Garveyism: An Assessment." The *Western Journal of Black Studies* 7 (Summer 1983): 103–12.
Mayberry, B. D. "The Tuskegee Moveable School: A Unique Contribution to National and International Agriculture and Rural Development." *Agricultural History* 65 (Spring 1991): 85–104.
McCall, Nathan. "How Herman Russell Built His Business . . . Brick By Brick." *Black Enterprise* 17 (June 1987): 176–84.
McGee, Leo, and Robert Boone. "Black Rural Land Ownership: A Matter of Economic Survival." The *Review of Black Political Economy* 8 (1977): 62–69.
McMurry, Linda O. *George Washington Carver: Scientist & Symbol*. New York: Oxford University Press, 1982.

McPherson, James M. *The Abolitionist Legacy: From Reconstruction to the NAACP.* Princeton, New Jersey: Princeton University Press, 1975.

Mecklin, John M. "The Philosophy of the Color Line." *Journal of Sociology* 19 (1913): 343–57.

Meier, August. "Booker T. Washington and the Negro Press: With Special Reference to the Colored American Magazine." *Journal of Negro History* 38 (January 1953): 67–90.

———. "Booker T. Washington and the Town of Mound Bayou." *Phylon* 15 (Winter 1954): 396–401.

———. "Negro Class Structure and Ideology in the Age of Booker T. Washington." *Phylon* 23 (1962): 258–66.

———. *Negro Thought in America, 1880–1915.* Ann Arbor, Michigan: University of Michigan Press, 1963.

———. "Toward a Reinterpretation of Booker T. Washington." *Journal of Southern History* 23 (1957): 16–24.

Meier, August, and Elliott Rudwick. *From Plantation to Ghetto.* New York: Hill and Wang, 1970.

———. *The Making of Black America: Volumes I & II: The Origins of Black Americans.* New York: Atheneum, 1969.

Meltzer, Milton. *Thaddeus Stevens and the Fight for Negro Rights.* New York: Thomas Y. Crowell Company, 1967.

Meyers, Gustavus. *History of the Great American Fortunes.* New York: Random House, Inc., 1936.

Miller, Basil. *George Washington Carver: God's Ebony Scientist.* Grand Rapids, Michigan: Zondervan Publishing House, 1943.

Miller, Perry. *The New England Mind: From Colony to Province.* Boston: Beacon Press, 1953.

Moore, Jacqueline M. *Booker T. Washington, W.E.B. Du Bois, and the Struggle for Racial Uplift.* Wilmington, Delaware: A Scholarly Resource Inc., 2003.

———. *Leading the Race: The Transformation of the Elite in the Nation's Capital, 1880–1920.* Charlottesville, Virginia: University of Virginia Press, 1999.

Morris, Richard B. *Encyclopedia of American History.* New York: Harper & Brothers, Publishers, 1953.

Moses, Norton H. *Lynching and Vigilantism in the United States: An Annotated Bibliography.* Westport, Connecticut: Greenwood Press, 1997.

Mtima, Lateef. "African-American Economic Empowerment Strategies for the New Millennium—Revisiting the Washington-Du Bois Dialectic." *Howard Law Journal* 42 (Spring 1999): 391–429.

Myrdal, Gunnar. *An American Dilemma.* New York: Harper and Brothers, 1944.

Norell, R. J. "Perfect Quiet, Peace and Harmony: Another Look at the Founding of Tuskegee Institute." *Alabama Review* 36 (1983): 110–28.

Notable Black American Women. Gale Research Inc., 1992.

Oak, Vishnu V. *The Negro's Adventure in General Business*. Westport, Connecticut: Negro University Press, 1970.
Ofari, Earl. *The Myth of Black Capitalism*. New York: Monthly Review Press, 1970.
O'Hare, W. P. "Black Business Ownership in the Rural South." The *Review of Black Political Economy* 18 (Winter 1990): 93–104.
Osofsky, Gilbert. *Harlem: The Making of a Ghetto: Negro New York, 1890–1930*. New York: Harper & Row, Publishers, 1971.
Painter, Nell Irvin. *Exodusters: Black Migration to Kansas after Reconstruction*. New York: W. W. Norton & Company, 1986.
Perkins, William Eric. "On Booker T. Washington: A Review Essay." The *Journal of Ethnic Studies* 1 (Spring 1973): 56–62.
Perlo, Victor. *Economics of Racism U.S.A.* New York: International Publishers Company, Inc., 1975.
"Personal, Anthony Overton." *Journal of Negro History* 32 (July 1947): 394–96.
Piehl, Charles K. "The White Use of Dr. Booker T. Washington: Rocky Mount, North Carolina, 1910." *Journal of Negro History* 70 (1985): 82–88.
Porter, Glenn. *The Rise of Big Business: 1860–1910*. Arlington Heights, Illinois: Harlan Davidson, Inc., 1973.
Potter, Richard. "Booker T. Washington: A Visit to Florida." *Negro History Bulletin* 40 (September-October 1977): 744–45.
Poxpey, C. Spencer. "The Washington–Du Bois Controversy and Its Effect on the Negro Problem." *History of Education Journal* 8 (1957): 128–52.
"Profiles." *Black Enterprise* 6 (June 1976): 121–26, 211, & 216.
Pryor, Theodore M. *Wealth Building Lessons of Booker T. Washington for a New Black America*. Edgewood, Maryland: Duncan & Duncan, 1995.
Puth, Robert C. "Supreme Life: The History of a Negro Life Insurance Company, 1919–1962." *Business History Review* 43 (1969): 1–20.
Pusateri, C. Joseph. *A History of American Business*. Arlington Heights, Illinois: Harlan Davidson, Inc., 1988.
Quarles, Benjamin. *The Negro in the Making of America*. New York: Touchstone, 1996.
Rashad, Adib. *Elijah Muhammad & The Ideological Foundation of The Nation of Islam*. Newport News, Virginia: U. B. & U. S. Communications Systems, 1993.
Record, Wilson. "Negro Intellectuals and Negro Movements in Historical Perspective." *American Quarterly* 8 (1956): 3–20.
Redding, Saunders. *The Lonesome Road: The Story of the Negro's Part in America*. New York: Doubleday & Company, Inc., 1958.
———. *They Came in Chains*. Philadelphia, Pennsylvania: J. B. Lippincott Company, 1950.
Robinson, Bernard F. "The Social Psychology of Negro-White Relations." *Phylon* 7 (1946): 47–57.
Rogers, J. A. *World's Great Men of Color: Volume II*. New York: Simon & Schuster, 1996.

Rome, Adam Ward. "American Farmers as Entrepreneurs, 1870–1900." *Agricultural History* 56 (January 1982): 37–49.

Rose, Willie Lee. *Rehearsal for Reconstruction: The Port Royal Experi*ment. New York: Oxford University Press, 1964.

Rudwick, Elliott M. "Booker T. Washington's Relations with the National Association for the Advancement of Colored People." *Journal of Negro Education* XXIX (Spring 1960): 134–44.

———. "The Niagara Movement." *Journal of Negro History* 42 (1957): 177–99.

———. "Race Leadership Struggle: Background of the Boston Riot of 1903." *Journal of Negro Education* 31 (1962): 16–24.

Sales, William W. Jr. *From Civil Rights to Black Liberation: Malcolm X and the Organization of Afro-American Unity*. Boston, Massachusetts: South End Press, 1994.

Schuyler, George S. "Madam C. J. Walker: Pioneer Big Business Woman of America." The *Messenge*r 6 (August 1924): 250–58 & 264.

Schweninger, Loren. *Black Property Owners in the South 1790–1915*. Urbana: University of Illinois Press, 1997.

Shaw, Francis H. "Booker T. Washington and The Future of Black Americans." *Georgia Historical Quarterly* LVI (Summer 1972): 193–209.

Sherer, Robert G. *Subordination or Liberation?* Tuscaloosa, Alabama: University of Alabama Press, 1977.

Simmons, Judy D. "Heman Perry: The Commercial Booker T. Washington." *Black Enterprise* 8 (April 1978): 41–48.

Simmons, Willis. "Maggie Lena Walker and The Consolidated Bank and Trust Company." *Negro History Bulletin* 38 (February/March 1975): 345–49.

Sisk, Glenn N. "Negro Education in the Alabama Black Belt, 1875–1900." *Journal of Negro Education* 22 (Spring 1953): 126–35.

Slade, William G., and Roy C. Herrenkohl. *Seven in Black: Reflections on the Negro Experience in America*. New York: J. B. Lippincott Company, 1969.

Smith, John David. *Black Voices From Reconstruction, 1865–1877*. Gainesville, Florida: University Press of Florida, 1997.

Smock, Raymond W. *Booker T. Washington in Perspective*. Jackson, Mississippi: University of Mississippi Press, 1988.

"Some Chicagoans of Note." The *Crisis* 10 (September 1975): 237–42.

Sowell, Thomas. *Race and Economics*. New York: Longman, Inc., 1975.

Spear, Allan H. *Black Chicago: The Making of a Ghetto, 1890–1920*. Chicago: University of Chicago Press, 1967.

Spencer, Samuel R. Jr. *Booker T. Washington and the Negro's Place in American Life*. Boston: Little, Brown and Company, 1955.

Spivey, Donald. *Schooling for the New Slavery: Black Industrial Education, 1868–1915*. Westport, Connecticut: Greenwood Press, 1978.

Sterling, Dorothy, ed. *The Trouble They Seen: The Story of Reconstruction in the Words of African Americans*. New York: Da Capo Press, 1994.

Steward, Gustavus Adolphus. "Something New Under the Sun." *Opportunity* 3 (January 1925): 20.
Stewart, Merah S. *An Economic Detour: A History of Insurance in the Lives of American Negroes*. New York: Wendell Malliet and Company, 1940.
Stone, Chuck. "Drop Your Bucket Where You Are." The *New York Age* (December 5, 1959), 79, no. 38: 6.
Stowe, Harriet Beecher. *Uncle Tom's Cabin*. New York: E. P. Dutton & Company, 1961.
Strauss, Anselm L. *Qualitative Analysis for Social Scientists*. Boston: Cambridge University Press, 1996.
Summers, Mark W. *The Gilded Age or, The Hazard of New Functions*. Upper Saddle River, New Jersey: Prentice Hall, 1997.
"The Great Divide." The *American Enterprise* (November/December 1998), 9, no. 6: 70–72.
"The National Negro Business League." *Black Enterprise* 2 (1972): 37–41.
"The National Negro Business League After 70 Years of More Downs Than Ups, NBL Looks for a Turning Point." *Black Enterprise* 2 (1972): 37–38 & 41.
Thimm, Alfred L. *Business Ideologies in the Reform-Progressive Era, 1880–1914*. Tuscaloosa, Alabama: University of Alabama Press, 1976.
Thornbrough, Emma L. *Booker T. Washington*. Englewood Cliffs, New Jersey: Prentice-Hall, Inc., 1969.
———. "Booker T. Washington as Seen by His White Contemporaries." *Journal of Negro History* 53 (1968): 161–82.
———. "More Light on Booker T. Washington and the *New York Age*." *Journal of Negro History* 43 (January 1958): 34–49.
———. "The National Afro-American League, 1887–1908." *Journal of Southern History* 53 (1961): 161–82.
Tolnay, Stewart E. and E. M. Beck. *A Festival of Violence: An Analysis of Southern Lynchings, 1882–1930*. Urbana: University of Illinois Press, 1992.
"Torture and Lynching." *Outlook* 71 (June 28, 1902): 533–34.
Tucker, David M. "Black Pride and Negro Business in the 1920's: George Washington Lee of Memphis." *Business History Review* 43 (1969): 436–61.
Tyler, Lawrence. "The Protestant Ethic Among The Black Muslims." *Phylon* 27 (Spring 1966): 5–14.
Upson, William Hazlitt. "A Great Negro Conservative: What Would Booker T. Washington Say Now?" *Human Events* 16 (October 21, 1959): 1–2.
Verney, Kevern. *The Art of the Possible: Booker T. Washington and Black Leadership in the United States, 1881–1925*. New York: Routledge Press, 2001.
Walden, Daniel. "The Contemporary Opposition to the Political Ideas of Booker T. Washington." *Journal of Negro History* 45 (April 1960): 103–15.
Walker, Juliet E. K. *The History of Black Business in America: Capitalism, Race, Entrepreneurship*. New York: Twayne's Publishers, 1998.
———. "Racism, Slavery, and Free Enterprise: Black Entrepreneurship in the United States Before the Civil War." *Business History Review* 60 (1986): 343–82.

"Washington and Du Bois Reconsidered." *Precinct Reporter* (April 16, 1998), 33, no 40: A-2.

Washington, Booker T., Emmett J. Scott, and Fred R. Moore. "Making Your Local League More Effective." *The Booker T. Washington Papers*, Washington, D.C.: The Library of Congress Microfilms: Reel no. 752: 1

Watkins, Ralph. "Voices Beyond the Dark Veil: Expanding the Boundaries of the inquiry into the Harlem Renaissance." Presented at the Monroe Fordham Conference at Buffalo State College, October 23, 1999, 1–16.

Weare, Walker B. *Black Business in the New South: A Social History of the North Carolina Mutual Life Insurance Company*. Urbana: University of Illinois Press, 1973.

Weber, Max. *The Protestant Ethic and the Spirit of Capitalism*. New York: Charles Scribner's Sons, 1930.

Weems, Robert E. Jr. *Desegregating the Dollar: African American Consumerism in the Twentieth Century*. New York: New York University Press, 1998.

Weiss, Nancy J. *The National Urban League 1910–1940*. New York: Oxford University Press, 1974.

Wesley, Charles H. *Negro Labor in the United States, 1850–1925*. New York: Russell and Russell, 1927.

White, Arthur O. "Booker T. Washington's Florida Incident, 1903–1904." *Florida Historical Quarterly* 51 (January 1973): 227–49.

Whitfield, Stephen J. "Three Masters of Impression Management: Benjamin Franklin, Booker T. Washington, and Malcolm X as Autobiographers." The *South Atlantic Quarterly* 77 (Autumn 1978): 399–417.

Wiener, Jonathan. *Social Origins of the New South: Alabama, 1860–1885*. New York: Vintage Books, 1974.

Williams, George W. *History of the Negro Race in America From 1619 to 1880*. New York: G. P. Putnam's Sons, 1885.

Williams, Vernon J. Jr. "Monroe N. Work's Contribution to Booker T. Washington's Nationalist Legacy." The *Western Journal of Black Studies* 21 (Summer 1997): 85–91.

Williamson, Joel. *After Slavery: The Negro in South Carolina During Reconstruction, 1861–1877*. New York: W. W. Norton and Company, Inc., 1965.

Wilson, Amos N. *Blueprint for Black Power: A Moral, Political and Economic Imperative for the Twenty-First Century*. New York: Afrikan World InfoSystems, 1998.

Woodson, Robert L. *On the Road to Economic Freedom: An Agenda for Black Progress*. Washington, D.C.: Regnery Gateway, 1987.

Woodward, C. Vann. *Origins of the New South 1877–1913*. Baton Rouge: Louisiana State University, 1951.

———. *The Burden of Southern History*. New York: Vintage Books, 1961.

———. *The Strange Career of Jim Crow*. New York: Oxford University Press, 1973.

———. *Tom Watson: Agrarian Rebel*. New York: Oxford University Press, 1972.

Wortham, John M. "The Economic Ideologies of Booker T. Washington and W.E.B. Du Bois: 1895–1915." PhD. dissertation, Boston University, 1997.

Wright, Elizabeth. "The Importance of Booker T. Washington to Black Conservatism." *Jacksonville Free Press* (June 24, 1998), 12, no. 24: 4.

Wright, Ellicott. "Section D: The Soul of Black Folk and My Larger Education." *Journal of Negro Education* 30 (1960): 440–44.

Yett, Samuel F. "Booker T. Washington: His Wise Words Still Apply." The *Philadelphia Tribune* (February 13, 1998), 114, no. 13: 2-A.

Young, Alfred. "The Educational Philosophies of Booker T. Washington and Carter G. Woodson: A Liberating Praxis." PhD. dissertation, Syracuse University, 1977.

———. "The Educational Philosophy of Booker T. Washington: A Perspective for Black Liberation." *Phylon* 37 (1977): 224–35.

Zangrando, Robert L. *The NAACP Crusade Against Lynching, 1909–1950*. Philadelphia, Pennsylvania: Temple University Press, 1980.

Index

Abstractions, 63, 74, 162
Academic education, 36, 58, 124–25
Accommodationist strategies, 27, 57, 74, 105, 149
Accounting principles, 28, 45–48
Adams, Cyrus F., 8
Adams, Lewis, 41–43, 104–5
A.F.L. *See* American Federation of Labor
African Americans: in agriculture, 10–13, 16–17, 156; businesses of, 14–15, *15*, *111*, 111–12, 186; capital investments of, 14–15, *15*; dimensions of life for, 131–43, 150; disenfranchisement of, 4–6, 24, 109, 154; economic nadir for, 9–18, 56, 94; employment statistics for, *11*, 11–14, *13*; as entrepreneurs, xi–xiv, 14–16, 29, 91–92, 148; equal rights and, 1; in Harlem, 131; in Macon County, 17–18, 44, 77, 82; nationalism of, 130, 133; opportunities for, 39, 59, 66–68, 73; political nadir for, 3–9; political power of, 2, 95, 150, 153; population statistics for, 10, *10*; during Reconstruction, 1–2, 18–19; rural/urban statistics for, 10–11, *11*; scholarship on, 112; social-cultural nadir for, 18–27, 74; in the South, 10, *10*, 27; violence against, 2, 153; voting rights of, 3–9; Washington and, 129–43
Afro-American Council, 93–94; Negro Business Bureau of, 93
Afro-American Realty Company, 131
Agreements, gentlemen's, 22, 158
Agriculture: African Americans in, 10–13, 16–17, 156; business development and, 87–88; education in, 80, 83; Tuskegee Institute and, 80–84, 124–25, 156; uplift activities in, 90
Alabama, population statistics for, 16–17, *17*

Alabama Constitutional Convention, 5, 24
Alabama Polytechnic Institute, 84
Alabama State Negro Business League, 24
Alabama State Teachers' Association, 45
Albon L. Holsey Collection at Tuskegee University Archives (ALHCTU), xv
Alexander, Mr., 65
Alger, Horatio, 49, 72, 166
ALHCTU. *See* Albon L. Holsey Collection at Tuskegee University Archives
American Federation of Labor (A.F.L.), 13
Armstrong, Samuel C.: Hampton Institute and, 35–37, 44, 52, 125, 161; Tuskegee Institute and, 116
Arts, 62
Atlanta Exposition address: content of, 4, 7, 16, 59, 68, 142, 148; reception of, 19, 31, 46; speaking tour after, 14, 87, 120–21
Atlanta University Conference on the Negro in Business, 41
Ayers, Edward L., *The Promise of the New South*, 19

Baker, Ray Stannard, *Following the Color Line*, 25
Baldwin, William H., Jr., 45–50, 52, 69, 117, 121–22
Baldwin Farms Colony, 69, 123
Banking, 51, 104, 107, 122, 137
Banks, Charles, 53–55, 101, 107
Barbour, Minnie R., 98
Beck, E. M., 25
Bible training curriculum, 70
Biblical teachings, 36
Birmingham Reporter (newspaper), 134

Black Belt, of South, 17, 20, 78, 156
Black Enterprise (magazine), 135
Black Star Steamship Line, 139, 195
Booker T. Washington (steamship), 139, 195
Booker T. Washington Burial Insurance Company, 134
Booker T. Washington Business College, 134
Booker T. Washington Collection at Tuskegee University Archives (BTWCTU), xv
Booker T. Washington Papers at the Library of Congress (BTWPLC), xv
Boston Riot of 1903, 94
Boy Scouts, 137
Brickyard, of Tuskegee Institute, 59, 124
Bridgeforth, George R., 81, 83, 85
Brock, Randall E., 142
Brown, E., 99
Bruce, Blanche K., 3–4
Bruce, Roscoe Conkling, 124
BTWCTU. *See* Booker T. Washington Collection at Tuskegee University Archives
BTWPLC. *See* Booker T. Washington Papers at the Library of Congress
Buffalo Criterion (newspaper), xii
Bullock, Rufus B., 19
Burroughs, Nannie H., 98, 107, 110
Business development: agriculture and, 87–88; community and, xiii, 42, 61, 73, 101; expansion and, 45–56; management in, 120–23; slavery and, 59, 74, 89, 112; in the South, 28–29, 38–40, 45, 73; Washington and, xiii, 37–41, 73
Businesses, of African Americans, 14–15, *15*, *111*, 111–12, 186
Butler, John Sibley, 142; *Entrepreneurship and Self-Help Among Black Americans: A Reconsideration of Race and Economics*, 15, 155–56

Cabinetmaking, 119, 124
Campbell, George W., 44
Campbell, Thomas Monroe, 83–85
Capital investments, of African Americans, 14–15, *15*
Capitalism, 145
Carnegie, Andrew: *The Gospel of Wealth*, 53; NNBL and, 100, 106; Tuskegee Institute and, 38, 49, 66, 118, 150
Carpentry, 36, 49, 124, 161, 196
Carter, William, 106

Carver, George Washington, 80–83, 86, 139, 174
Cash, Wilbur J., *The Mind of the South*, 66
Casneau, Mrs., 110
Caste system, racial, 18–19, 23
Cemeteries, segregated, 24, 26, 108
Census statistics, 14, 16
Character-building, 35–36, 70
Charities (magazine), 103
Citizens Federal Savings Bank, 134
Civil Rights Act of 1875, 3–4, 6
Civil rights movement: Douglass and, 3–4; entrepreneurs and, 131; self-help and, 143; in the South, 3–4; violence and, 147, 150
Civil War period, 14, 17, 53, 66
CMA. *See* Colored Merchants Association
Colonial period, 14
Color-blind markets, 60, 72–74, 97
The Colored American Magazine, 99
Colored Merchants Association (CMA), 184
Color line, 19, 25, 104, 157
Community(ies): business development and, xiii, 42, 61, 73, 101; education and, 30, 58–59; quality of, 23
Consolidated Bank and Trust Company, 194
Constitution, U.S., 112; fifteenth amendment to, 5
Constitutional rights, 2, 4, 71, 73
Convict-lease system, 75
Cook, George W., 100
Cooking, 81
Cooper, E. E., 95
Cooperation, racial, 68–69, 195
Cooperative ventures, 123
Core values, 29–37
Correlative method, of education, 58–59, 120, 125, 169
Cotton gins, 127, 156
Cotton industry, 38, 86
Covenants, restrictive, 22, 158
Credit: charges, 18; ratings, 44, 121
Criminal activity, 79
Crisis (magazine), 142
Crop rotation, 81
Crop yields, 17, 82
Crummell, Alexander, 95
Cruse, Harold, *Rebellion or Revolution*, 130, 140

Dairying, 81
Darwin, Charles, 38

Darwinism, social, 57, 162
Davidson, Olivia A., 31, 114–16, 118, 159, 186
Davis, Jefferson, 43, 53
Davis, Joseph, 53–54
Debt avoidance, 76, 79, 85–86
Debt peonage, 69, 75–77, 123
De-emphasizing grievances, 67, 73, 95, 99
De facto segregation, 148, 156
De jure segregation, 148, 155
DePriest, Oscar, 96
Dimensions, of African-American life: entrepreneurial, 131–36; intelligentsia, 140–43, 150; leadership, 136–40
Discriminatory hiring practices, 12
Disenfranchisement, of African Americans, 4–6, 24, 109, 154
Divide, racial, 19, 142
Dizer, Silas C., 190
Dizer Fund, 123, 190
Dorsette, Cornelius N., 43–44, 104
Dorsey, Carolyn A., 186
Douglass, Frederick: civil rights and, 3–4; death of, 160; Garvey and, 195; segregation and, 8; self-help and, 40–41, 147; Washington and, 31
Du Bois, W.E.B., xi, 21; Crummell and, 95; equality and, xi; in Ghana, 147; "The Negro in Business," 14–15, 93; NNBL and, 93–94; "Of Mr. Booker T. Washington and Others," 94; "Talented Tenth" program and, 70–71, 150, 172; Washington and, 53, 57, 105, 129, 132–33, 140, 146, 150
Duke, Washington, 38
Duties v. rights, 57

Ebony (magazine), 135
An Economic Detour: A History of Insurance in the Lives of American Negroes (Stewart), 15–16
Economic Detour Theory, 15–16, 155–56
Economic equality, 70–71, 128
Economic freedom, xi, xiii, 27, 70
Economic influence, of Washington, 129–43
Economic nadir, for African Americans, 9–18, 56, 94
Economic segregation, 102–5, 129–30, 133, 156
Economic slavery, xi
Economic uplift activities, 28, 61, 95, 141, 150
Education: academic, 36, 58, 124–25; in agriculture, 80, 83; community and, 30, 58–59; correlative method of, 58–59, 120, 125, 169; higher, 58, 71, 169; industrial, 29, 35, 47, 57–59, 62, 115, 124–28, 147; practical, 59, 97; public, 5–6; slavery and, 117; state, 67; in trades, 49, 58, 119, 124, 161; uplift activities in, 31, 59, 98, 115. *See also* Tuskegee Institute
Educational fund, of Tuskegee Institute, 66
Edwards, Thomas J., 18
Electoral statistics, 4–5
Elitism, 71, 172
Emigration, 79, 89, 147
Emphasizing opportunities, 95, 99, 108
Employment statistics, for African Americans, *11*, 11–14, *13*
Entrepreneurial dimension, of African-American life, 131–36
Entrepreneurial ideas, of Washington, 57–74, 97, 114, 127–28, 142
Entrepreneurs: African American, xi–xiv, 14–16, 29, 91–92, 148. *See also* National Negro Business League; civil rights movement and, 131; foreign, 156; women as, 109–11
Entrepreneurship and Self-Help Among Black Americans: A Reconsideration of Race and Economics (Butler), 15, 155–56
Equality: Du Bois and, xi; economic, 70–71, 128; social, 149; Washington and, xiii, 27, 85, 91
Equal rights, for African Americans, 1
Evolution, 38, 112, 186
Expansion: of business development, 45–56; industrial, 37–39; of railroads, 38
Extension work, 84

Faith, 69
Farm agents, 83–84, 175
"Farmers' College on Wheels," 83–84
Farmers' Institute, 81
Farrakhan, Louis, 140
Ferguson, Jane, 32
Ferguson, Karen, 85
Fisher, Isaac, 88
Fisk Jubilee Singers, 118
Fisk University, 116
Flynn, John, 54
Folk songs, 118
Folkways, of the South, 9, 74
Following the Color Line (Baker), 25
Foreign entrepreneurs, 156
Former slaves, 17, 41–42, 77, 155

Fortune, T. Thomas, 92–93, 95
"Forty acres and a mule" rumor, 9–10
Framingham Institute, 115
Freedom: economic, xi, xiii, 27, 70; land and, 9, 77; from slavery, 1, 112
Freedpeople, 9–10, 15, 17, 155
Frugality, 37, 95, 122, 127, 140
Fundraising: for NNBL, 100; for Tuskegee Institute, 99, 114–20, 122, 124, 146

Gambling, 23
Gardening, 86–88
Garvey, Marcus, 137–40, 194–95
Garveyism, 139, 195
Gaston, Arthur G., 133–35
Gentlemen's agreements, 22, 158
Get-rich-quick schemes, 64
Ghana, and Du Bois, 147
Gilded Age, 38
Gordy, Berry, Jr., xii, 193
"Gospel of hard work," 37
The Gospel of Wealth (Carnegie), 53
Great Depression, 123
Great Migration, 133; first, 13, 19, 148, 155
Greene, Charles W., 80–81
Grievances: de-emphasizing, 67, 73, 95, 99; protesting, 60
Group-advancement philosophy, 29, 159
Group consciousness, 29–32
Group v. individual interests, 57
Groves, Junius G., 61, 88–89, 123
The Guardian (newspaper), 179

Hampton Institute: Armstrong and, 35–37, 44, 52, 125, 161; Greene and, 80; industrial education and, 35, 124; Washington and, 29–30, 34–35, 54
Hampton Singers, 118
Harlan, John Marshall, 7
Harlan, Louis, 75, 84–85, 93, 120
Harlem, African Americans in, 131
Harris, Abram L., 147; *The Negro as Capitalist*, 186
Harris, Gilbert C., 95
Harris, Thomas, 26
Hayes, Rutherford B., 2–3
HBTWPVN. *See* Louis Harlan's Edited Booker T. Washington Papers and the Volume Number

Higher dimensions, of life, 73
Higher education, 58, 71, 169
"Hints and Helps for Local Negro Business Leagues" (NNBL), 109
Holsey, Albon L., xv, 184
Homestead Act of 1866, 10
Hope, John, "The Meaning of Business," 41
Huntington, Collis P., 51–52
Hutchinson, Earl Ofari, 143, 196

Immigrants, 156
Improvement associations, 76
"Indispensable-asset" strategy, 25, 42, 76, 91, 149
Individualism, 29, 57
Individual v. group interests, 57
Industrial education: Hampton Institute and, 35, 124; need for, 62; Tuskegee Institute and, 47, 57–59, 124–28; Washington and, 29, 115, 147
Industrial expansion, 37–39
"Industrial idea concept," 36
Industrialization, of South, 66
Industrial Revolution, 38–39, 148
Insurance, 15–16, 134
Intelligentsia dimension, of African-American life, 140–43, 150
Interdependency, between races, 149
Interracial commerce, 42–43
Iowa State University, 80
Iron industry, 38
Islam, Nation of, 139–40

Jackson, Deal, 88
Jackson, Giles B., 95
Jerkins, Henry, 141
Jesup, Morris K., 83
Jesup Wagon, 83
Jews, as role models, 69
JHPCTU. *See* John H. Palmer Collection at Tuskegee University Archives
Jim Crow era: legislation of, 4, 6–8; social conditions of, 24, 58, 62, 67, 70, 134, 137
John H. Palmer Collection at Tuskegee University Archives (JHPCTU), xv
Johnson, E. A., 95
Johnson, John H., 133, 135–36
Johnston, David L., 127
Jones, Allen, 84
Jones, Theodore W., 101

Kansas Exodus, 88
Kellogg, John Harvey, 157
King, Martin Luther, Jr., 135, 193
Kirklin, Henry, 88
Knapp, Seaman, 83, 175
Knox, James, 192
Knox, John, 192
Ku Klux Klan, 166

Laissez-faire capitalism, 29
Land: freedom and, 9, 77; ownership of, 12, 36, 62, 77, 84–87; purchasing, 76, 123
Leadership: dimension, of African-American life, 136–40; of race, 31, 138, 179
Legislation, of Jim Crow era, 4, 6–8
Liberal arts, 59
Library of Congress, 64
Literacy tests, 4
Lodge, Henry Cabot, 6
Logan, Rayford, 1
Logan, Warren, 44, 47, 52, 121, 189
Long Island Railroad, 47
Louis Harlan's Edited Booker T. Washington Papers and the Volume Number (HBTWPVN), xv
Louisville, New Orleans, and Texas Railway, 54
Lovejoy, George W., 26
Low, Seth, 53
Lumber industry, 38
Lynchings: nadir and, 20–22; race issues and, 25–26, 43, 67; Walker and, 137; Washington and, 73, 75; Wells-Barnett and, 147

Mackie, Mary, 34
Macon County (Alabama): African Americans in, 17–18, 44, 77, 82; segregation in, 26; Tuskegee Institute and, xi–xiii, 80, 126, 145; Washington and, 17, 30, 76
Malcolm X, 140
Management, in business development, 120–23
Mandle, Jay R., *The Roots of Black Poverty*, 12
Manufacturing statistics, 38–39, *39*
Marshall, James F. B., 44–45
Marshall Farm, 47–48
MARTA. *See* Metro Atlanta Rapid Transit System
Martin, Tony, 139
Martin Luther King Jr. Community Center, 135
Materialist business philosophy, 70

Mathews, Basil, 21
McDougall, Mrs., 40
"The Meaning of Business" (Hope), 41
Mecklin, John M., 157
Meharry Medical College, 127
Meier, August, 75, 94
Merit, personal, 65–66
Merriweather, Frank, Sr., xii
Message To The Blackman in America (Muhammad), 140
The Messenger (newspaper), 82, 85
Metro Atlanta Rapid Transit System (MARTA), 135
Metropolitan Mercantile and Realty Company, 99
Miller, Dora A., 110
The Mind of the South (Cash), 66
Ministry: as calling, 69–70; conditions of, 78–79
Mississippi State Convention, 4
Mixed business clienteles, 104
Mob action, 20
The Mobile Weekly Advocate (newspaper), 192
Mobility, upward social, 29, 35, 67
Montgomery, Isaiah T., 4, 53–54
Moore, Charles H., 102
Moore, Fred R., 99–102
Morality, 35–36, 73, 87, 98, 140
Moral training, 58, 70
Morgan, J. P., 38, 55
Mortgage system, in the South, 67, 69, 77–78, 85–86
Moton, Robert Russa, 189
Motown Records, xii, 193
Moveable School, 82–83
Muhammad, Elijah, 139–40; *Message To The Blackman in America*, 140
My Larger Education: Being Chapters from My Experience (Washington), 36–37, 55

NAACP. *See* National Association for the Advancement of Colored People
Nadir period, for African Americans: economic, 9–18, 56, 94; lynchings and, 20–22; political, 3–9; slavery and, 1, 27, 32, 146; social-cultural, 18–27, 74
Napier, James C., 132–33
National Association for the Advancement of Colored People (NAACP), 22, 137
National Association of Negro Insurance Men, 108

National Colored Conventions, 41
National Colored Immigration and Commercial Association, 25
National Educational Association, 3, 42, 45
Nationalism, African American, 130, 133
National Negro Bankers Association, 108
National Negro Bar Association, 108
National Negro Business League (NNBL), xiv; Adams, C. F., and, 8; analysis of, 102–13; Carnegie and, 100, 106; Du Bois and, 93–94; fundraising for, 100; "Hints and Helps for Local Negro Business Leagues," 109; history of, 92–102; impact of, 131, 148; Peabody and, 51; Scott and, 92–93, 99, 102, 107, 132; self-help and, 106; Washington and, 23, 28, 52–53, 55–56, 63, 74, 91–113
National Negro Funeral Directors' Association, 108
National Negro League, 53
National Negro Press Association, 108
National Urban League, 141
Nation of Islam, 139–40
Native Americans: acculturation of, 3, 37; population statistics for, 17
The Negro as Capitalist (Harris, Abram), 186
Negro Business Bureau of Afro-American Council, 93
Negro Business Men's Leagues, 93
Negro Factories Corporation, 139
The Negro Farmer (newspaper), 82, 85, 88
Negro Farmers' Conference, xiv, 75–90, 148
"The Negro in Business," (Du Bois), 14–15, 93
The Negro in Business (Washington), 61, 97, 110, 183
Negro nationalism, 130, 133
Negro Organization Society, 137
The Negro's Adventure in General Business (Oak), 186
Nelson, Ezekiel E., 132
Neo-slaves, 126
The New York Age (newspaper), 92
Niagara Movement, 94
Niches, economic, 60–61, 66, 72, 74, 97
Night school, at Tuskegee Institute, 124, 161
NNBL. *See* National Negro Business League
Normal School (Tuskegee), 42

Oak, Vishnu V., *The Negro's Adventure in General Business*, 186

Obama, Barack, 143
"Of Mr. Booker T. Washington and Others" (Du Bois), 94
Ogden, Robert, 52
Opportunities: for African Americans, 39, 59, 66–68, 73; emphasizing, 95, 99, 108; in South, 66–67
Opportunity (magazine), 141
Optimism, 60, 67
Orchards, 89
Order of Saint Luke, 136–37
Ownership, of land, 12, 36, 62, 77, 84–87

Palmer, John H., 123
Panic of 1873, 39
Payton, Philip A., Jr., 131
Peabody, George Foster, 51–52
Peanuts, 41, 88, 174
Personal merit, 65–66
Phelps Hall Bible Training School, 70, 120
Pig iron production, 38–39
Pioneering spirit, 71, 118, 126
Pitts, Emma L., 110
Plantation melodies, 118
Platitudes, 97
Plessy, Homer, 6–7
Plessy v. Ferguson (1896), 6–9, 15
Political nadir, for African Americans, 3–9
Political power, of African Americans, 2, 95, 150, 153
Poll taxes, 4
Population density, 22
Population statistics: for African Americans, 10, *10*; for Alabama, 16–17, *17*; for Native Americans, *17*
"Potato King," 88
Poultry-raising, 81
Poverty, 76–77
Practical education, 59, 97
Prejudice, racial, 66–67, 104, 175
Producer mindset, 148
Productivity, 85
The Promise of the New South (Ayers), 19
Protestant work ethic, 32–38, 161; Muhammad and, 140; Tuskegee Institute and, 117; Washington and, 28–29, 50, 53, 56–57
Protesting grievances, 60
Protests, 60, 150
Public education, 5–6

Public transportation, unequal facilities on, 6–9, 24, 75
Pusateri, C. Joseph, 37

Race issues: interdependency between races, 149; lynchings, 25–26, 43, 67; prejudice, 66–67, 104, 175; race leadership, 31, 138, 179; race relations, 27, 36, 58, 136, 147, 169; race riots, 20, 22–23, 43, 147; racial caste system, 18–19, 23; racial cooperation, 68–69, 195; racial divide, 19, 142; racial solidarity, 40, 132; racism, 108, 146, 156; uplift activities and, 27, 36, 72, 74, 124, 132, 142–43, 145–47
Railroads: expansion of, 38; travel on, 6–9, 24, 137
Real estate covenants, 22
Rebellion or Revolution (Cruse), 130, 140
Reconstruction, xiii; African Americans during, 1–2, 18–19; aftermath of, 3–9, 27, 53, 56, 58, 67, 70, 74, 94; end of, 2–3; failure of, 61
Reform nationalism, xii
Reid, Dow, 126–27
Reid, Frank, 126–27
Religion, 69–70
Renting, 17–18, 36, 77
Republican Party, in Alabama, 25
Restrictive covenants, 22, 158
Retaliatory violence, 147
Revenue-generating activities, 115–20
Richardson, George, 22–23
Right, to trial by jury, 71
Rights v. duties, 57
Riots, race, 20, 22–23, 43, 147
Robber barons, 70
Rockefeller, John D., Sr., 38, 50, 52, 150
Rogers, Henry H., 52–53
Role models, 57, 69
Roosevelt, Franklin D., 143
Roosevelt, Theodore, 24–25
The Roots of Black Poverty (Mandle), 12
Rosenwald, Julius, 53
Ruffner, Viola, 32–34, 44, 50, 52, 116
Rural/urban statistics, for African Americans, 10–11, *11*
Russell, Herman, 133, 135

Saint Luke's Penny Savings Bank, 137
Salesmanship, 33
Savings accounts, 122, 137

Scholarship: on African Americans, 112; on Washington, xii–xiii, 108, 140–43, 149–50
School year, three-month, 67, 78, 127
Scott, Emmett J.: Banks and, 55; NNBL and, 92–93, 99, 102, 107, 132; Tuskegee Institute and, 121, 189; Washington and, 65, 90
Segregation, 15, 75, 137; of cemeteries, 24, 26, 108; de facto, 148, 156; de jure, 148, 155; Douglass and, 8; economic, 102–5, 129–30, 133, 156; in Macon County, 26; self-help and, 54
Self-help: civil rights movement and, 143; Douglass and, 40–41, 147; NNBL and, 106; segregation and, 54; Tuskegee Institute and, 85, 114, 117; Washington and, 56, 58, 112, 129, 131–32, 136
Self-sufficiency, 59, 71, 105
Separate-economy thesis, 102–5, 129–30, 133
Separatism, 139–40
Sewing, 81
Sexism, 110
Shakespeare, William, 72
Sharecropping, 17–18, 77
Shaw, Nate, 23–24
Sherman, William T., 9
Shoemaking, 36, 41, 124, 161
Slavery: business development and, 59, 74, 89, 112; economic, xi; education and, 117; former slaves, 17, 41–42, 77, 155; freedom from, 1, 112; nadir period and, 1, 27, 32, 146; neo-slaves, 126; racial caste system and, 18–19; work and, 35, 42
Smith, Albreta M., 110
Smith, Daniel C., 46–48, 52, 122
Smith, Hoke, 24
Smith, Joseph R., 88
Smith, Wilford H., 5
Smith-Lever Act, 84
Social-cultural nadir, for African Americans, 18–27, 74
Social Darwinism, 57
Social equality, 149
Socialism, 145
Social mobility, 29, 35, 67
Solidarity, racial, 40, 132
South (southern U.S.): African Americans in, 10, *10*, 27; Black Belt of, 17, 20, 78, 156; business development in, 28–29, 38–40, 45, 73; civil rights in, 3–4; folkways of, 9, 74; industrialization of, 66; *The Mind of the South*,

South (southern U.S.)—*continued*
  66; mortgage system in, 67, 69, 77–78, 85–86; opportunities in, 66–67; *The Promise of the New South*, 19
Southern Christian Leadership Conference, 193
The Southern Letter (newsletter), 118
Spanish-American War, 122
Spaulding, Charles C., 108
Spencer, Herbert, 38, 53, 162
Spencerianism, 53, 72, 167
Spero, Sterling D., 147
Spirituality, 73
Springfield, Illinois, Riot of 1908, 22–23
Springfield, Ohio, Riot of 1904, 22
Standard Oil, 50–51, 53
State education, 67
Stewart, Merah S., *An Economic Detour: A History of Insurance in the Lives of American Negroes*, 15–16
Stock raising, 81–82
Stone, Chuck, 142

The Story of My Life and Work (Washington), 61, 166
Strategist role, of Washington, 72, 105–6, 145–51
Strauss, Anselm, 85, 176
Supreme Court, 3–4, 6–7
"Survival of the fittest," 70
Systematized work, 33, 37

"Talented Tenth" program, 70–71, 150, 172
TBLA. *See* Tuskegee Building and Loan Association
Tenant farming, 10–12, 16, 87–88, 156
Tennessee Coal and Iron Company, 134
Thomas, Jonas W., 88
Thornton, A., 110
Thrasher, Max Bennett, 5
Three-month school year, 67, 78, 127
Tilden, Samuel J., 3
Tillman, Ben, 24
Tobacco industry, 38
Tolnay, Stewart E., 25
Tourgee, Albion W., 6
Trades, education in, 49, 58, 119, 124, 161
Travel, on railroads, 6–9, 24, 137
Trial by jury, 71
Trotter, William Monroe, 147, 179
Tuckerman, Alfred, 157

Tuggle Institute, 134
Tuskegee Building and Loan Association (TBLA), 123
Tuskegee Experimental Station, 80–83
Tuskegee Farmers' Conference, 63, 77–80, 94–95, 114, 136
Tuskegee Institute: agriculture and, 80–84, 124–25, 156; Armstrong and, 116; brickyard of, 59, 124; Carnegie and, 38, 49, 66, 118, 150; educational fund of, 66; faculty of, 42; founding of, 30–33, 63, 65; fundraising for, 99, 114–20, 122, 124, 146; industrial education at, 47, 57–59, 124–28; Macon County and, xi–xiii, 80, 126, 145; night school at, 124, 161; Protestant work ethic and, 117; Scott and, 121, 189; self-help and, 85, 114, 117; trustees of, 42, 46, 51, 55–56, 69; Washington and, xi, xiv, 30, 114, 120; women's programs at, 120
Tuskegee Machine Thesis, 93, 178
Tuskegee Mission, 126
Tuskegee Negro Conference, 77–79, 174
Tuskegee Quartet, 118
"Tuskegee Spirit," 114–15, 127–28, 134
The Tuskegee Student (magazine), 101, 118
Tyler, Ralph W., 102

Uncle Tom attitude, xi–xii, 105, 150
UNIA. *See* Universal Negro Improvement Association
Union Drugstore, 127
Unitarian National Conference, 45
Universal Negro Improvement Association (UNIA), 138
Up From Slavery (Washington), xii, 49–50, 61, 69–70, 134, 137–38, 166
Uplift activities: agricultural, 90; economic, 28, 61, 95, 141, 150; educational, 31, 59, 98, 115; racial, 27, 36, 72, 74, 124, 132, 142–43, 145–47
Upward mobility, 29, 35, 67
Urban League, 137
U.S. Steel, 49

Values, core, 29–37, 56, 97
Vardaman, James K., 21–22, 24
Violence: against African Americans, 2, 153; civil rights movement and, 147, 150; in retaliation, 147
Virginia Interracial Commission, 137
Voting issues, 73, 75, 154; disenfranchisement, of

African Americans, 4–6, 24, 109, 154; voting rights of African Americans, 3–9
Vulcan Realty and Investment Corporation, 134

Walker, Maggie Lena, 136–37, 194
Walker, Sarah Breedlove, 110–11
Walker, Sherman L., xii
Wanamaker, John, 52, 111
Warren Logan Papers at Tuskegee University Archives (WLPTU), xv
Washington, Booker T.: African Americans and, 129–43; business development and, xiii, 37–41, 73; Douglass and, 31; Du Bois and, 53, 57, 105, 129, 132–33, 140, 146, 150; economic influence of, 129–43; entrepreneurial ideas of, 57–74, 97, 114, 127–28, 142; equality and, xiii, 27, 85, 91; Hampton Institute and, 29–30, 34–35, 54; industrial education and, 29, 115, 147; influences on, 28–56, 160; lynchings and, 73, 75; Macon County and, 17, 30, 76; *My Larger Education: Being Chapters from My Experience*, 36–37, 55; *The Negro in Business*, 61, 97, 110, 183; NNBL and, 23, 28, 52–53, 55–56, 63, 74, 91–113; private v. public behaviors of, 75–76; Protestant work ethic, 28–29, 50, 53, 56–57; scholarship on, xii–xiii, 108, 140–43, 149–50; Scott and, 65, 90; self-help and, 56, 58, 112, 129, 131–32, 136; *The Story of My Life and Work*, 61, 166; as strategist, 72, 105–6, 145–51; Tuskegee Institute and, xi, xiv, 30, 114, 120; *Up From Slavery*, xii, 49–50, 61, 69–70, 134, 137–38, 166
Washington, Margaret James Murrray (wife), 87, 160
Washington, Portia (daughter), 19
Wells-Barnett, Ida B., 21, 93–94, 147
"Whitecapping," 67–68, 87
White flight, 131, 149
White supremacists, 2
Wickersham, Charles A., 9
Wilcox, William G., 53, 69
Wilkeson, Frank, 40
Williams, W.T.B., 141
WLPTU. *See* Warren Logan Papers at Tuskegee University Archives
Women: as entrepreneurs, 109–11; treatment of, 79; Tuskegee Institutes programs for, 120
Women's Conference, 79
Woodward, C. Vann, 147
Work, and slavery, 35, 42
Work, Monroe N., 20, 73, 84, 101
Workers' Conference, 79
Work ethic. *See* Protestant work ethic
World War I, 1, 13, 122
Wright, Richard R., Jr., 13
X, Malcolm, 140

YMCA, 137

Michael B. Boston is assistant professor at Brockport State College. He is a member of both the American Historical Association and the Association for the Study of Afro-American Life and History in New York State. He has published several articles in the *Journal of Afro-Americans in New York Life and History*, including "Blacks in Niagara Falls, New York, 1865 to 1965, A Survey."